THEORY
OF REALITY

THEORY
OF REALITY

Larry and Diana Bogatz

To order additional copies of this book, contact:
Xlibris Corporation
1-888-795-4274
www.Xlibris.com
Orders@Xlibris.com
17329

TABLE OF CONTENTS

MATERIAL AND RELATIONAL SUCCESS

INTUITION AND BEYOND

APPENDIX

Theory of Reality is dedicated to our wonderful children.

To Sherilyn:

We admire your desire to achieve excellence in all that you do. You have continuously demonstrated that if something is worth doing, it's worth doing right; for you success is a way of life.

To Mitchell:

We are impressed with the confidence that exudes from your being, and how others instantly relate to you. We have also been amazed by your determination, which creates an energy force drawing the things you desire to you.

To Karalyn:

We are blessed by your gentle and loving spirit and your uncommon kindness toward others. You have continually astounded us with your imagination—where others see a pile of stones you see a castle.

To Spencer:

We are proud of your quest for understanding that has helped you stand strong against the tide of adverse thought. Your well thought out opinions on everything exhibit wisdom beyond your years.

We love each one of you beyond words. Your unique and special talents make us proud to be your parents. We are confident that you will take our knowledge and wisdom to a greater level in your own lives, and achieve a higher level of life than anyone ever dreamed was possible.

Acknowledgements

To David Selley, our friend and mentor:
We are grateful for your presence in our life. Without your encouragement and direction our desire to communicate the wisdom received from a lifetime of self-realization may never have blossomed into this book.

To Alan Heikens, our editor and friend:
We appreciate your astute understanding and sensitive application of grammar and punctuation, but we are most grateful for your thoughtful insight that aided us in our desire to bring the color of our experiences to the written page.

To the staff at Image Net:
We acknowledge those whose combined effort created our wonderful website at *www.TheoryOfReality.com*. We recognize Juli Land for her creative talent that made it possible to take the book cover that existed only in our minds and make it come alive exactly as we imagined. We also recognize Heidi Bautista whose talent as a programmer created an outstanding online store.

To our family, relatives, and friends:
We are especially grateful for the large part you played in the stories that are shared within these pages as well as the experiences we have shared. Our love is yours always.

To all the other individuals:
We acknowledge that you have touched our lives and given us new insight and direction, and that is why your stories are contained within the pages of this book.

Disclaimer

Most names contained in this book have been changed so that their identity could be revealed only at the sole discretion of that individual. All the stories contained in this book have been conveyed according to the authors' perception. Any inexactness in relaying the facts was not deliberate. Any perceived discrepancies with the personal stories contained herein are merely a difference in perception of the events as they took place. The stories are shared for the purpose of helping the reader understand the concepts contained in this book. At no time have the authors willfully intended to harm, cause emotional pain to, or sought to disparage the reputation of, anyone mentioned. The authors share these stories with the intent to help people change their perception of reality and ultimately achieve a greater level of life.

Foreword

(David Selley is the President of Target Management Services, the author of the "Health, Wealth, and Happiness" Series, a motivational speaker / teacher and an entrepreneur / investor.)

What if you woke up one morning to discover that almost everything you had been taught from the time you were born . . . was a lie? Just like your innocent discovery that Santa wasn't the one placing presents under your Christmas tree. Or a more serious discovery such as learning the myth and reality of our failing educational, employment, medical and social systems. From Socrates and Plato to Quantum Physics the authors take you on a roller coaster ride of self-discovery. As you contemplate, absorb, and implement the various approaches to your "reality" discovered in this book, you will realize that you have available all the resources and energy needed to create a new reality for yourself. Taking responsibility for your thoughts and actions is just one of the many valuable messages in this book.

Theory Of Reality contains oceans of discernment and pearls of wisdom. Knowing the authors on a personal basis makes writing this forward very simple for me. When I first met Larry, it was one of those very rare, instantly profound relationships. There he was, transformed from grease monkey into GQ executive, wearing an overstated brown three-piece suit replete with a gold time piece and chain. He stood out from the crowd of networking wannabes. He made his point of difference his point of advantage. Soon after we met, in his first burst of entrepreneurialism, Larry used up his military separation pay and was forced to move in with us. We loved, shared, learned, and bonded in a special way that will last forever. We already had one son— now we have two. Sonja, my wife, talked Larry out of the brown suit and proudly taught him how to dress for success with a great combination of Saks, sales and a wardrobe designed from a budget perspective. Over the years it has been pure joy mentoring Larry and Diana.

Through this book you can, if willing and eager to learn, permit the condensed wisdom of the ages to lubricate your brain waves for positive changes in your life. In today's hectic environment dealing with reality can be difficult. We get mixed media messages dealing with morality and spirituality, which result in a world where confusion reigns. However, your perception is your reality.

Larry and Diana have skillfully revealed their lives, adding an insightful analysis by incorporating concepts from ancient history thru the present and into the future, to create this very useful set of tools to help you. It has truly been a pleasure to watch Larry and Diana grow to a stature that is unparalleled among the masses. They simply choose to march to a different drummer. They walk-the-walk and talk-the-talk. From humble but diverse backgrounds they have blended their unique qualities and experiences to forge this positive, forward thinking book. They are living examples of how someone can change their lives forever simply by applying the solid principles described so well in this book. The old adage, "If they can do it, I can do it," still applies to those who are willing to step outside the box of conformity. *Theory Of Reality* is a must read and should grace the shelves of all those who are interested in improving their lives.

David Selley   June 12, 2003

Preface

When you understand its essence, the book you now hold is shocking. If you read it, your life will never be the same. No sooner will you open this book than you will find yourself thrust into the thoughts of great minds. You will be led to the realization of how thoughts take on form, how perception creates, and you will be shown how to launch yourself into the world of your dreams and how to live the way you want. From the parent—child and man—woman relationships to the God—you relationship, from physics to philosophy, from mathematics to money, as you read this book you will gain a sense of the magic that creates fulfillment in life. You will develop your own *"FUTURE CONFESSIONS"* that will create the reality of your imagination.

Herein stories abound, stories you will relate to and learn from, stories that will guide you and yours through the hardest of times, and bring you thru to your desired future. However, *Theory Of Reality* is much more than stories that illicit an emotional response. The reader is taken on a powerful path of discovery. Just as Newton's mind awoke in a *FLASH* to the wonders of gravitation by observing an apple fall, your mind will also be enlightened to the powerful truths shared within these pages.

- Discover the fundamentals of how your reality is formed.
- Realize the importance of overcoming fear and other negative emotions, and learn how to eliminate these resistors.
- Enhance your self-esteem and insure the prosperity of your soul.
- Rise above the challenges of time and money.
- Gain insight on what makes relationships successful.

- Investigate the mysteries of paranormal experiences, and uncover the practical benefits of sharpening your intuitive abilities.
- Avoid the pitfalls of the mid-life crises, empty-nest syndrome, and the hoarder's retirement mentality.
- Improve your health, your parenting, your marriage, and escape the paycheck-to-paycheck exercise wheel.
- Change your magnetism so that you no longer attract people or things that will hurt you.
- Examine light, subatomic particles, and the substratum of existence.
- Avoid caging your energy and understand deja vu.
- Explore the power within your spirit.

The impossible will become possible for you through the enlightenment you will receive. You will be empowered to change your reality as well as to influence the reality of others. *Theory of Reality* will help you turn your dreams into attainable goals. Start reading and the direction of your life will be altered forever.

*"Reality is merely an illusion,
albeit a very persistent one."*

Albert Einstein

Chapter 1

LAYING THE FOUNDATION

Reality is Our Perception of Life

The narrative of life oscillates between the appearance, the imagination, and the subtle inklings from some deep unknown place. Life pulses and vacillates, and man, from the dawn of time, has pondered the underpinnings of his perception of his essence. The truth lies somewhere amidst the hard factual world, the soft beating of the heart, and the glimmer of our awareness. As humans we continually seek to define reality, to distinguish between what is real and what is imagined, to answer the why, what, and how of our existence. From Plato's theories to modern movies, we strive for answers.

A bumper sticker displayed on a beat-up brown Toyota Tercel proclaims, "Reality is for people who lack imagination." Though clever, even humorous, this saying falls short of our need for a definition. So what is reality? Webster's dictionary gives this definition: the quality or state of being real; actual existence; the totality of things that actually exist. The bumper sticker and Webster's agree that reality is based on what is real. Webster's seems to love to use circular definitions so that you have to go back to look up yet another word to obtain understanding. Webster's defines "real" as: existing in fact or actuality—if used as an adjective—or, genuine, authentic—if used as an adverb. So "reality", according to Tercel and Webster, is based on cold, hard fact and "imagination" is something quite separate.

But where is the line drawn between the marrow and the bone? On a gray day where is the line between the water and the sky? And where indeed is the line drawn between genuine, authentic fact and the imagination? Life's reality includes the emotions of the heart and the desires of the spirit; if it did not, life's reality would be innate and without breath as a wooden table standing motionless on the kitchen floor. So if you're willing to give the boot to Tercel's and to Webster's thoughts on the subject of reality, then how do we define reality? We propose this definition: our perception of life IS reality.

Granted this understanding, reality becomes a living and changing concept that breathes with you as your perception changes from each vantage point in your journey of life. With this description the reality of life can include appearance, imagination, and intuition. If you accept this meaning and belief, you become empowered to send a ripple into the constancy of fact and you see motion, direction, and energy. Energy is the capacity for action or accomplishment. Energy is power. To be alive is to be flowing with energy.

Reality based on fact alone is fatalistic, dead, and lifeless. Reality based on life is active, mobile, and has the concentrated extract of energy. The three realms that comprise reality are material, intellectual, and intuitive. Our bodies are made to live in reality. The brain demonstrates our interaction with reality. The brain receives the sensory input from the five physical senses; but the mind utilizes reason, willpower, creativity, and emotions. Further still, the mind, utilizing the organ called the brain, reaches for subtle, instinctive understanding and knowledge of things that cannot be obtained by reason to fill in the blanks.

Whether we call these three realms the material, the intellectual, and the intuitive or the physical realm, the soul realm, and the spiritual realm, we are referring to the same three planes that intersect to make up our perception of life—which is our reality. There is a depth to you—beyond your autobiography—that whispers of a world beyond the facts of what you do. We need to examine the intrinsic properties of our reality and understand its governance, so that we can gain control over the direction of our lives.

No matter how factual, logical, and practical you might consider yourself, you can benefit from pondering these ideas. This theory of reality and the concepts presented here were formed by the authors, Larry and Diana Bogatz, two engineers seeking a comprehensive but practical understanding of life as they sought to change their lives from the unacceptable reality "fate" had handed them to a reality where dreams were attainable goals. The authors share candid, true-life experiences from their own lives as well as from others' lives to demonstrate how to use this theory of reality to actualize YOUR dreams.

Before examining the practical differences this theory provides, the authors suggest that you, the reader, by reading the appendix, may enjoy an excursion into historical and modern philosophical thought as well as examples of that thinking found in modern motion pictures and breakthroughs in research in physics regarding reality. Through the ages many theories have been proposed. Those theories of a theological persuasion have emphasized the spiritual realm; some have even claimed that the true reality is spiritual alone. As in Christian Science, sickness and death are refuted as not being real at all. On the other hand, mathematicians stress the logical reality created by reason. In the arena of "reason" the battlefield is the mind and no mystical thinking is given credence. It is 1) mind over matter and 2) levels of fact—as in a proven fact versus a possible theory. Finally, there are many shallow thinkers who contend that reality can only be contacted through the five physical senses. Predestination and fate are the commonality behind their thinking. What is, is; and what will be, will be. No hope is found among these ideas; you cannot cheat death. There must be more to life . . . and there is.

"As far as the laws of mathematics refer to reality, they are not certain, as far as they are certain, they do not refer to reality."

Albert Einstein

Chapter 2

LAYING THE FOUNDATION

The Fundamentals Of Reality

Remember this working definition of reality? Reality is one's perception of life. With this definition you are empowered to change your reality because reality is a living concept ever changing with your perception from each vantage point of your life. This theory of reality is unique because it outlines a view of life that goes beyond philosophy to practical application. The authors have lived the techniques that changed their reality and have proven that they work. A man that believes that he can and a man that believes he cannot are both right. Each is defined by his own beliefs. The one that believes he can succeed is empowered to do so. The one that believes he cannot, limits himself. By defining what you believe in regard to your reality, you take control of your life. A choice of inaction is still a choice that will bring consequences. Obviously, it is better to make deliberate choices toward your desires and reap the rewards in your life. Building a plan to succeed—and following it—leads to success; failing to plan is planning to fail.

If you believe that your reality is your perception of your life, you are empowered to make different choices and to alter your reality. But you need much more than a simple definition of reality to proceed. Therefore, the authors will examine the three realms that intersect to form reality. The three realms are the material or physical realm, the intellectual or soul realm, and the intuitive or spiritual realm. Also, the authors will delve into and analyze other factors that influence reality—like time, money, nature, government, and the impact of others' realities upon your own reality.

The material or physical realm is the easiest to understand. This realm is the sense realm where input comes from the five physical senses of sight, hearing, touch, taste, and smell. This tangible realm shouts its existence to all. Since all persons are bombarded with input from the physical sense realm, you often need to turn down or turn off what your senses are telling you if the messages don't line up with your desired reality. This action takes conscious and deliberate effort on a constant basis to overcome the negative input from this realm. The material realm is measurable and concrete. Many have proclaimed, "If I can't see it, I won't believe it." These individuals have limited their realities to the physical realm and have immobilized their imagination and intuition. Life happens to them and they whine, "Why me?" The answer is clear. Their narrow perception of life has limited their options.

The mental or soul realm is intangible. Reason and logic rule for the analytical individual, while emotions run wild for others. The soul is comprised of the mind, the will, and the emotions. Ideally, the will balances the emotions with reason. Within this realm a constant battle is raging which causes the input into our reality from this realm to appear inconsistent and unreliable. Maturity of character and/or a strong willpower is required for the soul realm to have a forceful impact upon one's perception of life, and to empower you to achieve a particular goal. It is within the mental realm that you possess the power to choose. Quality decisions can change your life. Inappropriate mental, and sometimes subconscious, vows can ruin your life. The mental realm is the interface between the physical and spiritual realms. Hence, the popular saying, "The battleground is in your mind".

The intuitive or spiritual realm is also intangible. Just like the wind, the mental and intuitive realms impact your reality without being seen. The intuitive realm is the hardest realm for many individuals to acknowledge. However, it is well documented that most of the great, scientific discoveries have their roots in the intuitive realm. For instance, Sir Isaac Newton made at least three discoveries through intuition: the law of universal gravitation, the law of the composition of light, and the mathematical method of fluxation. On one memorable day an apple fell and, seeing that, Newton's mind awoke. As if in a vision, he saw and understood that if the mysterious pull of the earth can act through space to the top of a tree then it might even reach so far as the moon. Many similar testimonies of intuition use phrases like, "Ideas come when I least expect them," "in a flash," "with a sudden leap of thought."

Intuition goes beyond physical or mental sensation. Intuition is inspiration, revelation, extrasensory perception, mystic experience. Intuition delves into levels beyond the limits of our normal conscious life. At some time you have likely experienced disorientation when you have returned to the parking lot to find your vehicle after a visit to a local department store or shopping mall. Like stepping across the portal of one reality to another, you step out of shopping mode into driving mode and feel a strange sense of confusion when adjusting— to another realm. The spiritual realm can be like that. Visiting the spiritual realm can be as simple as a stray thought received while daydreaming or a deliberate trip through meditation to tap into a deep unknown place. Though uncomfortable for many, access to the intuitive, spiritual, realm is an undeniable part of our reality. Each realm has its own structures and rules. Each realm has its own fundamentals. Persons focused in the physical realm sometimes feel their lives revolve around time and money. They live by the alarm clock and their paychecks. However, as you will read in later chapters, time and money are ideas created by man. Time helps provide order to your life, and money helps place a common value on things. Time and money can't control your life unless you let them. Similarly, more global forces like nature and government impact your reality. Like death and taxes, they seem impossible to avoid. However, you have more control than you may think. Focusing our energy on producing our desired reality can restrict the effect of outside forces and others' realities on our reality.

Your reality is constantly changing as you journey to different vantage points of your life. A child is easily impressed, easily entertained, and easily frightened. A small sphere of knowledge and understanding forms a child's reality. Though creativity, imagination, and intuitive thinking can be very strong in a child, children are quickly overloaded by sensory input and then display high levels of emotion. Parents are famous for saying things like, "You just don't know how easy you have it." Most adults think fondly back to the days when they were children. But if you think back you can probably think of several times in your childhood when you were overwhelmed by the pressures of your life. There were times in Diana's childhood when she was devastated because some boy wasn't interested in her, when she felt swamped with tasks her teachers assigned, or overcome with emotions because her father made some hurtful comment. At this point the experiences of life and her personal growth have brought her to a far different perspective, and that child's reactions seem silly to her now.

Though some individuals become derailed by painful experiences and stop their emotional growth, most people mature in their character and understanding such that each of their previous realities later seem simplistic to them. They puzzle as to the anxiety and difficulty they had during those past experiences. When Diana was pregnant with her first child, she was terrified of the formidable tasks before her. She was afraid of labor, afraid of changing diapers, and petrified of potty training. Today, as a mother of four, that previous paradigm seems ridiculous.

Just through the normal course of life, we make shifts in our reality through experiences, increased knowledge, and decisions we have made. For instance, who you choose to marry will have a profound impact on your life. Gaining the knowledge of how to drive changed your life forever. Experiencing the death of a loved one could change your outlook entirely. Once you've defined your dream life you can purposely make decisions, learn, and experience those things that bring new realities into being. You have the ability and a much greater power than you realize.

Life is like an onion. At the center is your goal. Each time you peel back a layer, you get closer to your goal. Some layers seem to fall off on their own; others require much effort and may even bring tears to your eyes. Like the pungent smell and flavor of this vegetable, life's experiences can be spicy, stimulating, bitter, or palatable. The core is there for the finding for those who are persistent and devoted to the task. The reward can be great and the quest can be fulfilling.

*"The whole of science
is nothing more than a refinement
of everyday thinking."*

Albert Einstein

Chapter 3

LAYING THE FOUNDATION

Energy Between The Realms

We have offered a workable definition for reality and explored the three major realms that make up perception of life. Our pilgrimage has just begun as we take our next excursion into how the material, intellectual, and intuitive realms interact.

Scientists have informed us that everything is made up of atoms, which in turn are made up of smaller parts—the nucleus, protons, and neutrons. The atomic bomb was produced by presupposing that these parts interacted in a way that produced energy, and that the greatest energy would be produced by breaking apart the elements of the atom. Likewise, the elements of conscious reality interact and exchange energy. If a change is produced in one element, there will be a corresponding reaction produced in the other elements. Most of us have accepted our perception of reality as a non-changeable part of our existence. This perception, however, is easily disproved. Our choices impact our reality every moment of every day. Our failure to plan and purposefully choose has given us a sense of fate; but truly our fate is in our own hands, heads, and spirits. We have the tools to change reality from the inside out. By understanding the basic principles and practicing those principles in our daily habits, we can change our lives.

To understand the energy between the realms of reality, picture the atom as a model of life. Technically, the nucleus of an atom has a positive charge and is made up of protons and neutrons. Negatively charged electrons are in constant motion around the nucleus. For this analogy the reality atom is made up of a nucleus, protons, neutrons, and electrons where all can have either positive or negative charges. In this analogy the nucleus is a cluster of sensory input from the material realm. The protons are reason, emotions, and willpower. The neutrons are intuition, imagination, and revelation; and the electrons are factors like time and nature. These elements make up the atom. How the atom is configured determines if it is gold, copper, or a multiplicity of other choices from the Periodic Table of Elements. In our analogy the configuration of our reality atom determines the substance of our paradigm or our perception of life. Everything is made up of these basic units. Every substance contains these components. Just as the elements of matter remain together through energy, the elements of the total reality also interact through energy. Energy is a synonym of life. Life is the flow of energy that separates the static, inanimate object from the vital being. Since reality is our perception of life, energy is the key force between the elemental components of reality.

The definition of energy found in our son's sixth-grade science textbook is, "Energy is the ability to make something change." The two basic kinds of energy are potential energy and kinetic energy. Potential energy is when the ability to make something change is stored but not actively producing change. Kinetic energy is the energy of motion. The law of conservation of energy states that the total amount of energy in a system is constant and that energy cannot be created or destroyed.

In your reality you have all the energy you need to live your dream. You have all the ability to make the changes to your life that you desire. All that is required is to change the stored or potential energy into active kinetic energy, or to redirect your negative kinetic energy to positive kinetic energy.

Albert Einstein introduced the famous equation $E=MC^2$. In layman's terms this equation tells us that mass and energy are two forms of the same thing. Theoretically, one can be changed into the other. This basic law of physics and the universe can open our understanding to the inner workings of life and our perception of life. Energy can be transformed into mass! The cold, concrete world of facts measured by our five physical senses is a form of energy. In fact not only the material realm, but also the intellectual realm and the intuitive realm are forms of energy.

A substance is made up of particles that are always moving. The kinetic energy of these moving particles is referred to as thermal energy. When the particles that make up water are slowed down, ice is formed. When these same particles are sped up, water will boil. The faster the particles in a substance are moving, the higher the temperature of the substance. The metal of our pots and pans are good conductors of heat that warm our food on a stovetop while the plastic or wooden handles are insulators or poor conductors.

When thermal energy is transferred through solids, the process is called conduction. Through liquids or gases, this transfer is called convection. When thermal energy is transferred through waves of energy, it is called radiation. Light energy is a form of radiation. When two objects come into contact, the energy from the faster moving particles is transferred to the slower moving particles. The transfer of energy will continue until all the particles in both objects are moving at the same speed. Eventually the objects will then have the same kinetic energy, the same thermal energy, the same temperature.

Human relationships can be thought of similarly. Some people even call this the "tuning fork" effect because relationships reach an equilibrium or harmony. These understandings provide a profound insight into the interaction of the three realms of reality. In the material realm, the five physical senses are constantly working to see, hear, touch, taste, and smell everything our bodies come in contact with. In the intellectual realm, our industrious minds are reasoning, exercising willpower, and monitoring emotions. In the intuitive realm, our spirits are actively imagining, seeking answers through intuition and revelation, and coursing with the energy of faith or fear. Every element is in constant motion. When we exercise our bodies become heated, and when we sleep our temperature falls. When someone is angry we say they are hot under the collar, or if they are emotionless we say they are a cold fish. Those that have experienced miraculous healing often described it as "a feeling of warmth in their chest or in the area that the healing took place". Heat is a byproduct of energy transfer in every realm.

Whether or not we are good conductors or insulators of the kinetic energy or thermal energy of life depends upon our choice. Consciously or unconsciously we decide through our beliefs to allow the energy we possess to be in cold storage or to be actively producing change. If you don't believe any of that mystical, spiritual mumbo-jumbo, you will be an insulator toward that kinetic and thermal energy that travels through the waves of thought and imagination. Yet, what you greatly fear may come upon you because the negative, kinetic energy from your spirit will produce what your imagination has generated through anxious thought. The three realms of reality—the material, intellectual, and intuitive realms—are in constant contact to produce our perception of life. The energy from one realm will transfer to the others until they reach equilibrium. Conduction, the transfer through solids, is occurring in the material or physical realm. Convection, the transfer through liquids and gases, is comparable to the transfer of energy in the intellectual or soul realm, and radiation, the transfer through waves, is like the transfer of energy in the intuitive or spiritual realm. We say, "I have seen the light," when we receive a revelation that deepens our understanding. How telling when light energy is transferred through waves.

A pure substance is made up of only one kind of atom which scientists call an "element". Our individual reality is comparable to a pure substance or an element. Molecules are units formed of two or more atoms. A small, close-knit group, like a family, is like the molecule; it has its own, small, group reality—in this case a family reality. Very large molecules called polymers can contain hundreds or thousands of atoms. Polymers are like large groups that have something in common. For instance, a person who lives in California is a Californian; or a group of people with the same religious beliefs has a group identification, e.g., Catholics. Each of these groups has their own larger group reality, i.e., a Californian reality or Catholic reality, respectively. The larger the group, the greater the variance between the individual realities contained in the group.

In nature, elements are not often found in their pure state. Most elements occur in combination with other elements. A non-pure substance is a compound. Since we are not isolated in this world, our individual reality will not always be the pure, ideal, dream life we would like. Our individual reality will be a non-pure substance like a compound with a destination toward the ideal, dream life, but always influenced by factors outside ourselves. Compounds are classified as acids or bases. Are the worries of life eating you up? If so, you're an acid. If you are stuck in the same place like soap scum, you're a base. If you have obtained a perfect balance, you're a seven like water with a neutral pH balance of seven.

A mixture is a combination of pure substances. An example is granola. The people of the world are like granola made up of fruits, nuts, and flakes. (Just a little scientific humor.) If in a mixture the particles are mixed as evenly as the people of the world are (more or less), the mixture is called a solution. It is reassuring after so many scientific analogies that we can conclude with a solution.

Through some practical examples of how the material, intellectual, and intuitive realms interact, we can bring greater understanding to our scientific analogies of life. Graham had developed high blood pressure from a stressful job and his life in general. His doctor prescribed a medicine that suppressed adrenaline flow that in turn lowered Graham's blood pressure. Over the course of using this medication the dosage had to be continually increased in order to have the same results. After ten years, Graham was taking the maximum dosage but it was no longer effective.

It was discovered that Graham's body responded to this blood pressure medicine in a very unusual way. Graham's adrenaline glands had tripled in size to compensate for their decreased ability to produce the adrenaline that his body insisted it needed. Now, Graham had an inoperable condition as well as high blood pressure. The condition in his body as well as the associated discomforts from his ailment caused Graham to respond with depression.

Graham sought answers from non-traditional avenues because the doctors could no longer help. He tried nutrients, acupuncture, and relaxation techniques. Then he turned to miracle healers, faith teachers, and spiritual gurus. Over many years hope faded until his pain led him to give up. He decided to throw out his medication and let fate decide. Graham died of a massive stroke from his unchecked blood pressure.

This is a classic scenario where long-term illness or disability results in the individual becoming discouraged, melancholic, and despondent. The energy of the physical realm becomes slower from sickness, which results in a corresponding transfer to the intellectual and intuitive realms. The intellectual/ soul realm becomes depressed and the spiritual realm becomes disheartened. The body slows down, the mind shuts down, and the spirit gives up hope. An equilibrium in the system is achieved, which is often a complete loss of kinetic energy or what is commonly referred to as death.

Another actual case study involves a determined family man named Michael. Michael lived from paycheck to paycheck supporting his wife and two children. His job was of vital importance to the maintaining of his reality. Unfortunately, the company that he worked for needed to downsize in order to survive. Faced with the possibility of being let go, Michael made a quality decision to make himself as valuable to the company as possible.

Michael worked in the circuit board test department. He reasoned that if he knew how to repair every one of the dozen, different circuit boards produced and maintained through his company, he would become the most valuable man in the repair department. First, he met with his superior and asked for the opportunity to become the lead technician in his department because he had the skill to repair all the company's circuit boards. His claim at this time was not yet true, but he proclaimed it as if it was the truth because he was resolute that this would indeed become fact. Next, he took home the schematics of each circuit board and studied them so that he would understand how each one worked. Next, each time he mastered one type of board, he picked a new type of circuit board to troubleshoot and repair. As his confidence grew, he volunteered to work on the pile of rejected boards that the other technicians claimed were beyond repair. He proved to his superior that he could indeed do the job better than anyone else in his department. Michael became the lead technician and survived layoff after layoff until he was the sole technician left in the company.

In this example the strength of a quality decision and the willpower from the intellectual realm was able to impact the physical and intuitive realms. The energy from determination transferred to the physical hard work of learning new things and acting upon that knowledge. The positive experiences in the physical realm reinforced a belief in his ability. With a newfound faith in his capabilities, Michael impacted the beliefs of his superior, changed the superior's reality, and achieved his goal of staying employed by proving his value to the company.

Again, equilibrium is achieved across the three realms that make up reality. In this case the whole system is at a higher, positive, kinetic energy level due to the initial, quality decision. The impact of choice in life is high, and the impact of a quality decision is even greater. Many goals are achieved simply by making a quality decision to pursue that goal.

History is filled with people who believed in something that the rest of the world did not believe in. Christopher Columbus (1451-1506) believed that the world was round. His strong, intuitive knowing set him on a course of action that changed his reality and changed the reality of the world. His belief affected his mindset and his actions. Columbus reasoned that he could find a faster route to Asia by sailing around the world because he believed the world was round instead of flat.

Columbus was convincing because he was convinced. After numerous rejections Columbus obtained the backing of Queen Isabella and Ferdinand V, King of Castile, and sailed across the Atlantic Ocean. On Columbus' second voyage he stopped at Puerto Rico—which is the closest he came to the United States. That discovery was the foundation for the claim that Columbus discovered America. He established the first European settlement in what he called the "New World" in his logbook. He became wealthy; but he never enjoyed his wealth. Yet, his story became a part of history because his beliefs impacted the world's beliefs. Because he did not have enough information, his reasoning led him to faulty conclusions. Columbus never found a shorter route to Asia; however, he became famous for his discovery of America. Columbus endured ridicule and hardships because of his convictions— convictions that were instrumental in disproving the belief that the world was flat.

A strong belief or an intuitive knowing generates energy in the spiritual realm. Acting on what we believe is commonly referred to as "faith". This faith is not faith as a religious faith, which is a set of beliefs, but faith as a powerful force. A simple definition of force is a push or pull. Faith and fear work in a similar fashion. Fear attracts the negative that our imagination generates. Faith attracts the positive, consciously desired experiences that our imagination generates, that which our imagination hopes or believes for. In the example of Columbus, he had a belief that the world was round. When he acted upon his belief, it generated the force of faith in his life. This force pulled toward him the ability to prove that his belief was true. The energy of his faith from the intuitive realm generated a mindset in the intellectual realm and corresponding action in the physical realm. Though he did not achieve his goal to find a quicker route to Asia, he did achieve the goal to prove that the world was round. Here the energy of the intuitive belief was transferred to the intellectual and physical realms until equilibrium was achieved.

Each of these actual case studies shows how the energy in one realm is transferred to the other two realms that make up our reality until equilibrium is achieved. Understanding how these three realms interact gives us the basis for understanding how to affect change in our life. The substance of our reality can be changed by changing one or more of the basic units that make up the whole. Each realm of our reality interacts and reaches a stable state to form our perception of the complete picture of our life at a given time. So now that we recognize our life is made up of energy, we must learn how to utilize and direct that energy to produce the longings of our heart. When we purposely harness the energy available to us and direct it toward a desired goal, we will achieve our objective.

"Any intelligent fool can make things bigger, more complex, and more violent. It takes a touch of genius—and a lot of courage— to move in the opposite direction."

Albert Einstein

Chapter 4

LAYING THE FOUNDATION

The Power From Harnessed Energy

It is common knowledge that energy is released by accelerating a mass to the speed of light squared ($E=MC^2$), but this mathematical equation doesn't even touch our every day understanding. Energy is better understood by turning on a light switch, eating a candy bar, or rubbing two sticks together. These kinds of energy are common to us, but there is another type of energy that is unseen. This energy comes from our words, our thoughts, and our imagination. Many have grasped that if by hard work they obtain a college degree and land a better paying job, they have changed their reality. Most have not grasped that by utilizing their words, thoughts, and imagination that they can also change their reality. Hard work in the physical, sense realm will impact the other two elements that make up our perception of reality. Similarly, changing our mindset will impact our logical realm, and grasping a new revelation will impact our spiritual, intuitive realm. Changes in these intangible realms will cause a change in our physical, tangible realm. What a person thinks is a reflection of what he is in the spiritual or intuitive realm. What a person says indicates where he will be in the future, which comes from his intuitive reality or from a purposeful choice of the mind. What we say and what we think come from our imagination. When discussing the fundamentals of reality we said that a man that believes he can and a man that believes that he cannot are both right. A person who can imagine success can have it, but a person that cannot conceive of the possibility will be limited by his own thinking. In school many people have a "mental block" when it comes to math. They are no less capable of succeeding in math, but that block in their minds won't allow them to grasp the concepts necessary to achieve their goal. Realizing that you have a choice in what you imagine, think, and say is the first step in changing your reality. Choosing and following through with a quality decision to imagine, think, and speak differently according to your desired outcome is life changing.

Remember the laws of the conservation of energy? In a system the total amount of energy is constant; the energy cannot be created or destroyed. We may not be able to create energy, but we can convert stored energy to kinetic energy. And we can redirect negative, kinetic energy to positive, kinetic energy. In addition, we can harness energy to power our goals.

Back before the days of light bulbs and outlets in our walls, electrical energy existed but man had not learned how to harness it. Current electrical energy is a flow of electrons. In other words, electricity is energy that moves from one place to another. In order to maintain this flow of energy, an unbroken circuit is required. Have you ever felt like you were so close to something you wanted, but there was a missing piece in your jigsaw puzzle? If you find that piece, the circuit is complete and energy flows.

Similarly, if you have a resistant attitude, that resistor will inhibit the flow of energy in your life. One approach to solving a problem in your life is to identify those things that cause you to be resistant to your goal. Change these things and you connect the circuit. Common resistors are guilt, unforgiveness, unbelief, bad attitudes, lack of self-control, and laziness. Deepening your thought, identifying your resistors and writing down things you can think and do to overcome them is a great way to begin the change.

For example, Larry entered the military service straight out of high school. Being a young man seeking independence and self-identity, many of the rules and regulations rubbed him the wrong way. The petty, little things were his pet peeves. He hated having to stencil his name on all his clothes and he especially hated having to lay his clean, stenciled, perfectly folded underwear out on the ground for some big wig to inspect. Who cared if everything was folded, pressed, and shiny? Larry sure didn't!

Larry had enlisted for five long years of naval service. He didn't like being told what to do, but he knew if he didn't change his attitude his life would be miserable. He wanted advancements to higher pay grades and the favor he needed to obtain the schooling he wanted. It wasn't the easiest thing for a teenager to do, but he chose to let go of his bad attitude and to do with excellence even the stupid things that were asked of him.

Larry's attitude change paved the way to preferential treatment and recognition. He got his pick of duties and was given leadership positions. He was awarded with special commendations. One award said, "In keeping with the highest traditions of the naval service". Letting go of his rebellious attitude brought a simple solution to his greatest pet peeves. Larry always kept an extra set of perfectly shined belt buckles, shoes, and perfectly folded, stenciled underwear and clothes. After all, no one said he had to wear the items that were regularly inspected, and without wear, they rarely needed any attention.

Eliminating the resistors will allow energy to flow in your life. Sometimes, however, the circuit just needs to be completed. For instance, Beverly wanted to work with children instead of clean houses. She had inherited a sizable house with a fenced yard; and she was blessed with a patient and jovial personality. The neighborhood needed another preschool facility. The stage was set. All she needed was a state board certification and the guts to make the change.

Beverly talked to some of her house-cleaning clients about her dream, but it wasn't until she stepped out and got the paperwork going on the board certification that things started clicking into place. Seeing her actions let people know that she was serious. She was given playground equipment and toys, offered free classes by the local university, and asked by acquaintances if their child's name could be added to her waiting list—before one even existed. She now has a prosperous, preschool facility and is very happy doing what she loves.

Unlike current electrical energy that requires an unbroken circuit for energy flow, chemical energy only requires a catalyst like heat to convert stored energy to kinetic energy. We can convert our stored energy by many kinds of stimulus. Like chemicals where the energy is stored in the bonds of the molecules or compounds, we have stores of energy available to use. Common examples of converting stored energy to kinetic energy are eating food, burning fuel, or using batteries. Our bodies store up energy for future events. Pregnant women store up for breast-feeding their newborn, and that dreaded middle-aged spread is storing up for old age when our bodies have difficulty processing food.

In the intellectual and intuitive realms, stores of energy are available which you may not have recognized that you have. Words, thoughts, and the imagination are containers that store energy. The apostle Peter compared the tongue to a rudder on a ship. To expand on this analogy, our imagination is like a sail; our thoughts like the rope used to trim the sail, and our words are like the tiller that steers the rudder.

Every day we use these tools. First, we conceive an idea in our imagination. Then, we define and expound on that idea with our thoughts. Next, we speak to people about our idea.

Finally, we do what we've been talking about. Loretta's story is a good example of how this process works.

Loretta worked in banking and raised her children all by herself. Sometimes her desire to get away was very strong. One day she imagined traveling all over the country in a recreational vehicle after her children were grown. She spent years thinking about how she could achieve this longing. Being in banking she recognized that a nice RV was expensive, and so was living without an income, so she began to save money for her retirement dreams. At times it was difficult since her resources were limited. However, the more she thought about her dream the easier it became to choose to sacrifice now for her future. As she got closer she found herself talking about where she was going to go and what she was going to do with everyone who would listen. She is currently enjoying her retirement in her RV, sometimes in sunny San Diego, CA, and other times on the cooler, but equally beautiful, coast of Maine.

How many people reach retirement age without planning and preparation? It took 41 years for Loretta to turn her dreams into a reality. Don't mistake wishing for a thing or idly talking about something as the power producing counterparts of focused imagination, critical thinking and planning, explicit confessions, and corresponding action. Precision and attention of the latter are like focusing a beam of light through a magnifying glass. Scattered light may seem exciting, but the convergence of light will start a fire.

Einstein's theory of relativity, $E=MC^2$, basically means that matter can be converted to energy and energy can be converted to matter. St. Paul penned this interesting sentence: "Faith is the substance of things hoped for and the evidence of things not seen". Faith is a force that pulls the things we desire toward us. Acting on what we believe *is* faith. The idea presented by St. Paul was that God conceived of the universe and by faith spoke it into existence. If human beings are truly made in God's image, then it is logical that we can use the same procedures to believe and to act on our belief to obtain our desires.

People have many differing views on when and how the universe came into existence as well as whether there is a divine being that started life. How fascinating it is that, approximately 2000 years ago, St. Paul would credit imagination, words, and faith as having such energy and power to bring what is unseen into the material realm. The process is taking an idea from the imagination, refining it through thought, speaking it through words, and acting upon your belief. This process outlines the steps of the force of faith that brings into substance the things that you have hoped for with your imagination.

The force of faith attracts what is hoped for just as fear repels what is truly desired and attracts the things we dread. Faith is analogous to magnetism. To become magnetized, all the electrons in a substance must be aligned in the same direction. In order for magnets to attract or repel another object, it must be in proximity to the object relative to the strength of the magnet. Many times we walk into a room full of people and are drawn to a particular person or repelled by another. We use phrases like, "He has a magnetic personality" or "I was drawn to something about him".

When we align our imagination, thoughts, words, and actions in a common direction, we become a powerful magnet with the force of faith. Our reality will move in the direction we have pointed our energy. Unless we redirect are imagination, thoughts, words, and actions, we will eventually obtain what we have focused upon. It is as simple as the magnets we were fascinated with as children but profound because our five, physical senses cannot see or comprehend the unseen. Nonetheless, what is unseen is real and powerful, and we can harness and direct this invisible energy.

When the authors were just beginning to grasp how the force of faith worked in their lives, Diana became pregnant with child number three. They were living in a small rented house where their family was crowded and uncomfortable. They were barely able to make the $650 payment each month and still eat. Larry decided to use his imagination and words for obtaining a one level four-bedroom house that they would own instead of rent. He consistently pictured his growing family enjoying the extra space and said out loud every night to himself, "We own a four-bedroom, one level home." Larry and Diana discussed what this dream home would be like—a big fenced backyard, large great room, spacious kitchen, three-car garage, the older children's rooms on the opposite side of the house from the master, and the baby's room near the master bedroom.

When Diana was about six months along, the couple whose house they were leasing gave them thirty days notice. That couple had purchased land to build on and had sold their primary residence to pay for their project. In the interim they wanted to live in their rental home. Since Larry and Diana had a month-to-month contract, they had no say in the matter. By faith they contacted a realtor and asked to look at all the four-bedroom, one level homes in the area. If they looked at the physical realm, they would have panicked. They didn't even have enough money for a move to a new rental property nor the ability to pay a security deposit. How could they possibly afford a new home? Looking at the cold, hard facts made owning a new home seem ridiculous. None-the-less, they acted on their confessions and sought to buy a house.

Walking into the fourth house they were shown was like walking into their dream. They were told later that the construction on the house started at the same time that Larry began his nightly confessing. They made an offer, which was accepted with no money down, based on Larry's VA loan. Diana went to talk to the loan officer and was told in no uncertain terms they would not qualify. After much negotiating their realtor received favor with a company which was willing to accept one year of profit in their business as proof of income instead of averaging the last three years, which included two years of loss. However, that company wanted $9000 down because Larry and Diana were considered high risk. Larry and Diana assured the lender that they would come up with the money at the time of closing—not having the vaguest idea where they would get such a staggering amount.

Then one of their regular customers called—coincidentally—and placed an order for product they had on their shelf and then paid for it in twenty-one days—just in time for the closing. The order was exactly $9000 in product. The loan payments were double what they paid in rent, but after such a miraculous experience, it was easy to believe for the payments. Personally, the authors don't believe in dumb luck or coincidence; they believe in consequences to actions. What happened may seem very puzzling and mystical to the mind, but, in actuality, what appears to be an unexplainable mystery is simply the force of faith drawing the thing hoped for into being.

Let's look at another example. When Larry was in the service his older brother died in a car accident. The incident changed Larry's outlook on life. Suddenly, life had greater importance and meaning. Larry wanted a long and quality life. He looked hard at his current habits and found many were counter-productive to life. He smoked and drank heavily and sometimes did drugs with his friends. He wanted to eliminate these bad habits and start new ones like weightlifting and regular exercise.

By the force of his will, he "cold-turkeyed" all his bad habits. He imagined himself being healthy, strong, and an exercise buff. He thought about what to do, and asked around to find a committed weightlifting partner that would be willing to train him. He joined a Tae Kwon Do class that met three times a week. He started taking vitamins and protein powder. What he hadn't expected was that as he realigned his life to an exercise focus instead of a party focus, all of his friends disappeared.

Larry no longer seemed like the great guy his party friends thought he was; instead they felt uncomfortable around him. The more serious crowd, especially weightlifters and exercise buffs, saw Larry as the kind of guy they wanted to hang with. Larry realigned his energy so he attracted a different crowd. Larry's goal for changing his lifestyle was achieved by aligning his imagination, thoughts, words, and actions in a common direction. The direction of his magnetism pulled what he desired to him and also had the by-product of drawing similarly aligned friends into his circle of influence.

You can purposely "hang with" the kind of people you want to become like and your energy will become aligned in a similar pattern to theirs. Remember how the magnet needed close proximity to be effective? Keep this in mind as you pursue new goals, and find people that you can network with to help accomplish your desires.

Another type of energy that scientists have tried to harness is nuclear energy. Nuclear energy comes from the stored energy that holds protons and neutrons together in the nucleus of an atom. Nuclear energy comes from either fission or fusion. Nuclear fission energy comes from breaking apart atoms and releasing neutrons. Nuclear fusion energy is released when atoms are joined together and is more powerful than nuclear fission. Nuclear power plants harness fission energy. Scientists have not yet been able to control nuclear fusion. As we've seen, scientific facts have enlightened our understanding of how the energy in our reality works and how we can use that energy purposefully to attain our goals.

With nuclear energy we see how a series of reactions occur because a single reaction happened. This process is called a chain reaction. We would like to harness this level of power like an atom bomb for a chain reaction in our lives. Fission is releasing a neutron by breaking apart an atom. In our lives this is similar to breaking a stronghold of negative thinking resulting in a positive and lasting change that will cascade through our lives. Fusion is joining two atoms so that they fuse together. In our lives this is similar to grasping a major, new revelation that impacts not only an individual but also a large group of people—or the world.

World War II pilots discovered in combat situations during high-speed dives that their planes would hit an invisible shockwave. This shockwave caused the airplane to shake violently as though it were being ripped apart and the cockpit controls would lock up. They discovered that when an airplane approached the speed of 760 miles per hour at sea level they would consistently encounter this shockwave. However, when flying at higher altitudes the pilots would encounter the same phenomenon at slower speeds. These pilots had discovered what became known as the sound barrier.

Pilots who approached the sound barrier would pull back in fear that their planes would be destroyed. Most pilots believed it was impossible to pass the sound barrier and any attempt to do so was suicide. However, Chuck Yeager believed that the sound barrier was like a bumpy road; once you get past the bumps the road is smooth again. Not only did Yeager believe it was possible to pass the sound barrier, he was determined to show the world that it could be done.

On October 14, 1947 over dry Rogers Lake near Victorville, California, Chuck Yeager broke the sound barrier at 662 miles per hour. When Chuck Yeager broke the sound barrier, he also broke a stronghold of negative thinking and fear resulting in a lasting change that affected the aeronautical world. Today, there's no such thing as a sound barrier. When a pilot reaches the speed of sound they call it "Mach I". In 1953 Chuck Yeager flew an airplane 1,650 miles per hour just over Mach II again breaking the world speed record. Today there are airplanes that fly in excess of Mach IV. One individual, Chuck Yeager, started a "fission"chain reaction by believing the impossible was possible and proving it to the world.

A fusion chain reaction is similar; it can affect people on a global level. The Wright brothers are a good example of fusion. Orville and Wilber Wright never formally graduated from high school, but they believed that powered flight was possible. First, they flew a kite that incorporated wing controls that were the forerunner of ailerons. Then, they built a small wind tunnel to test wing designs, and compiled the first accurate tables of lift and drag. Next, the Wright brother's first biplane made a successful flight. They patented their control system, including the elevator, rudder, and wing controls. In 1908 Orville kept his plane aloft for more than an hour. Later, they began manufacturing airplanes for the United States and Europe. Their common belief propelled them through many trials and experiments until they proved powered flight was possible. Their research affected the global mindset and had a chain reaction throughout history. Now man has flown on the Concord, and countless space missions have been successful. Flying has become a commonplace mode of transportation.

Bill Gates, another world-renowned individual, was first introduced to computers while attending Lakeside Prep School. Lakeside Prep School purchased computer time on the computer owned by the Computer Center Corporation. Bill Gates and Paul Allen, knowing that computers were the wave of the future, spent most of their time on the computer. They used up all of Lakeside's computer time in a couple weeks. Desiring more time on the computer, they hacked into the computers security system and altered the time files. When the Computer Center Corporation discovered what they did, they were banned from the computer for a while. However, the Computer Center Corporation decided to use their skills to beef up the computer security system, and in return, Bill Gates and Paul Allen received unlimited computer time. Having heard of the reputation of Bill Gates and Paul Allen. TRW Defense hired the pair to resolve the problems with their computer system.

The world of Bill Gates and Paul Allen was brought into focus when Paul Allen saw the cover of popular electronics advertising the world's first microcomputer kit. Knowing that their dream of personal computers was about to be realized, they decided to contact Micro Instrumentation and Telemetry Systems, the maker of the microcomputer kit, and announce to them that they had a software program that could be used with their system. Micro Instrumentation and Telemetry Systems were extremely interested in the product that Gates spoke of—which at that time was only a vision. However, Bill Gates and Paul Allen were determined to make their perception a reality. Bill Gates began writing code to produce the program they had promised, and Paul Allen began working on the system required to test the code. Two months later, Bill Gates' program was demonstrated at Micro Instrumentation and Telemetry Systems. They were so impressed with the program that they immediately sought to purchase this wonder program produced by Gates and Allen. The vision of Gates brought together hardware technology with his newly developed software technology causing a fusion chain reaction that has revolutionized the computing world bringing to pass his vision to make it possible for every individual to own a computer.

Examine your life. Are there resistors you need to eliminate or steps you need to take to close the circuit and let your energy flow? What about your containers of stored energy? Are your imagination, thoughts, and words negative or positive? Is there a faith project you would like to take on? Do you associate with people whose thinking is in line with the way you want yours to be? Can you let go of negative thinking that is holding you back? Are you open to new revelation? The energy has always been there. You now have a better understanding of the energy in your life and how you can harness it.

"A person starts to live when he can live outside himself."

Albert Einstein

Chapter 5

LESSONS ON HOW THE SOUL PROSPERS

Positive Virtue

To make a positive change to your reality you must focus on the positive. This is a habit that can be consciously developed. What is spoken from your mouth is the best place to start working on the positive. If you have a friend, family member, and/or co-worker who will agree to kindly remind you of your goal, your words will soon be consistently positive. Also, you need to become conscious of what you think. Catch yourself when you are mulling and daydreaming. Ask yourself what you were allowing your mind to dwell on. Replace negative thinking with positive words or thoughts. Choose to change the direction of your thinking toward your desired life. Self-talk must become positive and encouraging. This process is difficult at first, but soon becomes a new freedom that you will enjoy and benefit from. Worry and fear will be eliminated through this process and a new sense of peace will take their places in your mind. The weight of fear and worry that is lifted from your spirit will give place to using your imagination for positive outcomes. The container for receiving will be expanded and your reality will be changed.

One place most of us talk to ourselves is when we look in the mirror. After Diana's fourth child, she would stand in front of the mirror every morning and examine the state of her new stretch marks and the excess fat that had been stored for pregnancy and breastfeeding. Her self-talk was something like, "You still look pregnant", "I wonder if those marks will ever fade", or "I hate the way my body looks". She tried to solve the problem by dieting and exercising. She would lose a few pounds, look a little better, and quit. Before long she would be standing in front of the mirror saying to herself again, "You still look pregnant". Many dieters have this problem. They cannot change their physical reality because their mental reality is fixed on the negative. All their hard work in the physical would eventually net them nothing because their mental reality would bring them back to how they think of themselves. As Diana meditated on the problem of unwanted pounds and undesirable stretch marks, she realized the root was that she still saw herself as pregnant. She consciously chose to say from her mouth, "I am the ideal weight and shape. I look great and I feel great all the time". When Diana first started saying this, it was difficult for her not to burst forth with laughter. But over time as she spoke these words to herself out loud, to the physical image in the mirror, the image inside her mind and spirit began to change. She could see in her mind's eye that she could look as good as she did before she had babies. It was possible. When Diana's mindset changed, she lost the weight and kept it off. In addition, she found a great crème that caused those nasty stretch marks to fade away. If the physical, logical, and intuitive elements are not in agreement, the result is confusion rather than the desired goal.

Common knowledge suggests that at least twenty-one days are needed to develop a habit. After years of allowing negative images, thoughts, and words into your life, great commitment and consistency will be required to form a new habit. Start categorizing and analyzing what you say. Is it a curse, a blessing, or wasted words? When you begin to say positive things, you may feel like it's the biggest lie you've ever told. Indeed, if you look at your situation or material circumstances, your positive words probably won't be a present fact in your life. However, unless you are saying these confessions with the intent to deceive someone else, you are not speaking lies. You are harnessing energy to change your life. The energy of imagination, thoughts, and words will eventually make what you say true in your life. This happens when you become fully persuaded in your mind and in your spirit. The tendency toward equilibrium of energy will bring to pass the desired result if you do not quit.

These things probably won't happen overnight. However, when you continually apply this method on a consistent daily basis, the positive kinetic energy will change your present situation and bring a new reality into your life. If you exercise your will over your tongue, you can redirect your life. The words you say will affect what you think and will govern your subconscious causing you to achieve what you say. As your attitude changes to "can-do" instead of "not possible", you open up your mind to receive the answers and direction you need.

Naturally, we begin with imagining something, clarifying it with our thoughts, speaking out what we believe, and finally acting upon that belief. This is the process of faith, the magnetic force; we can use faith to draw our desires to us. We can consciously produce the desired result in our life by starting with our words. It will feel awkward to start at the middle of the process but it is just as effective. We make a purposeful decision to speak the end result, which in turn will open up our minds and spirits to new thoughts and imaginations in that area of life. Make a quality decision to control your speech. This can be focused on a particular goal, or you can make it a general principle of your life to only speak in a positive way.

The sense realm yells to us all the negative, cold, hard facts. To counteract this negative energy we choose to focus on the positive in every circumstance. Don't dwell on failure or negative past events. Choose to eliminate words of sickness, lack, disappointment, and words associated with feeling sorry for yourself. Listen to other people and become aware of how much they complain and speak curses over themselves and others. It is shocking how acceptable it is to say "I'm not feeling well, I think I'm coming down with a cold"; yet, it is weird if you say, "My children never get sick".

The turning point in the authors' family happened when their son was having a chronic ear infection. He was constantly sick and on antibiotics. Finally, the doctor said it was necessary to have tubes put in his ears. His suggestion was unacceptable to Larry and Diana. They began to look for an alternative. At that time they were learning that words were containers. Words express ideas, feelings, and create mental images. They decided to speak only positive words over their son in regard to his ears. Their search led them to a nutritionist who claimed that a particular herbal mixture would relieve their son's condition. They decided to believe that giving him this liquid in his juice would make a difference, and they decided to confess his freedom from ear infections. They told their son that this special juice would make him well. He was young enough to believe them without question. They told friends and family that their son wouldn't need tubes in his ears after all, since they had discovered an herbal cure. Within two months time their son's chronic problem disappeared. They really didn't know if the herbs worked on their own, or if the words worked without the help of the herbs, or if their words in combination with the herbs worked. It is a proven fact that sugar pills are often just as effective as medication. If the patient believes that they will be helped by taking a pill, they likely will be helped. After many other experiences the authors concluded that their belief and words were far more powerful than the herbs.

Like most families, up until this point, Larry, Diana and their family caught colds, flues, and everything that was going around. It is interesting to note that the common phrasing is to say "caught" which is an action taken on the individual's part to receive sickness. Larry and Diana decided to resist sickness and speak positively. If they felt something was coming on, they chose not to talk about the negative but to speak positively instead. In fact, they often would start singing a catchy tune like, "I feel good, nana nana na." In addition, they took some vitamin C or herbs to attack the physically undesirable reality and ignored the symptoms. They responded to their children in a similar fashion. If the kids skinned a knee, they said, "You're fine, go play". Because they were not given special attention for illness, they did not have positive reinforcement to complain or fake illness. A slight fever or ache was not an excuse to skip work or school. They guarded against the negative input in the world by muting the TV during advertisements for medicines like cough syrup. Notice the pattern; they changed their words, their thoughts, their imagination, and their actions. They then attracted health, instead of catching sickness. A new equilibrium was achieved in their lives.

Amazingly, Larry and Diana's family became very healthy. Symptoms rarely developed into any long-term problem, and occurrences of illness became less frequent. Their two youngest children have never needed to see a doctor except for preventative shots or teeth cleanings. Their oldest two children don't remember the days when they were sick. Not surprisingly, the adults had more difficulty resisting sickness since sickness had been part of everyday life for so many years. As a doctor friend once said, "I can't believe that sickness is not for today". Like his patients, he was always sick. Other people stay happy and healthy because they believe that "a laugh a day will keep sickness away".

George Burns is a great example of how "what you believe" affects the way you feel. People have jokingly said that George Burns was living proof that smoking 10 to 15 cigars a day increases an individual's lifespan. Someone once calculated that George Burns smoked well over 300,000 cigars in his lifetime. It is unlikely that the cigars increased his lifespan. So, the question is: if it wasn't the cigars, what kept George Burns alive so long? The authors believe the following quotes from George Burns will show his lifespan was increased by his attitude and his words not by what he smoked. "Age means nothing. I can't get old; I'm working. I was old when I was 21 and out of work. As long as you're working, you stay young. When I'm in front of an audience, all that love and vitality sweeps over me and I forget my age". "Retirement at 65 is ridiculous. When I was 65 I still had pimples", he said. And finally he said, "I'm going to stay in show business until I'm the last one left". The last quote of George Burns came to pass: everyone who was in show business from his generation had died before him, so truly, he was the last one left.

Sickness is very real, but it does not have to be part of your reality. You can eliminate great suffering from your life by changing your confession in regard to your health. Your words will be containers of images for your imagination and thought life. Finally, if your actions line up with your beliefs, you will be healthier than ever before.

Obviously, you can negate all these efforts by abusing your body with excessive drinking of alcohol or coffee, smoking, drugs, and other substance abuses. But even without the perfect eating, sleeping, and exercising routines, you can resist a multitude of illnesses through choosing to control your words, thoughts, imagination, and actions. The best would be to combine healthy physical habits with healthy intellectual and intuitive habits.

The words, "I can't", are considered curse words in Larry and Diana's family. During homework time, they correct their children when they say, "I can't" or "I don't understand". Phrases like this shut off the mind and the intuitive parts of one's being and create a block or resistor to learning. Larry and Diana have taught their children to ask for help without confessing negativity over their abilities. Ninety percent is attitude, and ten percent is ability. Remember the child's story about the little train that could. The train said to himself, "I think I can, I think I can", and then he did what he thought he could. A positive attitude and a confession go a long way toward a positive end result.

Another common area that most people speak negatively over is finances. People say, "We can't afford this or that". Of course, each needs to use wisdom, but budgets can be a death sentence to financial ability. You need to ask, "How can we afford?" or say, "I'll find a way to afford". A slight tweak to your words will have a profound effect on your ability. Open the thought processes and your imagination to find the answers, and your finances will magically increase. You can probably think of someone you know who sits on a wad of cash, but believes that they can't afford anything. This is a very common problem for people who lived through the depression or were raised in poverty. Even when they acquire the means, fear keeps them bound from enjoying their resources. Often, retirement age individuals take on a mentality that says, "I'll never earn another cent, so I better be extra careful." It is so much better to believe that "there is more where that came from" than to believe that "there's not enough".

If Harland Sanders had that attitude then no one would have known about his "finger lickin' chicken". When Harland was 40 he owned a service station in Corbin, KY. Harland noticed that many of the people who stopped at his service station needed to eat but there were no restaurants close by. To solve this problem Harland started to feed these hungry people his special recipe chicken. Later people started coming to Harland's service station just for the food. In honor of Harland Sanders good deed, Governor Ruby Laffoon made him an honorary Colonel. From that point forward people called him "Colonel" Sanders. Unfortunately, the interstate highway commission planned a bypass around the town of Corbin, and Harland lost his service station. All Harland's hard work was reduced to a $105 per month Social Security check. Instead of accepting that as his reality, Colonel Sanders went on a massive road trip to franchise his chicken recipe. In 1976, Colonel

Sanders was considered by an independent survey to be one of the world's most recognizable celebrities. Colonel Sanders believed beyond his Social Security check and forced the world around him to conform to his dream.

A common mistake is to trust in the income from a job or the savings in a bank account. By doing so, you limit your imagination and thinking. It takes courage to think outside the box, but in today's world it is an absolute necessity if you are to prosper financially. Besides using your time to make money, you can use your money to make more money. Fear can keep us from gaining more by keeping us from risking what we have in order to do so. The best place to start is to change your words and your thinking in regard to your finances. You need to remove the limitations on your thinking so that you can find new ways to increase.

Recently, when the authors started this process in their lives, they started with just speaking positive words over their belongings. Instead of saying, "I hate this lousy van; it's always got something wrong with it", they began saying, "This van runs like a charm." The result? They never have problems with it. They were amazed at how much money was spent repairing or replacing the things they had. It seemed as soon as something would be paid off, it would break and they would need to fix it or buy a new one. They were in a negative cycle that kept them from prospering. They took authority over what was happening with their words. Daily they confessed that their things lasted, and when they would choose to replace them, they would always upgrade to something better and pay cash. The negative cycle was replaced by a positive cycle. Their belongings improved in quality, and their department store credit cards were all paid off.

When they were at a point that they needed a new vehicle, they chose to take a different approach than ever before. They ignored the prices and focused only on what vehicle would meet the needs of their family. Then, they took an even bolder approach and asked which vehicle would meet their needs—that they liked the best—regardless of price. Thus, the BMW X5 came to the top of their list. Diana clipped a picture from the catalog and used it as a bookmark in her novels. Every time she took a moment to sit down to read for pleasure, essentially every night before bed, she would imagine driving her new BMW. Often Diana would say something like, "I'm enjoying my new car". Notice the present tense and a word that invokes an emotional response? When you purposefully confess positive for the purpose of attracting what you desire, use words that create a picture in your mind with as many of your senses involved as possible. In just a matter of a few months, they sold two investment properties that had been on the market for over two years and had the money to buy that BMW X5 for Diana.

Don't let present circumstances dictate your dreams. Let your dreams dictate your future through the use of positive words, thoughts, and imagination. We call this "Future Confessions".

Maybe you're thinking, "These people have gone off the deep end". Not only do they believe they can be healthy all the time, but they speak to, or about, inanimate objects and expect that will change their reality. The authors challenge you to take notice of what you say. How many times a day do you speak to or about inanimate objects? Most people find that they are unconsciously cursing things or complaining about things. Your cell phone cuts out on an important call, and you say, in frustration, "My phone always does this to me". You grab a pen to jot down a note, and it doesn't write. You say, "This pen is worthless. Why can't I ever find a pen that works when I need one?" Have you ever hit your computer and threw a fit when it froze up on the project you were working on? Suddenly, the object of great value became the object of your scorn. You can reverse this trend. You can choose to bless the objects in your life instead of cursing them with your words. A pleasant by-product will be an attitude of appreciation for the things you have.

Resist letting your mouth run when you are feeling sorry

for yourself. Watch a funny movie or exercise instead. Often lonely people talk constantly about their inability to find friends or a mate. Complaining generates counter productive energy. Soon they convince themselves that their situation is hopeless and depression sets in. You need only to attract one person into your social circle to fulfill a multitude of social needs. Can you believe there is at least one person in the whole world with whom you would be compatible? If so, use that belief to attract him or her. When Diana was a lonely teenager, she found a picture of a man standing in the shadows that looked fine to her. She pinned the picture on her bulletin board in her room. Whenever she was longing to be married, she would glance at the picture and say, "I know you're out there". As time passed, Diana made a speech about her ideal man to her Toastmaster club at work. This fine-tuned the image in her mind. She became choosy in regard to whom she would date. When she met Larry, he fit her list and that need was filled. Without knowing the principles, her positive words and imagination worked together to attract her desired mate.

Most people have not realized the energy in their words. As a child, when someone called you a hurtful name, you were told, "Sticks and stones may break my bones, but words will never hurt me." However, bones mend quicker than our emotions and our self-esteem. Words transmit energy. Words are containers of images, feelings, and forces like fear and faith. Words are very powerful. Solomon wrote in Proverbs, "Death and life are in the power of the tongue." Are your words producing negative or positive energy? Are your words attracting those things you desire or are your words complaints about the things you don't like in your life? Harness the strength of your words for positive gain. Have you wondered why this chapter was called Positive Virtue? Some synonyms of virtue are principle, benefit, advantage, value, and reward. The positive virtue of controlling your words, thoughts, imagination, and corresponding action is a great reward. Make a quality decision today to speak only positively. You can start with saying, your glass is "half full" instead of "half empty"; and it will lead to your glass being full and overflowing.

*"The fear of death
is the most unjustified of all fears,
for there's no risk of accident
for someone who's dead."*

Albert Einstein

Chapter 6

LESSONS ON HOW THE SOUL PROSPERS

Fear Not!

Fear is an emotion as well as a powerful force. Fear comes in many forms. There is healthy fear—a respect for things that can harm us. Healthy fear is not really fear at all because there is little or no emotion associated with this type of fear. Instead, proper, healthy fear is a type of wisdom or common sense that helps us to make logical decisions to avoid pain or bodily harm. Healthy fear, or common sense fear, will keep us from stepping in front of a moving vehicle or remind us to take a jacket if it is cold outside. If we do not have the proper balance with healthy fear, then we may do things like touch a hot stove or stick a fork in an electrical outlet.

The author's young son, who was supposedly in childcare, was attracted to the banister that surrounded the staircase descending to the bottom floor of the building. To him the banister appeared to be some kind of playground equipment resembling the monkey bars at the park. When pick-up time came, he saw the opportunity to sneak out unnoticed. He swung on the bars until he was tired and decided to let go. He fell approximately eighteen feet and dropped onto a hard concrete floor. Larry and Diana arrived just as the workers had discovered that he had fallen. Larry flew down that flight of stairs to scoop him up in his arms. Their son had only a slight swelling in his ankle. They attribute his good fortune to their daily confessions over their children—that the angels guard them and keep them from harm. Their son said that he would not have let go if he knew he would fall from "heaven to earth".

Most young children do not have a well-developed understanding of the power of the things that surround them. Healthy fear comes from an experience of understanding but can cross over to fear of death or pain when the emotions associated with what is common sense fear become exaggerated to an irrational level. Grandmother Bessie was plagued with the fear of pain and death. She was raised, impoverished, in West Virginia. She had witnessed many of her siblings die; that was probably the catalyst for her irrational response to everyday situations. Bessie's reaction to cold or even the slightest breeze was an unreasonable fear that pneumonia was lurking about ready to jump on someone at any moment. When Diana was a child, Bessie would insist Diana wear a sweater even when the weather was pleasant. Bessie continually said, "You'll catch pneumonia, honey, so wear your sweater." Bessie's ignorant ways actually brought that very thing to pass with the force of fear and her persistent confession. In sunny California Diana contracted pneumonia in the third grade for no explainable medical reason.

On another occasion Diana's brother, Michael, was stung by a bee in the park. Bessie grabbed Michael and began to scream, "My grandbaby's going to die!" If Michael's father had not pried open her death grip on Michael, he would have suffocated from her smothering embrace. Bessie would never have intentionally harmed her grandchildren, but her illogical responses derived from baseless beliefs did and could have caused exactly what she so greatly feared to come about. While the rest of the family enjoyed the lightning displays in the sky on a stormy night, poor Bessie would hide under the bed afraid for her life. While driving through the icy mountain roads, Bessie opened the passenger door with the intent to jump because she was afraid that the car would slide out of control and over the side of the mountain. She very nearly fell to her death trying to keep from falling to her death. Her fear of death and pain kept her from enjoying life.

Howard Hughes' mother had a very fearful life much like that of Grandmother Bessie. It is said that Howard Hughes also struggled with many fears later in his life. Howard Hughes was considered one of the most famous people of the 20th century. Hughes was one of the most successful industrialists, aviators, and motion picture producers of his time and was known as a cinema genius. Howard Hughes even made tremendous advances in aeronautical engineering. However, later in his life he was consumed by a fear of death. He insisted that his newspaper be delivered to him between two other papers so that no human would have touched the paper that he would touch. He was afraid of germs to such an extreme that he took unnecessary precautions to avoid any contact with the outside world. His fear of death and pain kept him from public interaction. Afraid that even his clothes had too many germs, Howard Hughes spent most of his time sitting naked on his germ free chair in a part of the room he called the germ free zone. He considered Kleenex to be germ free. Therefore, everything had to be given to him covered with a Kleenex, and a Kleenex box became his slipper of choice.

Fear of death or pain keeps people from living life to the fullest; instead, they exist—robbed of the vitality life can offer. Most people know the Biblical story of Job who suffered unimaginable things. In this story, what Job "greatly feared" came upon him. Job feared for his children's lives, so daily he sacrificed on their behalf just in case they may have sinned. One day, he lost all his children, all his belongings, and was inflicted with sores on his body. His wife encouraged him to "curse God and die"; but Job refused. God replaced seven fold all that Job had lost, and Job learned a valuable lesson about fear.

Fear is faith in the negative. Faith will bring what you desire to you. Fear will push away your desires and bring what you dread in its place. Fear and faith are like magnetic forces that push or pull on your desires. These forces are opposites of each other, but they work in the same way. Fear is an alignment of belief, imagination, thought, words, and corresponding action for a negative result. Other than a balanced, common sense fear that prevents harm, all other types of fear produce the very thing that is feared and drains a tremendous amount of energy from the individual.

For instance, fear of man is a fear of rejection or intimidation caused by the desire for approval. Stage fright is an example of the fear of man. Suddenly, when in front of the very people that you desire to applaud you, you freeze, fumble over well-rehearsed lines, and secure your failure publicly. Diana was so intimidated by a boss that during an unfavorable review of her performance on a particular assignment, she burst into tears. She wanted to be taken seriously in an all male working environment, but fear of man brought the very humiliation that she wanted to avoid.

Fear of failure is another common type of fear. Writer's block usually is a result of the fear of failure. Many people never attempt what they truly desire to do because they are afraid to fail. Of course, they secure their failure because they never act. Many talented individuals who have great potential for success hide their talents due to fear. Fear steals from them success, recognition, fulfillment, and all that their talent could provide.

Many advisors would recommend that you face your fears by doing the thing that you fear. Unfortunately, you cannot guarantee that you will overcome a fear by doing the thing that you fear. It might help the author with writer's block to start typing away, even if at first what he writes does not make sense, but in many cases doing the thing you fear can have negative consequences. Overcoming fear by "doing" may work if the experience is good, but if the experience is bad it can reinforce the fear.

Michael decided that the best way to overcome his many fears was to face one of his greatest fears. He decided to join his friends in a skydiving adventure. The day was a little windy. He jumped fine, but he landed poorly. Since he was headed toward telephone poles draped with electrical cords, he adjusted his descent the best his one day of training taught him. He managed to avoid the danger, but he was still twisting when his body met the ground. The twisting action broke his leg. He could choose to applaud his courageous effort, but the bleak incident could hardly be positive reinforcement that his fears were baseless.

Similarly, Diana decided to face her fear of roller-skating. She joined a friend to go weekly to the roller rink. On stiff and trembling legs Diana faced her fear by doing the sport she desired to learn but was apprehensive to try. Over time Diana became more comfortable and actually enjoyed skating—part of the time. One night she was asked to couple skate with a cute guy. He did all the work, and she was actually skating backwards. Unfortunately, when the guy saw a fallen individual in their path, he let go of Diana so they could skate around the obstacle. Diana didn't understand and collided with the fallen skater. She broke her tailbone. At the same time she lost all the hard work she had done of overcoming her fear.

Fear must be overcome by choice. We must choose to reject fear and resist the irrational thoughts associated with fear. We can take control of the emotion of fear just like we control other emotions. For instance, when we feel angry we can choose to yell and become violent, or we can choose to calmly deal with the source of our anger. Fear must be dealt with by consciously replacing negative thoughts with positive ones. For most of us, this will require speaking the positive. Have you ever noticed how difficult it is to think about something other than what you are talking about? Use this phenomenon to your advantage to control your thinking and your imagination.

When Diana was a teenager, she was bound by a stronghold

of negative thinking. For years she had been around a father that talked about committing suicide because of his constant pain from a terminal illness. Diana became depressed because her home life was filled with desperate struggle and pain. Her father was dying, her parents had marriage problems, and her brother had left home leaving her feeling alone and helpless. Diana started having suicidal thoughts and visions. She saw disturbing images of knives poking her or slicing her wrists. These images frightened her. She thought she was crazy: she felt destined to take her own life.

One day Diana listened to a preacher who claimed that all thoughts were either from the Holy Spirit or from demons. Those evil thoughts were not our own, but come from the devil. The preacher said that if we resist those thoughts, the devil would flee. Whether his theology was accurate is not the topic of this book; but these words empowered Diana to take action. She now thought, "I'm not crazy". "These suicidal thoughts are not my own". She could resist and overcome. Diana had hope for the first time in many years.

Constantly over the next year, Diana said, "That's not my thought, I will not commit suicide", whenever an evil thought or vision would come. The stronghold of negative thinking was broken and Diana's fear of suicide and the depression left. She learned to cope with her difficult home life and to separate that negative from the other areas of her life. She focused on her college studies and graduated top of her class. If this negative stronghold had remained, Diana would not be alive today.

Diana's unjustified fear that she was destined to take her own life was overcome by first believing that she could be free. Then, consistently saying words out loud to reject and replace the images and thoughts that had held her captive to the fear of death and pain. These words must be chosen carefully to invoke a positive image. Diana said, "I will not kill myself"; even though she was resisting, the image was still one of killing herself. Instead, Diana should have said, "I am enjoying a long and happy life." What image do you think if you are told, "It's not an elephant"? You think of an elephant. So avoid phrases like "I am not going to fail" and use "I enjoy success". You can attack the emotional aspect of fear with your mind by adding words like "enjoying" or "happy" to your word image. Emotional words invoke emotional energy. This energy attacks fear not only in the intuitive realm with imagination, but also in the mental realm with emotional energy. Further, it is more powerful to use phrases in the present tense than phrases utilizing the future tense. "I am going to impress the audience with my performance" is a wishful phrase that invokes hope but not faith. "I am delighted with my excellent performance" invokes the force of faith. Faith believes "Now!" for the thing hoped for; therefore, faith filled speech is always in the "Now".

We have discussed the major types of fear: 1) healthy common sense fear, 2) fear of death or pain, 3) fear of man, and 4) fear of failure; however, there are many other forms of fear that you may not have considered. Lower levels of fear also produce negativity in our lives by draining our energy and lowering the body's resistance to sickness. Lower levels of fear include anxiety, stress, worry, mulling over details of the past or a decision that needs to be made. If you are wondering if you did the right thing or if you said something wrong, you are worrying about the past. If you are concerned, apologize to the individuals involved. Most times you'll find they thought nothing about which you were worrying. Men especially love to mull over decisions while women prefer to talk over all the points with a friend. Perhaps men's tendency for anxious mulling is the reason they have a shorter lifespan, in general, than women. However, if either mulling or talking through decisions is done with anxiety, try another approach. Listing the pros and cons in two columns on a sheet of paper often makes clear cut what seemed to be a difficult decision. This method may also help point out what facts still need to be gathered to make the best choice.

Guard against stress. Physicians place stress as the number

one cause of sickness and disease. If stress, which is a lower form of fear, is that powerful, think how powerful the force of a major form of fear is in your life. Many of the things people attribute to heredity or generational curses may be caused by fear. Elvis Presley was a son of Vernon and Gladys Presley. Gladys Presley was a very fearful woman. One of her greatest fears was that of being left alone. Although Gladys desired to see Elvis prosper, her own unmet dream of stardom caused her to struggle with his success. Gladys died at the age of 46. Elvis was convinced that he was not better than his mother. To Elvis that meant that his lifespan would be shorter than that of his mother. What Elvis believed is exactly what happened. Elvis died of heart failure at the age of 42. Many people fear that they will suffer the same fate as their parents, grandparents, or siblings. When their fear brings to them the very thing of which they are terrified, doctors say it was genetic, and spiritual leaders claim it was a generational curse. Perhaps fear drew to them what they imagined, worried, and spoke into existence.

Jeff was named after his uncle Jeff who in turn was named after his grandfather Jeff. Grandfather Jeff died young in a horse and buggy accident. Uncle Jeff was hit by a car at the age of eight and died. Jeff asked his girlfriend if she really wanted to marry him since he would also die young in a car related accident. After they broke up, Jeff married Julia. Of course, Jeff named his firstborn Jeff Junior. Before Jeff turned thirty he was burned beyond recognition when his car mysteriously hit a tree and exploded. Jeff Junior is living in Minnesota. He is in his twenties. Is he destined to die young? Is he destined to die in a car related accident? Or is fate in his hands? If Jeff Junior chooses to fear not, then he should live a long life. But if Jeff Junior chooses to fear death at a young age in a car accident, the force of fear will most likely bring the same fate upon him as the previous three generations.

Beliefs profoundly affect lives. Your strongly held beliefs affect not only your own life, but the lives of those around you—even if the beliefs are not spoken. There is a reason and it starts in a profound connection between us all, a place that is fundamental to all awareness, a place fundamental to all life.

All matter shares a common fundamental makeup; therefore, all things are interconnected in some way. Sir Jagadis Chandra Bose, a physicist who in 1926 was appointed to a League of Nations committee, researched the boundary between the organic and the inorganic. Bose said, "In my investigations on the action of forces on matter, I was amazed to find boundary lines vanishing and to discover points of contact emerging between the living and the non-living." In his work he found that certain metallic objects exhibited fatigue characteristics similar to human and animal muscle tissue, which recovered full sensitivity after rest.

Several interesting studies have been done with plants. The five physical sense skeptics argue that though plants are living things, plants lack nervous systems or sensory organs and are limited to their cellulose cell walls to respond to their environment. However, according to *The Secret Life of Plants,* experiments with plants and music indicate that plants incline toward pleasant music, but harsh, highly percussive sounds stunted their growth and caused them to lean away from the source of the sounds. Many people claim the secret of their green thumb is speaking kindly to their plants.

One of the most fascinating studies claimed that, with a device similar to a lie detector, a plant was monitored as to its reactions while its owner was traveling. The owner, a woman, had an intense fear of flying directly associated with the take off and landing of aircraft. Her prized plant registered a violent reaction corresponding to its owner's take off and landing schedule. If a plant responds to the fear of its owner even at great distances, it is not difficult to believe that fear will affect our sphere of influence and our circumstances.

As a teenager and as a young woman, Diana suffered from the fear of rejection and hurt from men. Many people suffer from fears that affect their relationships with the opposite sex. Because Diana had been rejected and hurt by her father, she allowed that to carry over into a fear that men in general would reject and hurt her. This type of fearful belief becomes a self-fulfilling prophesy for many people. Their relationships repeat the same mistakes over and over because, with their fear, they are unknowingly attracting people who will do the very things they wish to avoid.

As a teenager Diana dated a boy with excess energy and emotional problems. When Diana wanted to end the relationship, the boy, Tom, threatened to commit suicide and vomited. Then he began to stalk her wherever she went. Tom hit Diana on eight different occasions—each time claiming he would never do so again—until Diana was able to break off the relationship. Ultimately, she convinced Tom, who claimed he worshiped her, that he was unworthy of her. Tom then joined the military service which, within six months, dishonorably discharged him for psychological reasons.

Diana moved on to a relationship with Brian. Diana and Brian shared their mutual childhood and home life struggles. As the relationship evolved, Brian revealed more and more disturbing facts about his family relationships including incestuous relations with his sister who had since become same sex oriented. Brian divulged one of his deepest secrets by showing Diana his collection of hand drawn pictures of naked women tied spread eagle—part of his warped fantasy life.

Next, Diana briefly dated Nathan who was actually attracted to a friend in her support group and not to her. He openly shared that he only asked her out because the girl he really liked wouldn't "satisfy" him.

Then a co-worker invited her to dinner, and Diana started seeing the man, Richard, from time to time. Richard seemed to be in a different category from the other males she had dated. He was a professional and a little older. When Richard bought his new house and asked Diana over to see it, she felt comfortable accepting the invitation. As soon as she entered the house, Richard attacked her and raped her.

At this point, many women would have come to the conclusion that all men were evil; but Diana knew that couldn't be true. Somehow she was attracting men that would reject her, or use her and hurt her. She uncovered the hidden truth that she believed that she was unworthy of love and that all men would betray her trust and hurt her like her father had. After recognizing this erroneous belief, Diana dealt with her past hurts, and chose to believe that she was worthy of love. She was more careful in her choices of who to date, but she was no longer fearful. She chose to believe that she would find a man who would love her and treat her properly. As a result, Diana's dating experiences changed. She dated several emotionally healthy men and had positive experiences. Eventually, Larry and Diana found each other and are still very happily married. And now they have four wonderful children.

Choose to live by faith and to fear not. You do not have to live in fear. Resist fear, and develop faith in your dreams.

"We can't solve problems by using the same kind of thinking we used when we created them."

Albert Einstein

Chapter 7

LESSONS ON HOW THE SOUL PROSPERS

Eliminating Resistors

When something bad happens, people have a need to place blame for the incident on someone or something. If we blame ourselves, we feel guilt. If we assign blame to another person or people, then we often experience unforgiveness, which can lead to bitterness. If we place the blame on God or the cosmos, the result is unbelief, doubt, and fatalism. If we manage to keep from holding ourselves, others, or God responsible, we still have painful memories and the associated hurt that remains.

Guilt, unforgiveness, unbelief, and hurt are the most common and potent resistors preventing us from changing our lives to a more positive reality. Other less enduring resistors include laziness, lack of self-control, and bad attitudes stemming from discouragement. All of these resistors obstruct the flow of positive energy in our lives. We must remove these obstacles and refrain from allowing new resistors to be formed in our lives. Eliminating resistors that have taken root in our lives takes considerably more effort then preventing new resistors from forming.

Guilt is a feeling of shame from a perceived wrongdoing.

Guilt goes beyond a healthy conscience that convicts us of misconduct. Instead, guilt forms a wound that never heals. Even if we have sought forgiveness or paid our recompense, guilt remains. Guilt keeps our minds and our emotions in bondage to the negative past. Guilt impacts our self-esteem and keeps us feeling unworthy of blessing. Many religious organizations promote the "unworthy worm" syndrome which keeps people in submission to the leadership by guilt manipulation. If this sounds too familiar to you, unshackle yourself; find a new place to worship. St. Paul said, "Whom the Son set free is free indeed". So seek a place that teaches a doctrine that you are clean after you have repented. "Repentance" means "to turn from an evil way". If you are no longer acting improperly and have made things right to the best of your ability, you should have no guilt.

Something very bad happened when Melissa was only a young girl, and her life irrevocably changed forever. She lived in a cold climate with a furnace in the basement. Her mother had instructed her to hang the laundry up to dry and to watch her baby sister. Her sister was playing in a playpen near the furnace in order to be kept warm. Melissa was only eight. When the room became engulfed in flames, she panicked. She ran from the basement calling for her mother. To their horror it was too late to save her baby sister who died in the fire that destroyed their home. Melissa's mother reasoned that Melissa must have been responsible for the fire, and she blamed Melissa for the death of her baby daughter. Most likely, the mother was truly responsible since she left her two young girls alone near a furnace; but the mother could not accept the shame upon herself. No one will ever know what actually started the fire.

Nothing Melissa could ever do would right the death of her sister. She accepted the heavy burden of guilt. Now Melissa is in her fifties, and she is still trying to overcome her feelings of inadequacy and shame. She has worked hard to put behind her the pain of rejection caused by her mother's accusations.

She still weeps bitter tears and wonders if she could have done something to have saved her sister or whether she was somehow at fault for the fire that destroyed so much. Childhood experiences of this magnitude leave enduring scars of hurt and guilt that may never be removed. Logic says that even if she was responsible, she should not have to pay emotionally all her life. But, unless she makes a choice to forgive herself and put the past where it belongs, she can never heal.

Larry and Diana's two oldest children were competing in the swim team during a hot and humid Arkansas summer. Diana never attended the Saturday swim team competitions that summer because she was in her third trimester of pregnancy with their fourth child. The heat and humidity added to her discomfort by making her feel bloated. Trim, suntanned mothers, who looked especially sexy in their bathing suits, surrounded Larry. Larry began to feel guilty that he noticed these scantily clad women. Finally, Larry confessed to Diana his "all too natural" reactions to the bathing suit beauties. After bringing his guilty feelings out into the open and asking Diana to forgive him, he felt clean again. They agreed that he needed to take some reading material with him to distract his attention away from the parade of ladies. Expression of guilt, to an understanding and non-judgmental party, will help rid you of guilt.

At one time Jane was Larry's supervisor. Jane's sad story was aired on 20-20. Jane had developed bitterness towards men. She had several unsuccessful marriages and distrusted all men. Upper management required her to hire a token male in her all female department; Larry was the top pick. While complaining one day, Jane remarked, "All men are scum", then hastily added, "No offense, Larry". Larry replied, "None taken". Jane hoped to one-day land a rich husband so that she would no longer have to deal with the rat race of competitive sales. She accomplished just that. While the couple was still newlyweds, they had a bitter fight. Jane's husband shot her six times with a .38 caliber handgun. Jane had attracted men that would hurt her because she believed that men would. She let unforgiveness turn to bitterness that eventually led to her murder. Deal with unforgiveness and don't allow it to fester. When you harbor unforgiveness or bitterness toward someone, that unforgiveness and bitterness hurts you. Usually the person who hurt you does not even know there's a problem.

In this all female working environment, Larry had the opportunity to take offense on several, different occasions. Larry shared a common cubicle wall with Debbie, a co-worker, who purposely told lies about his performance to his supervisor Jane. Debbie knew Larry could hear every word. She was jealous that Larry had been hired at the salary level she had worked years to attain. Larry had a choice. He could confront Debbie in an accusatory fashion or he could apologize to her for accidentally offending her. Larry chose the humble way, and they became good friends after Debbie realized Larry was not after the promotion she was seeking. Larry had nothing to apologize for, but "a soft answer turns away wrath". He chose wisely not to take offense and enter into the unforgiveness, blame game of that competitive, corporate structure.

When you have practiced changing your speaking and thinking to be positive, it will become clear that certain areas are a struggle for you personally. Most of the time, an incident or multiple incidents in your past have formed a stronghold in your thinking. These past memories often involved emotional pain that has not been properly dealt with. In order to break that stronghold, forgiveness toward the one who caused the pain is necessary, and any internalized vows need to be renounced.

While growing up, Larry was repeatedly slapped on the back of his head by his father; he was told he could never do anything right. He made a vow that he would prove his father wrong. The pain of these incidents caused Larry to bury the memories. He was left only with the overwhelming feeling that no matter how hard he tried he would never succeed. He strived and strived but the stronghold of fear that he could not succeed kept him in a cycle of failure. As Larry attempted to confess the positive in regard to his success, he realized that each confession was accompanied by negative self-talk that he was bound to fail. At this point, the spiritual or intuitive side needed to reveal the hidden truth in the past that would set him free. Larry sought the answer earnestly. By pondering, meditating, or praying we can open up our minds to receive what is in our spirits. When attending a family dinner, Larry's father, in a frustrated but teasing way, slapped his new son-in-law on the back of the head because he was displeased with him. Larry nearly became sick to his stomach as he observed this incident because a flood of memories came up from his spirit to his conscious mind. Larry dealt with those memories, had a heart to heart chat with his father about these incidents, and forgave his father. Larry recognized that he had unconsciously made a vow to prove his father wrong. He then renounced that vow and formed a new goal to become successful, for healthy and positive reasons.

Many people are convinced that they are unable to forgive. Here we are not talking about whether the one who has inflicted pain is worthy of forgiveness or trust. Most often it is unwise to trust or form a close relationship with someone who hurt us. Instead we are referring to consciously making a choice to forgive to free ourselves from the bitterness of the hurt emotions that remain because of unforgiveness. We can make a choice to forgive that person, and because we have forgiven, we can refuse to entertain bitter thoughts or bitter feelings from the past. Through the process we free ourselves of pain and negative energy expended toward keeping us in an unwanted reality. Often close relatives are the guilty parties, so we should desire to mend the fences in order to have the best possible relationship with these people. However, trust is earned by a consistent track record. Do not lightly give your trust to those who have not proven their trustworthiness. Trusting is not required to prove that you have forgiven, and forgetting is not necessary to forgive. The goal is to free our emotional energy from the bitter memories of past wrongs or perceived wrongs.

Larry and Diana had another opportunity to become trapped in the unforgiveness cycle when they added a sunroom onto their home. They hired Alex, a friend from church. He estimated the job at approximately one-third the final cost. He failed to supervise one of his workers who used the expensive tongue in groove boards bought for the wood finish ceiling for the rooftop. They replaced the boards at their own expense. Alex claimed to need extra money to pay his workers during the final week, but then the workers complained that they had never been paid. Alex confessed that his brother had stolen the money, and he didn't have any left to pay his workers. Though they didn't have to do so, they chose to give him the extra money. Larry and Diana learned several valuable lessons about having estimates in writing and hiring friends to save money. They chose not to harbor unforgiveness over the incidents and remained friends with Alex.

As Drew was growing up, his mother displayed a split personality. Drew's mom was a hypocritical and judgmental, religious woman. She spoke of the virtues of love, but she displayed anger and vindictiveness. Drew blamed his mother when his father committed suicide. Drew blamed God for the hurt and painful memories; therefore, Drew chose to believe in fate instead of God. His mother's God was someone he didn't want to know. He never considered that God might be a different entity than the God of his mother, a God he could love and trust. When people blame God or the cosmos, they become trapped in a cycle of hopelessness, doubt, and unbelief. They can't exercise faith or take any control over their lives because they have chosen unbelief. Unbelief is not non-belief; instead it is a belief that God or the cosmos is against them and they will fail regardless of what they do.

Diana had a miscarriage. It was very devastating for her. She wanted to blame God, since she couldn't find anyone else to blame. Instead, Diana pondered, meditated, and prayed.

She sought the truth as to why this event took place. The answer was intuitively revealed to her. Unknowingly, Diana had spoken that she did not produce enough of a particular hormone to show up pregnant on an early pregnancy test. Diana was tested after becoming pregnant with their first child and told that she was not pregnant when she actually was pregnant. Though she was relating an interesting story, which seemed innocent, to her friends, the words produced enough negative energy to become a problem for her current pregnancy. Without producing enough of that hormone, the pregnancy could not be maintained. Knowing the truth was liberating for Diana. As she came to know that she could speak positive words over her next pregnancy, she didn't need to fear losing another baby. Diana had two more children after this miscarriage.

Guilt, unforgiveness, unbelief, and hurt can be removed from your life by identifying them and choosing to deal with these resistors. The deeper the wound that brought on these reactions, the more difficult the process to heal that wound and remove the resistors. By a choice of our will, we can refuse to allow new resistors into our lives in the future. Ask yourself if blocking your energy flow is worth indulging in one of these resistors. Pass up every opportunity to be offended and make it a habit to forgive quickly. You will experience a freedom from the burden of these resistors, and your life will become happier because of that freedom.

Other less enduring resistors include lack of self-control, laziness, and bad attitudes stemming from discouragement. For most people these are momentary resistors, but for other people they are ingrained habits that permanently hold them back.

Bob lacked self-control. He hated to be told what to do, and he hated to think that anyone had the right to tell him what to do. He reasoned that everyone had to put his or her pants on the same way that he did in the morning, so no one was better than him. Bob was pulled over by a police officer. He argued with the policeman that coasting down the hill had caused him to go over the speed limit. He let his mouth run with disrespect. He told the policeman that he should be out protecting people instead of hassling them. He talked himself right into a ticket and nearly into being arrested. Bob even bragged about the incident because he felt that standing up to the police was proof of his manliness.

Amazingly, Bob's oldest son, Eddie, had observed how his father's lack of self-control had often resulted in trouble, so his son chose to exercise a high level of self-control. Eddie had a live-in job as a hired hand on a farm. The farmer's wife didn't like him and convinced her husband to fire him. Eddie came back from working in the fields to find all his stuff lying in the dirt. While the farmer cursed him, Eddie loaded his stuff into his truck. At one point the farmer pushed him, but Eddie just said, "Grow up", and resumed collecting his things. Eddie proved that he was better than his father by choosing to live a lifestyle of self-control.

Larry once picked up a hitchhiker named Jack who told him at length about his life. Jack chose laziness as a way of life. He had beachfront property that he shared with his women and their two children. Jack was a beach bum. He paid no taxes, lived off handouts, and thumbed his way around. He seemed quite content to let the rest of the world support him.

Most of us fall into a pattern of laziness from time to time. Larry and Diana had a great bedtime routine with their children. After the children brushed their teeth, they told their children character building stories every night before they covered them with kisses and sent them off to bed. The burdens of life interfered with their routine and bedtime stories went by the way side for a time. Eventually, Larry and Diana recognized the lack in their nightly routine and reinstated the ritual. It is easy to be lazy, but it is not better.

Robert dreamed of owning his own business. He started a small restaurant that served fresh fish. He kept the fish in a large, glass tank. Because start up costs ate up much of his profits, he neglected to insure his business and its assets. His restaurant was vandalized and his fish tank was smashed. When Robert went to open up the next morning he was greeted with a floor full of dead fish. He was so discouraged by the incident that he gave up. He did not replace the tank, the fish, or ever reopen his business. We are often tempted to have bad attitudes when we become discouraged. Left unchecked we may even quit trying because we lose hope.

Larry and Diana have been involved in a trademark case for six years. Another company has been using their trademark, and they were determined to see justice done. Many times they have felt discouraged and desired to quit, but they know better than to give in to discouragement. If you quit, you fail. Resist negative attitudes especially when you are discouraged. Choose to be courageous. Treat yourself to a "pick me up", like a movie or day off, but keep your attitudes positive. Resist the resistors, and you will have more, positive energy flow through your life.

*"Two things are infinite:
the universe and human stupidity;
and I'm not sure about
the universe."*

Albert Einstein

Chapter 8

LESSONS ON HOW THE SOUL PROSPERS

The Impact Of Self-Esteem On Your Reality

Self-esteem is the primary mindset that governs your life. Self-esteem is how you esteem or evaluate yourself. Self-esteem has two major components—your estimation of your capabilities and your assessment of your worthiness to receive happiness. Since self-esteem is based upon your judgment of your capabilities and your worthiness, your actual abilities and worth may be totally different from your opinion of the two. An arrogant, narcissistic individual will have an inflated self-esteem; an individual who has contempt for himself will have a diminished self-esteem. A balanced, ideal self-esteem includes high self-confidence, high self-worth, but a reasonable assessment of one's competences.

Many people mistakenly believe that the self-esteem you acquire in your childhood is the self-esteem you have for life. However, most people constantly re-evaluate themselves so their self-esteem fluctuates with their circumstances and their reaction to their circumstances. In times of loss, sickness, or failure, most people's self-esteem plummets, and in times of victory their self-esteem will momentarily soar. Allowing circumstances to dictate your self-esteem is unadvisable. You'll be tossed about with the ebbs and flows of life, and this painful roller coaster is unnecessary. Your self-esteem should not be an ever-changing thing, nor should your self-esteem be fixated on your childhood or past.

Your image of yourself has a tremendous impact on your reality. If you reject yourself, you will not be able to believe that you are worthy of happiness, acceptance, and love. If you judge yourself beneath your capabilities, you will not be able to rise above that faulty visage. Even with an accurate self-appraisal, we need to be careful not to limit our future potential by our present capabilities. Thomas Edison said, "If we did all the things we are capable of, we would literally astound ourselves." We must choose to believe we are worthy of great happiness, and we must choose to believe we are capable of producing any desired result in our lives. If we maintain these convictions regardless of circumstances, we will not limit ourselves to a lower life.

While growing up, Diana had damaged her self-esteem. Many things were spoken over her that she received as a young girl. In kindergarten Diana was given glasses with "Coke bottle bottom" thickness. Her teacher remarked, "It's such a shame that she has to wear those ugly things; she might have been pretty without them." Diana was constantly looking for affirmation from those around her. She strongly desired her parents' acceptance and love. She always had to be teacher's pet. In fact, her mother claimed she would do anything for a gold star. Education and grades seemed very important to her parents, so Diana strived until she succeeded in getting all "A's". The first time she brought home a perfect report card, she expected that she would be wrapped up in her father's arms and told what a good girl she was and how very proud he was of her. Unfortunately, Diana's father took one look at the hard earned grades, tossed the report card aside, and said, "Of course, you're my daughter. That's exactly what I've been expecting all the time." Diana was devastated that even perfection did not gain her the love and admiration that she so desired.

Because of Diana's father's health and her mother's unwillingness to do things without him, Diana's family lived like hermits. The family dynamics were dysfunctional. Diana's mother refused to be the taxicab for her two children. Other than going to school, Diana had few outside activities. She never joined girl scouts or belonged to groups outside of school. Once she was allowed to walk to a neighbor's house and take a few piano lessons. To her first enthusiastic attempts her dad's response was degrading. He said, "You have no rhythm, but maybe with a lot of practice you might sound okay." Similarly, her father and her brother made fun of her physical activity. "You suck at ping-pong. I don't want to play with you; you're no challenge at all," her brother said even though he was five years older. "It's amazing you don't trip over yourself, you look so awkward when you run", her father remarked. Diana's mother was too busy cooking, doing laundry, or puttering in her garden. To Diana it seemed that her mother rarely noticed she existed. Nothing she did seemed good enough for praise.

As children we often allow those around us to determine our self-worth and we accept their evaluation of our capabilities. When children do not grow up in a nurturing and supportive family, their self-esteem is usually poor. As adults we need to overcome this mentality. We should not allow what others think of us to determine how we think of ourselves. When people reject us and put us down, it can hurt, but if we internalize their opinions, we hurt ourselves even more. Never allow the cutting comments of others to affect your self-esteem. You can choose to accept or reject their assessment. If they have valid points, you can choose to change. Maintain control over your own self-esteem.

If you expend today's energies on yesterday's mistakes or past emotional aches and pains, you are robbing yourself of a happy future. Take your mental eyes off the past and focus on the future you desire. Failures in your past reinforce internal beliefs that you can't do what you desire today. The sting of parental criticism and broken promises of loved ones can leave you bruised and beaten on the inside. Time will not heal these wounds. In fact, over time most people relive these experiences over and over reinforcing the past failures, disappointments, and emotional distress. The wounds fester and become infected with unforgiveness, bitterness, resentment, and self-loathing. If you are beating yourself up about something in your distant past, rejoice that there is no new material your mind can conjure up and move on.

If you are having problems with your past, make a list of your past successes. Include not only the meaningful accomplishments but every small success too. Not everyone learns to ride a bike, graduates from high school, or overcomes the adversity that you have. Take the time to review your list and recreate the joy and satisfaction you experienced the first time. You have been doing this on the negative side for a long time. Next time, the negative past comes to your mind, choose to rehearse one of your positive, past experiences instead.

Once you have put the past behind you, you will need to form a positive and healthy self-esteem for your present. Most of us have an impossible, perfect image that we hold up as a standard for our achievements. We continually fall short of our demanding, perfectionist standards; therefore, we view ourselves as failures. We'll call this perfect image the *"should"* model. It comes from all the *"shoulds"* we impose on our lives. This is how I *"should"* act, this is how I *should* feel, and this is how I *should* be. All day long we evaluate ourselves with self-talk, "I *should* never raise my voice to my children", "I *should* be more attentive to my spouse", and "I *should* always be prepared for the weekly staff meeting at work, so I can impress the boss".

The problem is having so many goals that even Superman couldn't achieve them all. Many times being the best in one area makes it impossible to be the best in another area. For instance, the man who wants to be the best possible provider for his family may find he doesn't have the time to be the best possible husband and father. Defining what are your most important goals and knowing what you're willing to give to achieve them are necessary steps to maintaining a healthy self-esteem. The authors invite you to set high standards for yourself, but to keep them in perspective to your goals. Then you can make choices to eliminate the unnecessary for the vital.

Ryan is an example of a man who didn't know how to balance the drive for professional achievement with his desires to be a great father and husband. His career was extremely demanding. Ryan was a successful litigator. He spent long hours preparing and litigating his cases. He felt a genuine responsibility to his clients. He even took cases for drastically reduced fees because he believed in giving to humanity. Ryan had a soft heart and an admirable moral code. Unfortunately, he found that the urgent needs of his clients consumed all of his time. He found it hard to say no, and he paid the price on the home front.

No matter how intense his case preparations, Ryan was faithful to call his two girls nightly before they were put to bed. His wife enjoyed the luxuries of his profitable career, but it was not enough. Her complaining turned to fighting, which turned to resignation and contempt. Ryan loved his family. He was convinced that he was doing the best that he could to provide for his family, and he didn't see any options available to him to solve this problem. He would try to set aside a day here and there to devote his time to his family, but some emergency always arose to draw him back to the office or to cancel his commitments at home. Without a significant change, Ryan could lose, through divorce, his family, which he honestly values more than his career. He just doesn't know how to satisfy the needs of both.

Underlying his situation is a self-esteem problem. Ryan is underestimating his capabilities to balance both career and family and assessing himself as unworthy of the love of his family. These buried beliefs are closing his mind to the solutions available to him. If Ryan set aside time for his family with the same determination that he gives to meeting a court appointed deadline, he could enjoy a relationship with his wife and two girls. He might not be good at saying "no" or at scheduling, but a secretary can just as easily juggle in family time at a specified minimum amount as she does court dates. Ryan can use his secretary as a buffer between his clients and himself so that she can say "no" for him for the sake of his family. This way he preserves the vital not just the urgent.

Larry had a similar problem when he and Diana started their fastener company. So much was required to get the company off the ground, and the resources were not available to hire out the work. Larry became a workaholic. Diana would say, "Dinner will be ready in half an hour." Larry would respond that he would wrap things up. Diana would call "Dinner's on", and Larry would answer that he would be there in a few minutes. Hours would pass and Larry would not show up for dinner. Often Diana would prepare the meal, feed their two babies, clean up, and perform the entire nightly routine to bathe, change, and tuck the little ones into bed before Larry would arrive.

What bothered Diana the most was that Larry was not following through with what he said. So Diana confronted Larry with her specific expectations: if you're not joining the family for dinner, explain why; have the courtesy to be honest; don't try to pacify with words that you have no intention of following with action. Larry was so wrapped up in his work that he didn't take the time to focus on Diana's interruptions and evaluate his true response. Since Larry valued his wife more than his work, he decided to make a conscious effort to focus his attention on her when she would interrupt his work. It was difficult to change gears, but the reward was great. Larry took the time to evaluate her requests and to answer as honestly as possible. Good communication kept their marriage together during that demanding time at the start up of their company.

If Larry had chosen to continue pushing off his wife to do the urgent, his actions could have undermined his self-esteem as well as his wife's self-esteem. When you don't do what you say you will do, when you say you will do it, you are disrespecting the one who you gave your word to and you devalue your own ability to respect yourself. There are times when you can't keep your word, but you can still keep a clean conscience by apologizing or explaining. Showing respect to yourself and to others, particularly by keeping your word, is important to maintaining a healthy self-esteem.

Another important component to maintaining a healthy self-esteem is safeguarding your self-talk. Start by uncovering and analyzing the self-statements that you habitually make. Eradicate the negative self-talk, and create new, positive self-statements that foster a healthy self-esteem. Use affirmations to boost your self-esteem. Whenever you say an affirmation, allow yourself to experience positive feelings about your affirmative self-statements. "I believe in myself", "I am loved", and "I look good and I feel good about myself" are examples of positive affirmations.

Visualize living your dream life. What choices do you need to make today to live your dream tomorrow? Set higher standards in your priority areas and give yourself some slack in secondary arenas. You can be the best, but no human being has ever achieved being the best at everything. Your positive affirmations should focus on your goals. If one of your top goals is to feel better about your body, say, "I am the ideal weight", "I am healthy and strong", or "I like the way I look". Goal oriented self-talk is better than passive self-talk. An example of passive self-talk is "I accept myself exactly the way I am". This statement is obviously a step up from self-rejection, but it is not proactive toward change. Being proactive/goal-oriented is the difference between a "positive affirmation" and a "future confession". The authors recommend a "future confession" based on your ideal, in present tense with a reinforcing, positive emotion.

Also, choose to associate with positive and supportive people. Being accepted and encouraged will provide a positive environment to raise your self-esteem. Drop from your life as many negative people, who constantly put you or your ideas down, as you can. Concerning those negative people you can't get rid of, like your mother-in-law or your boss, learn how to banish their unwarranted criticism immediately and how to look objectively at criticism that may have some merit. Find support groups for your specific goals. If you're not receiving enough hugs, volunteer someplace where you can hug others or splurge on regular back rubs. Establish groups, places, or friends in your life that build you up. Don't expend negative energy on self-criticism.

Carol was a widow and lonely. She looked for support groups and found that the singles groups were filled with people either too old or too young to make good friends. She was a retired teacher who had a lot of time on her hands. She swam at the gym regularly, walked her dog daily, and attended church. But she wasn't finding people to spend time with on a quality, one to one, basis. Being proactive, she started her own support group for widows and single women like herself. She convinced her church to print her monthly activities and meetings in the weekly bulletin. Within a short time, she found a friend who was willing to help in the planning and to share the responsibilities for organizing the group. Now her group is several years old and enjoys a full membership. Carol has people to talk to, and to do things with, and she feels good that she is able to contribute to the lives of the other women in her support group. Like Carol, you can be proactive and create your own support network if one does not exist to meet your needs in your area.

If you have a healthy self-esteem, it will show up in the

way you take care of yourself and the way you take care of your responsibilities. Be clean. Groom your body, organize your space, and keep your conscience clean. Be responsible for your actions and choices. Do what you say you will do, keep your word, be on time, and be reliable. Give yourself the respect and courtesy you would give your favorite person on the planet. Excuse your imperfections and failures quickly. Always have the attitude that you'll do better the next time.

On the road to recovery from childhood-induced, poor self-esteem, Diana was involved in support groups, changing her self-talk, dealing with past hurts, and learning to respect herself and others. She was making progress, but she was still in a delicate state of mind. She was attending college and making good grades while living at home with her parents. It was at this pivotal juncture in her life when her parent's marriage reached its pinnacle of difficulty. After years of neglect, Diana's mother had found comfort in the company of another man. Her mother had reasoned that she could not desert a dying man, but she needed something more for her own needs to be met. Unfortunately, Graham became aware of her frequent absences and discovered the truth. Graham threatened to follow his wife and kill both her and her lover. Diana's parents were not talking to each other; instead, they talked to Diana and used her like a ping-pong ball to relay information to one another.

Being naïve, Diana allowed herself to be used in this manner. The result was a plummeting of her self-esteem. She felt like neither of her parents could truly love her and still use her in this manner. Diana relayed Graham's threats to her mother to protect her, and her mother eventually ended the affair. Though years later Diana's mother asked forgiveness from Diana for her thoughtless behavior, Diana's father never did. Diana felt trapped in the position of warning her mother and playing the go between, or refusing to play the go-between and risking Graham killing her mother. If Diana had been wiser and stronger in this situation, she could have found a friend to live with, to put distance between her and her parent's struggle, and she could have ended the go-between scenario by involving the police or communicating with each of her parents that she would not be their mouthpiece.

Many times in life we feel we have no choice, so we do the thing we feel forced to do. This is the time to seek council and find out all your options. Because of our intense emotional involvement and fear, we close our minds to solutions that are readily available. Learn to think that there is always another way. Seek council or meditate to open your mind to your options. Think outside the box and remember that even people in respected positions may be close-minded. The best council will come from your spirit if you will diligently seek it.

Only you have the power and authority to change your self-esteem. You control your response. A healthy, positive self-esteem and a healthy, positive response to the circumstances of your life will actually change the equilibrium of your energy to be more positive; and you will attract positive people and positive circumstances in your new life.

*"I never think of the future.
It comes soon enough."*

Albert Einstein

Chapter 9

MATERIAL AND RELATIONAL SUCCESS

Time Matters

Some interesting facts about sound, light, and subatomic particles relate to time. Sounds are produced by the vibration of molecules in a material. The vibrations of the person's vocal cords produce the sound of a person's voice. These vibrations cause vibrations in the molecules in the air. The vibrations of sound travel in waves made up of kinetic energy. This kinetic energy is transferred from molecule to molecule in matter as it moves farther away from the source of the original sound. The kinetic, sound energy is lost to thermal energy as it travels through matter so that the sound diminishes until it can no longer be heard. The frequency of the sound wave determines the pitch, and loudness is the perception of the amplitude of the wave. The louder the sound, the more energy the sound wave has and the further it will travel.

Light is believed to travel in electromagnetic waves—waves of oscillating electric and magnetic fields. It is a fact that all objects emit an aura or glow of light. All objects glow regardless of temperature. The difference is that hot objects like charcoal briquettes glow with visible light and objects at ordinary temperatures glow predominantly with infrared light, which cannot be seen. Einstein believed that light was made up of particles called "photons". When light hits a metal surface, electrons can be ejected from the surface. This process is called the "photoelectric effect". Light behaves as a wave or as a particle depending on what we do with it and what we try to observe. This wave-particle duality and quantum theory currently mystify scientists. The determination of reality concerning the way electrons behave is purported to be via the act of observation. Particles produce effects by somehow "sensing" the presence of a field. This process is called the Ahranhov-Bohm effect.

In the case of photons, particles retain their original speed and kinetic energy. The kinetic energy, light wave does not diminish like the kinetic energy, sound wave. Sound waves cannot travel through a vacuum, but light waves can. Since the photon retains the same phase across its whole existence, it is as if the photon experiences no time when it moves from its start to its end. The Bogatz' theory is that light and subatomic particles are not subject to time. Light exists in both the seen and unseen realms. Light is made up of subatomic particles. The Bogatz' theory agrees with Einstein's conjecture that a substratum exists that is not subject to time. Also, according to the Biblical representation, God is Light and exists everywhere and has always existed and will always exist, not subject to time.

All matter is made up of atoms, which in turn are made up of subatomic particles. Matter shares a common fundamental makeup. This fact implies that all things are interconnected in some way. As scientists have studied the atom, they have discovered that electrons, like light, exhibit the phenomenon of wave/particle duality. The electrons appear as a cloud around the nucleus of the atom. It is believed that the electrons travel in a wave pattern with a fixed radius around the nucleus. What is so very fascinating is that when observed by a scientist, the electrons appear as a particle rather than a cloud. Many scientists believe that electrons are somehow "aware" or "sense" that the scientist is observing it. So, in layman's terms, looking at an atom affects its appearance. Is it too far fetched to believe that our imagination, thoughts, words, and actions can combine to create a powerful force that can change matter, when a mere look affects its appearance on the subatomic level?

Though time is not considered one of the elements that make up our perceived reality, time does matter. Time is a factor that influences our reality. Time can provide the framework for our goals or time can be the poison of discouragement that causes us to give up on our goals. When choosing our words, our thoughts, or the direction that our imagination takes us, we need to define the time as being now. If we think, "Someday I will be rich", we do not create the energy that will result in the change. "Someday" reduces the level of energy to that of hoping and wishing. We must imagine in the present, speak as if it is, and think as if it's done. Wisely the writer of Hebrews said, "Now, faith is".

Time is considered to be one of the world's most profound mysteries. In his special theory of relativity Einstein proved that time was not a physical constant. Einstein showed that time was affected by both motion and gravity. In one experiment Einstein utilized two high-speed aircraft and three atomic clocks. One atomic clock remained at the place of origin, and one atomic clock was placed inside each aircraft. One aircraft flew east and the other aircraft flew west. The aircraft that flew east lost time, but the aircraft that flew west, opposite the earth's direction of rotation, gained time in relation to the stationary clock. What Einstein was able to prove by this experiment was that speed, altitude, and gravity all affected how much time was lost or gained. Most have taken for granted that time exists, but no one can truly tell you what time is. The Russian mathematician, Hermann Minkowski, called it the fourth dimension. The space-time continuum is comprised of space—measured in length, width, and height—and time—measured in "units of time".

Although time is a mystery, imagine the chaos there would

be on the earth without some standard measure of time. Without a uniform structure through which an event could be planned, it would be virtually impossible to coordinate anything with another individual. People would see changes taking place around them in nature and know that there was something different from one point to the next without having a way to gauge or understand why those changes were taking place. The physical world is continuously changing. Every day you can see the ocean tide recede, and then, later in the day, you can see the ocean tide return. There are many recurring events in nature that allude to the passing of time.

The primary indication of the passing of time is the relationship between the earth and the sun. The first recorded information about time measurement is in the scriptures. Genesis 1:3-5 says, "Then God said, 'let there be light'; and there was light. And God saw the light, that it was good; and God divided the light from the darkness. God called the light, day, and the darkness He called night. So the evening and the morning were the first day." Then Genesis 1:14-18 says, "Then God said, let there be lights in the firmament of the heavens to divide the day from the night; and let them do for signs and seasons, and for days and years; and let them do for lights in the firmament of the heavens to give light on the earth; and it was so. Then God made two great lights: the greater light to rule the day, and the lesser light to rule the night. He made the stars also." Obviously the greater light referred to is the sun and the lesser light referred to is the moon.

Time was originally measured by observing the moving patterns and changes of stars, planets, and other objects in the sky. For example it was observed that the moon has a cycle of change. The moon appears to take on many different shapes before it starts the pattern all over again. It takes twenty-nine and one half days for the moon to complete one cycle. The cycle of the moon became known as one month. It was also observed that the sun had a cycle of change. The sun appears to travel in a circular pattern in the sky. It takes the sun three hundred sixty-five and one quarter days to complete a full circle or one cycle. This cycle of the sun became known as one solar year.

The observance of the sun and moon stimulated the creation of the first calendar. The ancient Babylonians created one of the first calendar systems based on the solar year. It was called the lunar calendar. Then in 45 B.C., Julius Caesar created a new calendar system that he called the "Julian" calendar. This calendar was also based upon the solar year. Julius Caesar wanted to have smaller chunks of time than one cycle of the moon, but there was nothing in the solar system that indicated such a timeframe. Julius Caesar knew about the Jewish custom called the Sabbath where the Jewish people rested every seventh day, and he decided to apply to his calendar that seven-day time frame which became known as one "week". One year after the Julian calendar was created Julius Caesar believed that at least one month should be named after him, so he renamed one of the original months to Julius or July. Then when Augustus became the new Caesar, he believed he should have a month also so he renamed to August the month immediately following Julius's month. However, his month was shorter than Julius's month. Augustus Caesar couldn't stand having a month that was shorter than Julius's month, so he robbed a day from February to compensate for the shortfall. The Julian calendar was the calendar of choice until the late fifteen hundreds when Pope Gregory the thirteenth decided to modify the Julian calendar. Pope Gregory was not pleased that the Julian solar calendar didn't correspond with religious holidays; some years these holiday festivities were met with inclement weather. Pope Gregory found that by adding one day to February every four years he would be able to keep the calendar year based upon seasons, instead of the cycles of the sun and moon; thereby, the calendar would maintain some level of weather consistency for the religious holidays. This extra day added to February became known as the leap year, and this new calendar became known as the Gregorian calendar—named after Pope Gregory, of course. Although there are a number of different calendars available, each having a different perspective with regard to days, weeks, months, and seasons, the four primary calendars are the Jewish, Muslim, Julian, and Gregorian calendars. The Gregorian calendar is the most popular calendar today and will remain the standard until someone in a position of authority over such matters decides it should change again.

Over the years many methods have been used to measure time. The first recorded time measurement device was the sundial. No one knows the exact date of the first sundial, but it is believed that the ancient Egyptians had portable sundials as early as 1500 B.C. At that time only the wealthy could afford a sundial. The scriptures refer to the sundial in Isaiah 38:8, "Behold, I will bring the shadow on the sundial, which has gone down with the sun on the sundial of Ahab, ten degrees backward." This statement shows the unreliability of the sundial, indicating that the sundial requires direct sunlight to work properly.

Other ancient methods of time measurement included: 1) the water clock that would drip water from one container to another, 2) the hourglass that allowed sand to pour through a narrow opening that supposedly measured one-hour, 3) a rope with knots spaced at even intervals that, when on fire, supposedly took one hour to burn from one knot to the next, and 4) the Chinese candle that was marked at one hour intervals. When the Chinese candle was combined with a nail, it doubled as the first known alarm clock. As the candle burned to the bottom, the nail would fall into a pan beneath it and make a loud noise waking up its owner.

The first mechanical clocks were not created until the fourteenth century. These clocks were extremely large and were mounted in towers that were designed to support them. "Bell" was the original term for clock. The name referred to the bell that would sound once every hour. These clocks were not very accurate and they only had an hour hand, this would explain why many people referred to them as the "hour teller". The first, portable, mechanical timepieces were designed by a locksmith named Peter Henlein in the early fifteen hundreds and like the large, tower clocks these timepieces only contained an hour hand. Portable mechanical timepieces did not contain a minute or second hand until the late seventeen hundreds. The general populace wasn't concerned about time until the building of the railroad. Most people didn't even own a timepiece because they were expensive and time was of little consequence to them. If they were challenged to a showdown, they scheduled it at high noon because everyone knew when that was, and high noon just happened to be the optimal position of the sun for that type of endeavor.

The railroad found it extremely difficult to develop any kind of schedule. Because in the mid-1800's every town set its clocks based upon local solar time, and there were more than a hundred different, local times on the railroad route. There was constant confusion as to when the trains would arrive or depart from the station because of all these time zones. The railroads recognized that there needed to be a standard schedule; but in order to have a standard schedule there had to be a standard time. So in 1883 the railroad decided to divide the United States into four, standard time zones. They called these time zones Eastern Standard Time, Central Standard Time, Mountain Standard Time, and Pacific Mountain Time. The United States Congress approved these time zones and made them part of federal law.

Just like the United States Congress, the rest of the world liked the idea of time zones. Hence, the very next year an international conference divided the world into twenty-four time zones. The starting point for the new time zones was the Royal Greenwich Observatory in Greenwich, England. The ending point for the new time zones was on the opposite side of the world at an imaginary point called the International

Date Line. When an individual would cross the International Date Line they would either gain one day or lose one day depending on which direction they were traveling.

In 1966 the United States Congress decided to divide the United States into eight time zones instead of the original four created by the railroads. The current United States standard Time zones consist of the Atlantic, Eastern, Central, Mountain, Pacific, Alaska, Hawaii—Aleutian, and Samoa time zones. Benjamin Franklin was the first to suggest a daylight savings time; however, it wasn't until the creation of the eight time zones that the United States government enacted daylight savings time as a standard procedure.

With the increased focus on time and the time zones instituted by the railroads came an increase in the demand for accurate and portable timepieces. As new timepieces were being created, the manufacturers found new ways to increase the accuracy of the timepieces. In 1889 clocks were considered accurate to one-hundredth of a second; today the cesium atomic clock is accurate to within, plus or minus, one second every million years. In addition, a new phenomenon known as "time pressure" came with the increased focus on time that prior to that point did not exist.

Today many people have their schedules honed down to the nanosecond, and they can't even laugh unless they have a time allotted for it. Unfortunately, without realizing it, these people have become slaves to time. They have a time to get up, a time to get ready, a time to go to work, a time for meetings, a time to pick up the children, a time to go home, a time for dinner, and then a time to go to sleep, so they can get up and start the process all over again. Although a heavy schedule can be stressful, some people find comfort knowing what they are going to do every second of the day. The drawback for these people is that they don't have time for the unexpected, which undoubtedly will come.

How have people progressed to the point that they place so great an importance upon time, and where did they develop their concept of time? Prior to the perception of time people would wake up to the crowing of a rooster. They would work until it was too hot then they would eat and rest to regain their strength. They would go back to work in the afternoon when it was cooler and they would work until dark. They knew the difference of seasons by the migration of birds and environmental changes such as the growing of wildflowers, or the falling of leaves. Their entire schedules corresponded with the rising and setting of the sun.

The concept of time in its present form is an illusion created in the minds of men. It requires years of training to bring an individual to the point that he can be controlled by time. As a child grows his perception of time becomes primarily based upon a schedule of events, such as breakfast, lunch, dinner, playtime, and bedtime. As a child grows older his perception of the schedule becomes associated with a day.

What parent hasn't made the mistake of telling their child that they were planning a special event in the future, thinking it would give the child something to look forward to, only to discover that the child had no concept of time. The event they had planned may have been two months in the future, but every day, like clockwork, the child asks them again if it's time for the event yet. The parent responds to the child saying, "No, its two months away", then the child asks the parent if that means tomorrow? Because even though they have an idea of what a day is, they have no concept of weeks, months, or years. By the age of ten most children have a fine-tuned concept of time. They can parrot back to you exactly what they have been told with regard to time. However, because time is not a physical constant, there is no intuitive understanding of time; instead what you will hear is what the child has learned through memorization.

Even though people have become so accustomed to the perception of time, most people have experienced periods of freedom from time at some point in their lives. For example, an individual on vacation may lose track of what the current day of the week is because their focus is to just have fun. Their only concern about time is to make it to the next, scheduled, fun activity.

Time is relative. When a person is bored, time goes by very slowly. When a person is participating in something they find exciting to them, the entire day goes by in a flash. Everyone has experienced this phenomenon and there's even a famous cliché that describes it: "Time flies when you're having fun." Two months to an adult could seem like a blink, but that same time frame to a ten-year-old could seem like an eternity. Einstein described this phenomenon another way, "When you sit with a nice girl for two hours, it seems like two minutes. When you sit on a hot stove for two minutes, it seems like two hours. That's relativity."

Many people have talked about the appearance of time slowing down during a traumatic event such as a car accident. From the time of the initial impact, the participant perceives the accident as if everything is traveling in slow motion and that they have plenty of time to take responsive action. However, if you were to ask someone who witnessed the accident without being directly involved they would tell you that to them the vehicles appeared to be traveling at a normal rate of speed.

Most people have heard someone speak the phrase, "My whole life flashed before my eyes"; and it is usually associated with a traumatic experience in a person's life. Experiences that took an entire lifetime to accumulate are in-an-instant relived in their mind. This time distortion is possible because the body is subject to time, but the mind is not. People are capable of seeing events from the past, present, and future because the mind is timeless. Most people train their minds to focus only on what they physically see with their eyes, that is what is in the visual present. However, the mind can also be trained to receive input from the past and the future with astounding clarity, but before one can receive input from these different avenues of perception, they must first believe that it is possible.

In 1982 a research team at the University of Paris led by physicist Alain Aspect discovered that subatomic particles are able to communicate instantaneously with each other regardless of the distance between the particles. Einstein believed that no communication could travel faster than the speed of light. However, if Aspect's research is correct, it would contradict Einstein's theory with regard to communication at the speed of light. In order for communication to travel faster than the speed of light, both the time barrier and the light barrier would have to be superseded. If Aspect's research is correct, this is further evidence of the Bogatz' theory that subatomic particles travel at the speed of light or greater and are not subject to time.

Physicist David Bohm from the University of London believes that Aspect's research is proof that objective reality does not exist, and any apparent separation of objects is an illusion. True reality to Bohm is a holographic world where all objects are interconnected, each object containing all the elements of the whole as it has been observed through the study of holographic images.

Bohm believes that subatomic particles are contained within a super hologram, which is the core, or matrix, from which reality is formed. In this underlining matrix the past, present, and future all exist simultaneously. To have a universe that is all interconnected as parts of one, enormous hologram is to say that time and three-dimensional space is nothing more than an elaborate, perceptual illusion.

Whether time is an illusion or not is somewhat inconsequential since at least in the United States time is a vital part of the fabric of our perceived reality. For most people the situations that cause the greatest level of stress in their lives are those situations that involve both deadlines and poker chips, or if you prefer time and money. Have you noticed that people use the terms "time" and "money" as almost synonymous terms? In many ways time and money are the same. When you have money you can buy time by hiring others to perform tasks that you don't want to do, giving you more time for the tasks that you desire. Of course, everyone knows it also goes the other way because most people trade their time for monetary compensation.

One of the largest sources of time pressure is related to money, more specifically bills. Mortgages, car payments, credit card payments, life insurance policies, loans and lines of credit all specify time frames for payment. Most people have borrowed money from a friend or relative at some point in their lives, and have experienced firsthand the pressure that can be applied by an individual who wants their money back in a specified, time frame. Of course, unless you have borrowed money from a loan shark, most professional institutions do not apply the same level of pressure; but you can still sense the presence of the pressure. If you're late making a payment, they slap your hand by charging you a late fee. If you forgot to make your payment before you went on vacation, they might freeze your account until payment is made. Obviously, the greater the amount of your financial obligations, the greater is the level of time pressure associated with those obligations. You can start to reduce the time pressures in your life by focusing your attention on the obligations that create the greatest level of stress and working towards eliminating those obligations. A common method is to eliminate the smallest obligation first. Once the smallest obligation is fulfilled, add the amount of money that was once paid to the smallest obligation to the amount being paid on the second smallest obligation until it is paid. Repeat the process until every obligation is eliminated, or until the level of pressure is reduced to a manageable and acceptable level in your life.

If you're the type of person that can't stand monthly bills, there are ways around them. For example, if you don't like to pay a water bill, then dig your own well. If you don't like to pay an electric bill, then you can do like Clint Eastwood did and install solar panels for your electricity and sell the excess energy back to the utility companies. The options are limitless. It's amazing what can be accomplished with a little creativity.

To some people the greatest source of stress in their lives is the time they spend at work. Many people look for work so they can trade their time for money while instead they should be looking for a situation that matches their personality. It's not difficult to know when the right match has been achieved because time goes by quickly and it doesn't seem like a sacrifice to give up the time. That was not the case for Graham. Graham realized from a young age that mathematics was not a difficult thing for him. However, what really excited him was chemistry. He decided to be a chemistry major in college so that he could pursue his desire. Unfortunately, he was allergic to most chemicals, which discouraged him from pursuing chemistry as a career.

Graham decided to focus on his mathematic ability and chose nuclear engineering as his new profession. Graham was very good at his work, but he found it to be extremely stressful. As the time went on Graham realized that the work he did was starting to affect his health. Graham wanted to start his own bicycle shop because he liked to tinker and believed that it would eliminate the stress in his life. However, when he approached his wife with the idea, she told him of all their financial obligations and how he would never be able to make the level of money needed to support their family if he quit his job. Graham wanted to be a good provider for his family and chose to continue working at the company that was causing his primary source of stress. The stress associated with his working environment turned into a fear of going to work, and then he became afraid of even going out the front door. Graham later had to retire with a medical disability, and then he became afraid that he would lose the money allotted to him for medical retirement if he earned money in a different occupation. It would have been better for Graham to have taken a chance on a bicycle shop than to spend the rest of his life stressed and suffering from a stress-related illness.

No matter what the approach, the goal for everyone should be to reduce the amount of time spent on things they consider to be negative, and spend more time on those things that are positive by eliminating those things that cause you stress, or eat up your time. In most cases the more positive issues are also the most important ones. For managers or business owners the rule of good time management is to delegate those things that can be done by someone else to someone else, so that they can spend more time on the things that are productive, and that create greater cash flow.

In most cases time pressure is self-induced. Because time has been fine-tuned to the nanosecond, people feel like they have to schedule their day in specific, time frames. For example, a common scheduling scenario would be to say, "I will meet you at 8:15 a.m." When the appointment is made they think to themselves, "I will have no problem being on time for that appointment", but they have to put out a fire at the last-minute and that makes them fifteen minutes late for their appointment. On a consistent basis being late for appointments can erode a person's self-esteem and give them a bad track record. One way to reduce time pressure is to pad the appointment time. Instead of setting an appointment for 8:15 a.m., the appointment could be set for sometime between 8:15 a.m. and 8:30 a.m.; that way even though the intention is to be there at 8:15 a.m., if they are a little bit late, they still look good. Manufacturers use this method all the time with their just-in-time programs. Even though the buyer may not like the lead-time upfront, they are always happy when they receive product early.

Another way to reduce time pressure is to set goals without timeframes. One of the biggest, self-esteem destroyers is to consistently not live up to your own expectations for meeting long-term goals. Larry had filed all the trademarks for their company himself, but he had never written a patent. Larry set a twelve-month goal for himself in which, during his off work hours, he would write patents on four of the products for his company. Larry, being an engineer and having designed products, believed that this was an easily attainable goal. It was eighteen months before Larry completed this project. Everyone except Larry was excited that he finished in that time frame. However, for Larry every day past the twelve-month mark was a continuous source of stress due to the time pressure associated with his unmet expectation. If Larry would not have associated a timeframe with his goal, he too would have been pleased with the result. If you must have a timeframe associated with your goal, then at least pad the timeframe to reduce your chances of unnecessary, time pressure. If you're a Star Trek fan, you can take a lesson from Scotty. He never ceased to amaze Captain Kirk because he always padded the time frame required to make the necessary repairs.

Another way to reduce time pressure is to do your best not to focus on time. Larry made a five-year commitment to the government. The first four years seemed to fly by in no time at all; the last year seemed to slow down quite a bit; but the last month seemed to move about as fast as molasses in January. Larry had the clever idea that he would put a countdown calendar on his wall so that he could witness first hand the final days until his commitment was fulfilled. Larry was working in Adak, Alaska. The single runway in Adak accommodated one flight per day. Larry had the privilege of working in the building that overlooked the runway. Every day Larry would imagine himself being on that flight. Needless to say it wasn't a positive reinforcement to his attitude or self-esteem. To focus that closely upon a timeframe is to subject oneself to the unnecessary torment of time pressure.

Like the railroads, corporate America has established their own "time zone", the corporate, standard, work time. This standard work time is from 8 AM to 5 PM and the standard workweek is from Monday to Friday. Most people are able to adjust their body clock to conform to these standard, time frames. However, some people find it very difficult to conform to these timeframes. For some, these timeframes create a consistent stress due to the time pressure associated with getting to work on time. Because these people find it difficult to conform to the standard timeframe, when others apparently have no problem doing so, makes them feel as though they are abnormal, usually pushing their self-esteem into the danger zone. To Diana, this scenario was all-too-familiar.

Diana has always been a night owl. As far back as she can remember she found it difficult to get up early; but in the evening when everyone else was exhausted and all they could think about was sleep, Diana was just getting her second wind. It was great when Diana started college because she was able to choose her class schedule. Of course she chose the classes that accommodated her preferred sleeping cycle. Diana always believed she could adjust her body clock to conform to the standard work time like everyone else. When Diana was getting close to receiving her bachelor's degree in mechanical engineering she was hired by a large aerospace company. Her schedule was flexible because she was only working part-time while she was obtaining her degree. The company that hired her was impressed with Diana's scholastic record. When she had received her bachelor's degree with honors, the company she worked for encouraged her to go on for her master's degree.

Diana admitted to herself that the thought of conforming to the standard, work time was a little scary. Even though she didn't like the idea of pursuing a higher degree, she believed it could only help her career and would give her more time before she would have to conform to the standard, work time. After Diana received her master's degree, that time for conformance came. Up until that point the company she worked for believed that Diana was brilliant. However, Diana's body refused to conform to the standard, corporate, time frame. She was less productive in the mornings and cranky in the afternoons because she got up before her body was ready. She made sure to go to bed at a reasonable hour, but she found it difficult to go to sleep. The cycle became very wearing.

If Diana had continued to work for that company, her self-esteem would have been completely destroyed. Then something wonderful happened, Diana found out that she was pregnant. During Diana's maternity leave Larry convinced Diana that she should find something else to do that could be done on her own schedule. Diana has never returned to the corporate time zone, and she is a much happier person because she has alleviated that time pressure from her life.

The concept of time only applies to those who choose to accept its constraints. As amazing as it seems, some aboriginal and some African tribes still base their day upon the sun, and have never seen, nor even heard of, a watch. France and some other European countries focus on productivity instead of time. The standard is a two-hour lunch and most people can set their own time schedule as long as they complete their projects and continue to be productive in their line of work. Obviously the concept of time in other parts of the world is totally different from that which is common in the United States. Recognize what is causing time pressure in your life and find a way to eliminate it.

"The hardest thing in the world to understand is the income tax."

Albert Einstein

Chapter 10

MATERIAL AND RELATIONAL SUCCESS

Money Is Just An Idea

Many people are stuck in the paycheck-to-paycheck rut. They work to exist and spend most of their lives working at jobs that barely meet their needs. They think if they only had more money, their lives would be great. Unmet desires are the norm instead of the exception. Often they hate their jobs until they lose them, and they blame the system for all their frustration and unmet expectations. Hope may exist in unlikely lottery winnings or inheritances from some tightwad relative. But, the day-to-day routines are unfulfilling, disappointing, and seemingly futile.

Monetary obligations consume the thoughts of those individuals participating in the rat race. In fact, financial pressure is the primary cause for divorce. Most people today have many different kinds of debts always associated with time frames for payment. The most common of these are house loans, car loans, unsecured loans, home equity loans, and revolving credit lines or credit cards. The companies providing you with the privilege of credit are the ones who impose the time frame for payment. If you don't provide payment to the company within the specified time frame they use pressure methods to force you to pay. The most common collection tactics of these companies are stiff penalties, increased interest rates, lowering the credit limit, and notifying credit reporting agencies of the individual's credit history. All of these tactics are forms of pressure to get you to conform to the specified time frame of payment. If you're working from paycheck to paycheck and are having difficulty meeting these financial obligations, here are some ways you can alleviate some of the pressure.

Many times knowing what the company looks for can help you plan your payment strategy. For instance, most credit companies look at two factors: One factor is how many "late pays" you have made, and the other factor is how long you have been making the minimum payment. Both factors indicate to a credit company that you're a higher risk. In most cases a credit company will not raise your interest rate if you have consistently paid on time, or if you have always paid more than the minimum payment even if your payments were not received on time. Paying over the minimum, even by a dollar each time, will buy you favor.

If a company has imposed stiff penalties you can contact the company and ask them to waive the penalties. In most cases the penalties will be waived unless they see that it's a recurring problem. One method of lowering the interest rate is to borrow from one credit company to pay off another credit company. In other words, use credit company A to pay off credit company B, then call credit company B, threaten to cancel the card if they are unwilling to lower your interest rate, and ask what is the best rate they are willing to offer you to keep your business. Credit companies are always more willing to negotiate interest rates and credit limits when your balance has been paid. If all your primary, financial obligations occur at the first of the month, you can alleviate some pressure by contacting the companies that monitor your car or house loan and negotiate a different time of payment. Most credit companies don't care what day of the month they receive payment as long as it is the same time every month.

If you need to get a handle on your bills or have an emergency, like losing your job, most mortgage companies are willing to accept interest only payments for a specified, time frame. This is expensive in the long run but may alleviate some pressure temporarily. Every loan institution would rather receive something instead of nothing. Negotiating amounts and time frames is always possible, but it may be frustrating to try to reach a person, in large and impersonal companies, with enough authority to authorize a special deal. Of course these methods are only short-term fixes. Real progress can only be made by attracting prosperity with the proper mindset and stopping the cycle of buying non-income producing items on credit. To solve the long-term problem you need to collect assets that put more money in your pocket than you have to pay out.

Being part of the "rat race" is the standard for most Americans. Just like rodents or hamsters stuck in a cage, the paycheck-to-paycheck crowd jumps on their exercise wheel and runs with desperation—attempting to go somewhere. Most frantically hasten to work, hustle each day, and scramble to fit some living into their non-work hours. When they're not working for their paycheck, they're spending it on mortgages, utilities, car payments, and food. Precious little is left for pleasure or their future. If this sounds too familiar, be encouraged. There is a way to get off the seemingly, perpetual exercise wheel.

Why do Americans work so hard? Because they want to acquire more poker chips to use in the game of life! However, all it achieves is just another turn on the exercise wheel. This is faulty logic. To understand why this is not correct thinking we need to look at the inception of the monetary system. It all started with the barter system. The barter system is still the primary method of trade in Africa, Asia, and Latin America. Although barter is sometimes used in the U.S, because of its rigid form, it is not a popular method of trade. For example, the barter system requires that all parties have items acceptable for trade. In other words, if you wanted to purchase a new suit, you would have to have something the merchant considered to be of equal value in order to trade for the suit. If you didn't have something the merchant wanted, you would have to acquire something that was acceptable in order to trade for the suit.

Out of necessity, something had to be designated as a common unit of value for trade. If the fur trader, didn't need the farmer's eggs, for instance, then he could accept that common unit to be exchanged for what he did need or desire. Common units of trade used prior to printed money included beads, cocoa beans, furs, livestock, cloth, tobacco leaves, grain, musket balls, nails, and items made of precious metal. The Chinese used shovels and other tools for trade and later made miniatures of those tools out of bronze that were considered acceptable units of trade. Tribes have designated a certain size and shape of bone for their common unit of trade. The Roman government paid their soldiers salt. The English word, salary, comes from the Latin word for salt, "salarium". Spices, shells, beans, silk, even woodpecker scalps have been used as currency.

Around 650 B.C., the first coins came into use in Lydia, current day Turkey. The coins originally were made of precious metals like gold, silver, bronze, and copper. The coins were shaped like a bean and had the seal of the king stamped on them. They were easier to carry around than chickens, and people used them as a common unit of trade or currency. In the thirteenth century, the Chinese decided that coins were too heavy to carry around so the emperor issued paper money. The paper had value only because the emperor's word was law, and he said it had a certain value. Laws were put in place to make counterfeiting punishable by death to insure that the emperor had control of this new form of currency.

When Marco Polo traveled to China he was astounded that the people accepted printed-paper for trade because it had no value as a commodity. At that time, the Europeans only used commodity money as a common unit of trade. Commodity money was made from a precious metal so it had value. However, paper had no value in itself, and the Europeans believed only a fool would accept paper in trade. It wasn't until much later that paper was considered to be of value and used as money in Europe. Paper was first used in Europe for bank notes. A bank note was similar to a checking account. Gold, silver, or other acceptable forms of money were deposited with the bank, and in return for that deposit the bank issued notes that could be used to draw against the money that was deposited. European governments later used this method to create their own monetary system. France was one of the first to adopt this system as a method of trade. It took too long for the currency to be shipped from France to the French soldiers in the colony known today as Canada, so instead they were paid for over seventy years with playing cards issued and signed by the Governor as a common unit of trade.

When the United States colonies declared their independence from Great Britain, the new United States Congress issued paper currency that was called "Continentals". The war effort cost so much that Congress had printed almost $250 million in "continental" money. The gold reserves were not large enough to back the amount of printed money, and continental money became essentially worthless. Thus, the phrase "not worth a continental" was popularized. This phrase was commonly used by the people to describe anything they considered to be worthless. After the continental, the United States colonies reverted back to bank notes. The United States Congress chartered two national banks that supported their bank notes with a gold reserve. This method was used until the Civil War at which time both the North and South began printing paper money to pay for the war effort. The Northern colonies printed money called "Greenbacks" because the back of the note was printed in green, and the Southern colonies printed money they called "Confederate dollars". The value of the paper money was dependent upon who appeared to be winning the war at any given point. At one point the greenback dollar was only worth 35 cents. However, after the war the greenbacks increased in value, and the Confederate dollar became worthless. The printed money used in the United States today is a continuation of the greenback.

Until 1969 the United States printed $500, $1000, $5000, and $10,000 notes. All money in the United States was backed by gold until 1971. In 1971, the amount of currency issued by the United States government was five times greater than the gold reserves. President Richard Nixon was concerned that the United States gold reserve would be depleted by foreign entities and the United States dollar would again become worthless (like the Continental had been), so he stopped all payments of gold in exchange for the dollar and eliminated the gold standard.

Today, though gold, silver, and precious stones still have value as a commodity, we don't use these to make currency; instead, our currency is primarily paper money and coins that have no real value. Today's currency only has value because the government says it has value. Money with no value as a commodity is called "fiat money". The government, not the material the money is made from, determines the value of each form of money whether it's printed paper money or formed coins. These common units are just different forms of poker chips. Just like a casino determines the value of a specific color of poker chip, the United States government determines the value of the currency issued. However, in and of themselves these poker chips have little or no value. Money is just an idea, a way to barter in an easier manner, and a way for the government to assure they get a share.

What happened to the Confederate money that the government of the south had printed when they lost the civil war? It became worthless, mere souvenirs of the past. Money is only as good as the entity that backs it. Often we can find ways to save money by bartering like our ancestors did. If the college student across the street will do your yard work for some homemade meals, you can both benefit tax-free. Be open to win-win scenarios. Exchange the things you love to do for the things you'd rather not do, and free up monetary resources as well as energy.

In the days when merchants used gold as currency, they would entrust a goldsmith to store their gold. The merchant would write a letter to the goldsmith to give an amount of gold as payment to an individual who they owned. In essence, today's check system is a simple letter, dated and signed, telling the amount to take from our storehouse in exchange for goods or services to pay the individual(s) whom we owe. Americans write over thirty-five billion checks a year.

In addition, the credit system was started to allow people to buy on their future earnings. These plastic cards originally represented a revolving bank account backed by money, called a secured line of credit. Today most credit cards are unsecured lines of credit that charge exorbitant interest rates. Obligations that require you to pay money are called debts or liabilities. A liability is anything that requires you to pay money. The two main types of liabilities are unsecured debts and secured or leveraged liabilities. The word "leveraged" comes from "levy", which means, "If the object that is leveraged is sold, you have a duty to pay your debt that was secured by that object."

The opposite of a liability is an asset. An asset is anything that requires that money be paid to you. The two, main types of assets are cashable possessions that are free from leverage, and financial resources that make you money. To become wealthy and free from the rat race, you must accumulate assets and reduce liabilities. In other words, you need to reduce things that cost you money and increase the things that make you money. Many people mistakenly believe their house is an asset, but at best it's only a potential asset. Even if you have paid off your mortgage you still have outgo in upkeep, insurance, and taxes. Your outgo may be minimal, and the value of the house may be great, but it still is not an asset until it makes you money. However, that same house can become an income producing financial resource or asset if it is rented to someone else.

To increase your portfolio of income-producing assets, you can use secured and unsecured credit to get you started. A common mistake is to use secured and unsecured credit to buy things that are not income producing assets. Most people use credit to buy living essentials or for recreation; this increases liabilities without increasing your income to pay off those liabilities.

Religious institutions are preaching against debt and are advising people to live on budgets while still giving generously to their programs. This mentality will keep people in bondage instead of setting them free. People become fearful of risking what they have for what they want. Their conscience is tainted by even the thought of debt because they are led to believe it is a sin to be in debt. If they don't give a tithe of ten percent or more, they are taught that they are robbing God or living in sin. Let's examine each of these mentalities in depth.

First, debt comes in different forms, some debt is unwise and other debt is wise. However, if you believe debt is a sin, search your scripture to discover if what you believe is truly backed by what you believe is God inspired text. When we accepted this challenge, we found that in many places there was advice concerning money and usury (charging interest), but there was nothing saying 'debt was a sin.' Debt to buy consumables and non-income producing items is unwise, but it is not sin. Non-income producing debt is leveraged against your future earnings; this kind of debt drains your future resources without providing a means to repay the debt. However, debt incurred to gain incoming producing assets is wise. In essence this kind of debt uses someone else's poker chips to earn you income in the future, and the debt is leverage against an asset that can be sold to pay the debt if necessary. Making wise financial decisions, and using debt wisely, will eventually set you free from lack and free from unwise debt.

Second, living on budgets can be death to your creative thinking. Diana's grandfather used to say, "If your outgo is more than your income, then your upkeep will be your down fall". Budgets can be useful tools to monitor spending and assure that you meet your financial goals. However, most people limit their thinking with their budgets. They say, "I can't afford this or that," because their budget tells them so. If your budget doesn't have enough available to do the things you desire, look outside the box to bring in more resources. Most budget manuals specify what percentage should be allotted to each category of spending, savings, debt reduction, and giving. There is no category for obtaining income-producing assets. At best, a percentage is set aside for investment. Traditional investment strategies are no longer affective in today's market and economy. Even mutual funds and blue chip stocks are no longer a wise investment. The key to financial freedom is obtaining income producing assets and eliminating income-draining liabilities.

Finally, religious institutions preach that you must give generously of your time and money to support their programs. Most would gladly allow you to clean their toilets, but they wouldn't think of offering you the opportunity to teach from the pulpit. Most institutions would drain you of your time and money without thinking twice about the sacrifice to your family. They call it a ministry, but when is the last time you heard them offer you their time, money, or even their help? Not all religious institutions are self-serving, but many are.

The temple of olden times was a community asset that belonged to everyone in the community. Those who served in the temple were prohibited from working outside the service of the temple and needed to be supported by the community they served. Most of today's religious institutions are privately held, tax-free businesses. They say they are ordained by God, but it's their personal names on the incorporation papers. If you give to their building fund, you are giving to the personal, financial empire of the individual who owns that business. What happens to the assets if the pastor or leader dies? The spouse or siblings inherit the business, the land, the buildings, and all the other assets of that business. Even larger organizations have someone at the top reaping the benefit of your hard-earned dollars. The members have little or no say in most of today's religious institutions. To receive the value of your hard-earned income, it must be given to places and things you believe in. Don't let anyone use guilt to manipulate you into giving or tell you how much to give. If they're passing the plate, their primary purpose may be to guilt manipulate you into giving at least as much as the person next to you. If they truly believed God was their source of supply, they would put a box in the back of the room so that people could give what they wanted without manipulation.

The interwoven thread in the philosophy of many religious institutions is the belief that "money is the root of all evil" and you should avoid it at all costs. Amazingly it's not evil if you give it to them; it's only evil to keep it for yourself. For the record, scripture doesn't say, "Money is the root of all evil"; instead it says, "The love of money is the root of all kinds of evil." Money is not good or bad; it is neutral. The people who spend the money determine whether the money will be used for good or evil purposes. If you can't trust yourself with money, don't be concerned about it because you'll never have any. Money only comes to those who attract it. In order for you to receive monetary wealth you have to give yourself permission to receive it. Those who have a positive attitude towards money, and believe they can be trusted to do good with it, are those who now have or will have an abundance of money.

Religious institutions should be there to help and support their members. Their teachers should help lead the people to greater levels of freedom and growth. If a teaching promotes bondage, question its validity. Horses eat the hay, but spit out the sticks; you should do likewise. In other words, teachers are fallible human beings. Learn and grow from the good they share, but don't assimilate everything taught without question. Reject teachings that put a yoke of burden about your neck. Like scripture says, "You have to judge a tree by its fruit"; and "Every good tree bears good fruit, but a bad tree bears bad fruit. A good tree cannot bear bad fruit, nor can a bad tree bear good fruit." If the fruit it produces looks good to you, then you are in the right place for you. If it does not, then you should look elsewhere.

We believe that one plus one makes two, and two plus two makes four because we were taught that these concepts are true. But someone at some time made up the names, the concepts, and the rules that go with them. Just tell your average, young, married couple that one plus one makes two, and they will promptly tell you, "only in math". One plus one in a marriage often produces a multitude of children, grandchildren, and future generations.

If you're not truly wealthy yet, it is because of your attitude toward money. For example, think of a person you know who consistently has a negative attitude and speaks hurtful things about you either to your face or behind your back. Do you desire to go to that person's house when you need to talk to someone? Money is the same way; you need to have a proper attitude toward it before it will come to your house. If you are already wealthy, but refuse to look at new methods of increase, you will become poor. The world is drastically changing around us, and in order to become wealthy or stay wealthy in the future, you will need to change too. First, let's examine how to make money, and then we will look at how to keep it.

Have you ever wondered why just about everything a truly, wealthy person touches turns to gold? You may say to yourself that they are wealthy because they received a better education, because their parents created a loving environment for them, or because they were born with a silver spoon in their mouths. You may think of a thousand reasons why they were able to become wealthy, and you were not. Although these points may be factually correct, the only way someone becomes wealthy or stays wealthy is by having an attitude that attracts wealth. When an individual has a positive attitude towards money, he/she becomes a money magnet. Suddenly all the great deals are spread out before them like an enormous banquet of possibilities. However, before you can be invited to the banquet table, you must have an attitude toward money that makes you worthy of such an invitation.

The key to changing your attitude is to become aware of the words that you speak. Your words are an audible indication of your heart attitude. Be aware of phrases like "I can't afford", "I can't see how", "I can't believe", "I don't think", and "But what if" because these words cause your mind to shut off. Spoken on a consistent basis they will be disastrous to your financial portfolio. Remember the famous statement, "Be careful what you say, you just might get it?" Indeed, if you have been saying it, you already have it. The reality you are currently living is a result of what you have spoken.

If you want to be invited to the banquet table of blessings you have to speak the language. You may have already been invited, but you just couldn't read the invitation. If you change the negative words, that you speak, into positive words like, "I have the ability to purchase anything I desire", "I always have the time and resources to pursue my desires", "I can afford", "I can see how", "I believe I can do", and "I will", you can open your mind and spirit to attract wealth. When consistently spoken, these positive words cause you to become wealthy in your mind. Like a magnet, opportunities will be drawn to you that will form the words you have spoken into your new reality.

For those who are already wealthy, the authors would like to propose a question. What would happen to all your wealth if the monetary system were to collapse today? Two previous monetary systems have collapsed. The current monetary system may have again collapsed in 1971 if President Nixon had not abolished the gold standard.

Historically the monetary systems collapsed in association

with war and the overprinting of money to support war. The monetary system is particularly susceptible when war takes place during a bad economy. It is the authors' opinion that the monetary system in the United States has a high probability of collapse within the next decade. Let's examine the reasons why.

The Federal Reserve Board was created to monitor and control the economy. When the economy is bad, the Federal Reserve boosts the economy by lowering the interest rate the banks pay to borrow money from the Federal Reserve, by increasing the amount of printed money, by increasing governmental spending, or by reducing taxes. The United States economy has become so poor that the Federal Reserve has been forced to use all means available to stimulate economic growth, yet the economy still falters. As additional money is pumped into the economy, inflation increases. As inflation increases, the value of the dollar decreases. America is at the brink of what could be a long and costly war against terrorism. Based on the historical cycle, if historical methods are used to fund the war effort, the United States dollar will become essentially worthless, causing the monetary system to become an unfortunate casualty of war.

If the monetary system fails and you have kept all your money in the bank, the stock market, or non-income producing real estate, you will see your financial portfolio wash away like the man who built his house on the sand. The secure investments of yesterday such as interest-bearing accounts, CD's, blue-chip stocks, mutual funds, and 401(k)'s are soon-to-be investment strategies of the past. The secure investments of the future will be businesses with an Internet presence, commercial investment properties, apartment complexes, intellectual property (patents and trademarks), and royalties (movies, songs, and books). There is still time to build a barricade against this future, financial storm, but don't be like the friends of the little red hen, don't wait until winter to build up your reserves.

There are several things you can do to secure your financial future. Buy a business, and be sure to incorporate your business. Having your business incorporated gives you much more flexibility, creates a protective umbrella against legal bombardment, and allows you to purchase many items with pre-tax dollars. Develop an Internet presence for your business. Your business or businesses should be represented on the World Wide Web because the days of face-to-face sales and handshakes have been taken over by computers, video media, voicemail, and e-commerce. Regardless of the type of business, whether you own an ice cream shop or an aircraft manufacturing facility, it's important to have an Internet presence. Many businesses can be managed by someone else; thereby you gain freedom of time while the business provides you with income and tremendous tax advantages.

Purchase income properties. Commercial investment properties will always be a valuable and secure asset because there will always be businesses that require space to rent. Apartment complexes will always be a solid investment as long as people need a place to live. The great thing about commercial, investment properties and apartment complexes is that they are income-producing properties; therefore, you can use them as collateral to obtain a bank loan to purchase them. Additionally, for a small fee you can hire someone to manage the properties for you.

If you have a valuable product or process, then have it patented. You can license other manufacturers to make the product or use that process, and each time they do, you receive royalties. Develop a unique trademark. When your product or process becomes popular, you can create a win-win situation with another company which wants to use your popular trademark to boost sales in their business.

If you believe the strategies we have just described are currently beyond your reach, follow the example of the southern people who maintained their wealth through the Civil War. Secure your future by investing in those items that have maintained value over the course of time such as paintings, rare coins, gold, diamonds, jewels, and real estate.

If you believe that real estate is too expensive and the chances of you ever owning any fall under the category of slim to none, then you need to think more creatively. The first investment properties the authors purchased were bought with credit cards. The Secretary of State's office was selling unclaimed properties, properties that were repossessed by the state for non-payment of taxes. The authors offered the minimum bid (approximately the amount of tax due) on twenty properties, and received accepted offers on thirteen. They deposited several checks from different, credit card companies into their personal account and wrote the checks for the properties to the Secretary of State's office. The interest rates on the credit cards were high, but the authors sold all thirteen properties. The profit not only paid back the credit card companies but also gave Larry and Diana the ability to purchase other income-producing assets.

Protect the assets you have. Open your mind to new ways of investing and the image of your reality will change. As you're collecting assets to increase your financial portfolio, remember to focus your attention primarily on those assets that will maintain value regardless of what happens to the monetary system. A solid, financial portfolio requires good planning. Refer to the appendix for recommended reading. These books do an excellent job of describing in detail many other options that are available to you as you journey toward a solid financial future.

*"Not everything that counts
can be counted, and not everything
that can be counted counts."*

(Sign hanging in Einstein's office at Princeton)
Albert Einstein

Chapter 11

MATERIAL AND RELATIONAL SUCCESS

True Prosperity

America's forefathers thought of true prosperity as being health, wealth and wisdom. Being healthy alone is not true prosperity. Though you may have your health, a constant bombardment of financial stress would probably chip away at even the strongest, positive attitude and would also eventually erode your health. A homeless man may be healthy, but he probably doesn't enjoy relationships with a loving family, keep his belly satisfied, or keep his body warm on cold nights. The homeless man may be free from debt and avoid paying taxes, but he is not successful or prosperous. A lonely teenager may be in perfect health but so emotionally distressed and discouraged that he ponders hanging himself to end his life.

Being wealthy alone is not true prosperity. Many men have set their course on achieving wealth at any cost, sacrificing the relationships with their mates and children only to find that the riches they obtained were a monument to incorrect thinking. They strived for riches believing that wealth would bring them happiness, but instead they found emptiness in material things. Many have regretted the loss of loved ones who were left behind in the consuming pursuit of riches. In fact, many wealthy people would trade all their riches for love, health, or family.

For instance, many Jewish families bought their way to freedom to escape the Holocaust. Most people would place money below family, spiritual values, health, and their close friendships. Paper money and stamped coins are poker chips that can be used as tools to build financial success and free up time by hiring out things you would prefer someone else do. Money can buy you a level of freedom of time and even a level of happiness by buying you some of the things your heart desires. But the most important things in life cannot be bought with money.

Being wise alone is not true prosperity. Would you listen to a wise, poor man? Many would not. Having wisdom may bring you wealth and may even bring you health, but only if the wisdom is applied through diligence. Having wisdom but being bound by fear or low self-esteem may equate to nothing at all. Solomon was said to be the wisest man that ever lived, but at the end of his life he was miserable and unhappy. Solomon was extremely rich, yet he sacrificed his children to gods, accumulated many wives, and believed "all is vanity".

Even having a harmonious combination of health, wealth, and wisdom is not true prosperity. Being healthy, wealthy, and wise is not enough if you are a man in the desert without water because the need for water is not being met. Therefore, we must expand our concept of true prosperity to include always having what we need. Certainly, true prosperity includes being content, being happy, and having your desires fulfilled. Prosperity includes every area of the body, mind, and spirit, as well as, social, economic, and even global arenas that may affect our well-being.

Most people don't take the time to evaluate their lives and what they need or desire. So, many people find themselves at a point in their lives where they get a shocking, wake-up call that they could have avoided with a little thought and planning. Mid-life crisis and empty-nest syndrome are the norm for the average American. If somehow they avoid these pitfalls and work steadily to retirement, many find their "dreamed of" retirement is lacking the excitement they had hoped for. True prosperity for one person may not be the same for another, but the heart of true prosperity is having your needs and desires met to a level of contentment.

Dale worked at various jobs. He was not a slacker, but he had little to show for his working years. When his oldest son started talking about applying to college during his senior year of high school, Dale experienced an emotional hit to his ego. He hadn't saved a penny for any of his children. He couldn't afford to help his son with his college expenses because what Dale brought home was hardly adequate for the necessities. Dale felt like a failure, and he slipped into a mid-life crisis. He reasoned that he had failed his oldest, but he had two years to somehow build up a college fund for the next, oldest child. To make himself feel better he bought a motorcycle. Age had crept up on him, and he wanted to feel young and free. Overestimating his abilities, Dale pushed the limits on his bike and ended up in a hospital. He lost his manual labor job and his insurance ran out. His knee required multiple surgeries to repair the damage. He found that he lacked the education for a desk job, and he would never be able to return to his previous line of work. He was deep in debt and even deeper in despair. Unfortunately, many people make poor decisions when their emotions are running high during a mid-life crisis, making their unsatisfying life even worse.

Career moms have a mid-life crisis of their own called the "empty-nest syndrome". Anita was a pastor's wife. Her life revolved around her three boys. She worked hard to provide the perfect home environment for her family. She made exquisite, large meals for her hungry boys. She took pride in a spotless house where her boys could bring their friends without shame. She even kept their closets and drawers full of clean clothes. On top of cooking, cleaning, and laundry, she prided herself on her parenting. She made sure her boys were respectful and well-mannered. She tried hard to meet their emotional needs. But, when her youngest son packed his bags for college, Anita's life fell apart. She no longer had value in her own eyes now that her children were grown and gone. Though there were no apparent problems in her relationship with her husband, he didn't share her feelings of emptiness. His work provided him with ample opportunities to help others, and he felt fulfilled. Anita sank into depression and longed for death since she had fulfilled her life's ambitions. When Anita saw the doctor to help her through this difficult time, she was diagnosed with breast cancer. Since she had no will to live, Anita quickly succumbed to the life threatening disease.

Marge worked and raised her large family of six children. When her last child left home, she was devastated. When she was at work she was occupied and didn't think about it, but when she came home, the house was too quiet. She was lonely, and she found she didn't share her husband's interests. She took long walks and found herself crying. One time she spent all day sitting by the railroad tracks weeping. She wondered how her husband could be so glad that he was free from the noise and hassles of having children around, and she could be so unhappy about the same event. Caring for her children had been an important responsibility that made her feel needed and gave her life meaning. It took Marge a long time to adjust, but she found projects that interested her and filled her time. Soon there were grandchildren who required occasional babysitting, and her need to care for someone was again filled.

George may have avoided a mid-life crisis if he hadn't been laid off. He had worked twenty-three years for the same company. He enjoyed his family and his work. His mortgage payments were high, and he had borrowed against his 401K-retirement plan to pay off some rising credit card debts. He thought that he was in a good position until he discovered that all his compensation package would do was pay off his retirement plan so he wouldn't lose it. Since his family lived from paycheck to paycheck, living from unemployment check to unemployment check seemed impossible to manage. He thought that they might lose their home. He considered selling his house and moving to a less expensive area, but he realized his chances of qualifying for a new mortgage, while he was unemployed, would be extremely low. George had never taken the time to examine his life. Immediately after being laid off, George felt depressed, hopeless and suicidal. After months of searching for a new job, he found he was overqualified for what few jobs were available and the employers would rather hire someone fresh out of school than an "old" man. For the first time in his life, George considered getting off the dead-end, rat race, job wheel. He bought a small café with a down payment borrowed against his house and a small business loan. Now, he is working for himself. He earns more money and works fewer hours. Through creative thinking the worst point in George's life became the catalyst for the best change to his career.

Many individuals find a rude awaking at retirement. Especially men have a tendency to derive their self-worth from their work. When they retire, the importance of their life is challenged, and many do not recover from this potentially stressful time. Many die soon after retiring.

When Margaret retired from teaching college students, she was excited about spending her retirement years traveling the world. She had planned several trips to historical sights that she had researched and studied. Margaret had to wait for her husband to be willing to retire to fulfill her dream with him. Unfortunately, Margaret's husband, Bruce, considered his electrical engineering firm to be his life's work. He had no desire to stop working; but eventually he capitulated to his wife and retired. Together they enjoyed a trip to England. When they returned, Bruce's health failed rapidly and he died. After fulfilling his life's work and giving his wife one of her dream vacations, his duties were done, so Bruce had nothing more to live for.

After Bruce died, Margaret managed to find a widow who was willing to travel with her. They enjoyed many trips together and saw most of the historical places that Margaret had planned on seeing. Interestingly, Margaret was willing to pay large sums of money for these trips, even though she had the "hoarder's" retirement mentality. In her mind she and Bruce had saved this money for trips, but otherwise, each penny needed to be carefully monitored to insure she would have enough to last.

Eva had the typical "hoarder's" retirement mentality. She would say things like, "My income-producing years are over; I can't dip into my savings because I may need it in the future; I can't be generous to my children, but at least I won't be a burden to them." Typically this type of person has saved all their life for retirement, but they are afraid to spend any of their money. Their savings represent security, so they don't want to touch any of it. Often these individuals will deny themselves the niceties they can easily afford, downsize to smaller houses under the guise of not needing as much space, and end up spending every cent to keep themselves alive without ever really living.

If an individual had properly prepared for their financial future, they would have numerous, income producing assets; therefore, they could not say, "My income producing years are over". Having no debt, a small pension, and social security income is not the ideal financial future. If the monetary system, mutual funds, or social security system fails, these individuals have no financial security at all. However, the individual who owns several income-producing assets, like apartment complexes, businesses, or royalties on artistic works (a movie, a book, a patent, etc.), will likely weather any financial upheaval, even the collapse of the monetary system.

The hoarder's retirement mentality often includes a fear of lack. Their mind is not free. They often refuse to enjoy new technology when the old way worked just fine. No microwaves, no DVD players, no computers—are they afraid to learn something new or are they just afraid to spend the money? Diana's Grandmother Bessie refused to use a clothes dryer since hanging the clothes up on the line worked just fine. When her son bought her one and showed her how easy it was to use, she felt foolish that she did without for so long. Margaret refused to buy a computer even though her family insisted that by email she could keep in touch with family so much easier. When Diana offered to buy Margaret an email machine that would only cost $20 a month to maintain the on-line service, Margaret refused the gift insisting that her old typewriter worked perfectly fine.

Often these retirees downsize their housing. "It's too much upkeep; we don't need that much space anymore", they say. When they bought their homes forty years ago they paid $20,000 for it. When they retired that same house was worth $400,000. Often these individuals see the property tax and the present day worth of the house and balk at the dollar amounts. Their mentality is still in the days of old, so they sell their houses to build up their security, their savings account, and they settle for lesser homes. What is the logic in striving all your life for a more spacious living space to downsize in your old age? Ideally, a larger house can provide space for visiting family and for all the possessions accumulated over a lifetime. If the maintenance is too tasking, hire a housekeeper and a yard service—that even helps the economy of the community.

Those with the hoarder's retirement mentality are tight with their money when they should be most generous. They justify that they are able to not be a burden to their children by selfishly keeping their resources to themselves. If these individuals were generous with their children, their children would feel loved and respond by giving them help that no money can buy when it is needed. But when these individuals ignore the needs of their children and keep a tight reign on every dollar, their children feel that the parent(s) love money more than them and they are not as inclined to help these individuals. Our government will step in and help when all your money is gone to keep you alive in a convalescent home. No inheritance is passed on to your children in this scenario. It is better to give and find favor so that your last days will be spent with loved ones, instead of in a sterile and lonely, convalescent home.

If you took Psychology 101, you may remember discussing the pyramid of needs. At the base of the pyramid are the basic necessities—food, clothing, and shelter. The pinnacle of the pyramid is the need to understand the purpose of our existence and to fulfill that purpose. Between the base and the pinnacle is everything from social needs to recreational needs. Psychologists say that people are consumed with meeting the base needs first, and then they move up the pyramid level by level as each need is met. If you reach the top of this pyramid, all your needs are meet.

True prosperity is meeting your needs as well as your desires to such a degree that you are content. However, you can have a false sense of contentment if you have not examined your heart's desires or planned for future events. Parents eventually have to deal with the empty nest. Most employees will have to deal with unemployment. Middle age often brings the mid-life crisis to those who aren't pursuing their true passions. Retirement from your life's work is in most individuals' futures. Each one of these points puts a magnifying glass to our lives, and if you deal well with these events then it is a testimony of your living a truly prosperous life. A little thought and planning can go a long way in avoiding crisis at these junctures.

Not many get a wake up call like David and Sonja when their son, Steven, nearly died overseas. Steven contracted shingles and was misdiagnosed by the military, medical facility in Germany where he was stationed. David devoted his life to saving the life of his son. Through a long process of talking to congressmen, writing letters, and making phone calls, David was able to get his son transferred from Germany to a state of the art research facility at UCLA. David fought for government funding and disability income for his son—who is still alive today because of the effort of his father. David and Sonja had to drop their pursuit of wealth and all their personal goals in exchange for keeping their son alive. They had to make tough choices that cost them personally for what they valued more.

Don't wait for a crisis to begin taking stock of your life. Are you putting the effort into building the relationships that you value? Or will you be singing, "The Cat's in the Cradle", over your misspent efforts in pursuit of less important things? Are you investing in yourself through books, tapes, seminars, and time alone to think? Is there "lack" in any area of your life? What are you doing "today" to change your "tomorrow"? Are you pleased with your mental and emotional maturity? Are you prospering socially? Physically? What do you lack to find peace and contentment in your life? Ponder these questions to discover what "course corrections" you need to make to be on the road of true prosperity in your life.

If you are free from fear, free in your thinking, emotionally healthy, and have your needs satisfied, if you have a plan that brings hope that those needs will be fulfilled, then you will truly have found prosperity. True prosperity takes place first in the mind and then it is transferred to all areas of your life. True prosperity is far more than just having money. The only person that can keep you from being truly prosperous is you.

*"Gravitation is not responsible
for people falling in love."*

Albert Einstein

Chapter 12

MATERIAL AND RELATIONAL SUCCESS

Relationship Success

True prosperity cannot be achieved without social prosperity. The relationships that make up our lives are more important to most of us than all the money in the world. Having the best relationship that is possible with yourself is the primary key to all other relationships; therefore, much of our focus has been on learning to be positive thinkers, on overcoming fear, on eliminating resistors, and on achieving an ideal self-esteem. When we are whole, we are able to bring something into our other relationships. Yet, it is important to address some key issues in regard to our interaction with the people we choose to love as well as the people who are a part of our lives who we did not choose.

Our primary, social relationship is the relationship with our spouse. In order for our spouse to be the soul mate we long to share life with, we need to find someone with whom our fundamental beliefs and attitudes toward life are compatible. If you are seeking that soul mate, look for a person who already possesses the same mentality and purpose that you possess. If either of you have to significantly change or compromise for the relationship to work, keep looking. A key to a good relationship with your soul mate is having the same mentality and fundamentally compatible beliefs, goals, and purposes. Your primary relationship must be founded upon mutual trust, respect, and friendship. Physical attraction should not be the sole basis for this relationship, but rather an added plus to the package deal.

Many people find themselves in marriages founded on physical attraction, fear of being alone, or some erroneous belief. If these individuals are not fundamentally compatible, it is unlikely that the marriage will be healthy or satisfying for either person. If the relationship does not foster growth, provide support, and fulfill your basic needs for companionship, the relationship needs help. If both parties desire to make the relationship work, then there is hope. But if either party is unwilling to work for a better relationship, the relationship may be doomed to misery. People often think that a marriage that ends in divorce is a relationship that has failed; however, a much greater tragedy is to live a lifetime with a person when there is no joy, contentment, or pleasure.

When considering the question of fundamental compatibility, it is important to understand that opposites attract. When we are lacking in a specific area, we are naturally drawn to people that exhibit confidence in this area. We admire those people that do not struggle in areas that are problematic for us. The very thing that attracts us can drive us crazy later. Each quality trait has, like a coin, two sides; that coin has a positive side and a negative side. If we are quiet and reserved, we may be attracted to the most outgoing personalities in a crowd. This same individual may be such a social butterfly that they have difficulty having serious and deep conversations. If these two individuals will learn from each other, then they can balance each other out. However, if they are unwilling to change, the very traits that were admired in the beginning will strain the relationship.

Tara's first marriage ended in divorce due to the accumulating credit card debt that created too great a financial strain on the relationship. Tara was determined never to be in that position again and admired that her future husband had his financial act together. What she didn't realize until after they were married was that her husband's security blanket was his stash of cash; therefore, he refused to spend anything unless he considered it to be absolutely necessary. The choice before them was clear; they could learn from each other and both achieve healthier attitudes toward spending, or they could argue their way toward divorce.

When Larry and Diana met, Larry was an extreme risk taker. He pushed his physical limits and sought the thrills of physical challenges. Since Diana was raised in a sheltered environment with family that feared life, she admired Larry's self-confidence in this arena. She was impressed by the long list of activities he had mastered or tried, like scuba diving, riding motorcycles, or Tae-Kwan-Do. Similarly, Larry admired Diana's boldness in speaking her mind. Diana could "cut to the quick" and dig deep into an emotional arena with a tenacity that Larry had never been allowed to do. Larry had been raised by an abusive father who would strike out if verbally challenged. There was no room for expression of emotion.

These differences could have driven a wedge between Larry and Diana, but instead they learned from each other. Larry recognized that he took unnecessary risks to feel alive. Once he honestly considered the risk to himself and his family, he refused to participate in activities that jeopardized the welfare of his family. Diana chose to join Larry in physical activities like weight lifting and sailing that she probably would never have tried without Larry's influence. Diana learned from Larry the art of diplomacy in conversation, and Larry learned from Diana the art of expressing his inner feelings. They balanced each other out, and both gained from the process. Differing character traits can add to the strength of a relationship if handled properly, but both parties must be willing to make minor compromises for the sake of the relationship.

Marriage, like all relationships, requires time and effort. A marriage that lacks spark can easily be rekindled by choice.

You can choose to love anyone with your will and be committed to that individual. The will is a strong tool that can bind together a relationship for a lifetime, and willpower applied properly can even make a relationship satisfying. By a choice of your will, you can choose to think only positive thoughts about your mate and take captive negative thoughts. Feelings will follow your thoughts. So affection and even passion can be developed by diligent control of your thought life. This journey is more difficult, though not impossible, for the couple whose fundamental mentalities and life priorities are inharmonious. Most people, however, cannot even agree to disagree on fundamental issues with their mates. Ideally your mate will have the same mind, the same will, and the same emotional frame of reference making them the soul mate that complements you as a life partner. However, if each partner understands the basic mentality of the other and believes they are compatible, willing to learn from each other's character traits, or willing to accept their basic differences without trying to change those fundamental aspects, then the relationship has enough in common to make it a happy and healthy relationship. Willpower, choice, and a positive thought life are fundamental keys to any good relationship.

In addition to controlling your thought life, positive feelings can be fostered toward another by simply spending quality time with that individual. Time spent together in recreation and in fun activities builds positive associations with that individual. Even difficult times can bring people together if caring and support is mutually offered to one another. Many relationships are greatly improved just by proximity. Proximity 'love' is the basis for most male friendships as well as for the relationship between parents and their young children. If you are never together, then there is no relationship. Time is a valuable gift to give any relationship. If your marriage needs help, find activities to do together and lessen activities that only one partner enjoys. Though some time apart can bring interest into the relationship when you are back together, too much time apart will bring separation and discord when you are together. Therefore, quality time is a fundamental key to any good relationship.

Since time fosters closeness, it is important to guard your time with the opposite sex. Most extramarital affairs started as innocent friendships that met a basic need that wasn't being met in the marriage. If you're not careful, this kind of relationship will evolve into a love relationship that endangers your primary relationship.

Diana worked as an engineer surrounded by male co-workers. She was given an assignment that required riding the company van to another location every day—an hour each way. Naturally, since another person from her department was assigned the same task, they gravitated toward sitting together on the van and having lunch together at the remote location. Steve was a single, lonely man. He wanted to be happily married like Diana, so he started asking Diana questions about dating and marriage. Diana felt honored by his asking her advice, which created warm feelings of compassion for Steve. Soon Steve started making comments like, "I want to marry someone just like you." As Diana talked about Steve at home, Larry was wise enough to recognize the danger signs, and advised Diana to spend less time with Steve. Diana took a book to read on the van and found a woman to have lunch with at the remote location. Steve confronted Diana with her avoidance, so Diana explained her concerns about his growing affection toward her and her desire to guard her marriage relationship. Steve admitted that he would jump at the chance to have a relationship with her, but he would respect her wishes. Even the best marriages can be put in jeopardy if we don't guard our hearts and use wisdom in our interaction with the opposite sex.

Another fundamental key to good relationship is trust. Trust is built through understanding and consistency. When we understand the position and feelings of another, we respond with compassion. Trust is built over time when we gain a sense of security in knowing another person and feeling comfortable that we understand how they will act and respond to the situations of life.

Even relationships outside our inner circle require a level of trust for success. For instance, an employer must be able to trust an employee to perform his duties and to value the goals of the company. An employee may find that taking a few stationery items for personal use will lead to unemployment because trust was violated by his actions.

Few marriages can survive infidelity because unfaithfulness shatters trust. Security is a basic need that is on most women's lists of their top, five, relationship needs. Additionally, many men equate love and sex, so the unfaithfulness of their spouse destroys their feelings of being loved.

Understanding fosters feelings of closeness. Without communication, understanding cannot be achieved. Therefore, good communication is a fundamental key to good relationships. Good communication requires listening, not just hearing. Good communication requires honest disclosure and expression, not just speaking. Openness, with the desire to share intimacy, fosters closeness; but openness with blunt disregard for the feelings of another will foster discord.

To understand communication, it is helpful to recognize that people primarily communicate from three, different perspectives. Visual people require eye contact and assimilate information better with visual aids. Auditory people tend to turn their heads so that their ears face the speaker; auditory people look away from eyes and visual aids because they find that too much visual input is distracting to listening. Kinesthetic people desire hands-on demonstrations.

Parents can, and should, tailor their communication to their child's primary, communication style. Look into the eyes of a visual child. Talk while walking with an auditory child. Hold a kinetic child in your lap for best results. Don't demand, "Look at me when I'm talking to you." Auditory and kinesthetic children don't need to look at you to receive the message.

Instead, ask your listener to parrot back what was said to discover if the message was correctly received. All communication styles can benefit from this exercise.

When emotions are high, people often add destructive tags to what was actually said, such as, "You don't love me because I made this mistake." Over eighty percent of communication comes through nonverbal means like body language and the unseen energy from our thoughts, feelings, and imagination. People sense anger and other strong emotions easily, but they may misinterpret the true message because they sense this aura of feelings. Children are particularly sensitive, so guard against raising your voice or trying to communicate a message when your emotions are overly strong.

There are people who are part of our lives that we probably would never have chosen as associates. We need to have peaceful interaction with these people and learn to get along for the sake of family or career. Choosing to show respect even when it has not been earned, or giving unconditional love to the unlovable, are two powerful ways to achieve harmony with these people.

Larry found that simply addressing his in-laws as "Mom" and "Dad" showed them respect and expressed his unconditional acceptance of their relationship to him. Diana's mother was particularly touched by Larry's use of such a term of endearment, and she responded by accepting him as a beloved son. Their relationship improved greatly.

Diana found her new father-in-law was intentionally doing things to negatively provoke her. He gave her painful, squeeze hugs when greeting and he criticized her openly. Diana asked him to be gentle, but he became rougher instead. He enjoyed getting a rise out of her and seemed to be on a power trip. Diana decided to unconditionally love her new father-in-law. One day Diana told him, "I choose to love you no matter how big a pain in the ass you are to me." Her unconditional acceptance brought an end to his antagonistic behavior. Despite their completely different personalities, they now enjoy a mutual respect for each other and a peaceful relationship.

Since there is no vested interest to resolve relationship difficulties in some situations, like in a work environment, avoidance may be the best solution. Don't allow others to provoke you. Be consistent in being kind, respectful, self-controlled, and mature in your responses to others. It will become obvious that you are not the problem when you do not treat people differently even when they are unkind to you. Do not condone or facilitate another's inappropriate behavior, but you can stand up for yourself without emotions driving your actions. The person with high self-esteem and strong self-control can deal with negative relationships in a productive and intelligent manner. Choose to think through or gain an intuitive insight for the best course of action instead of choosing immediate reaction based on emotions.

There are many important keys to good relationships. Having similar mentalities and fundamentally compatible beliefs, goals, and purposes are the key to strong, soul mate or best friend relationships. All relationships require a choice and a positive, thought life to maintain positive feelings. Time, trust, and communication are all key factors to any good relationship. We can have good relationships with people we normally would not associate with by showing them respect, unconditional love, acceptance, and by being mature in our responses.

"There are two ways to live your life—one is as though nothing is a miracle, the other is as though everything is a miracle."

Albert Einstein

Chapter 13

MATERIAL AND RELATIONAL SUCCESS

Define Your Ideal Paradigm

To achieve any goal you must clearly and concisely define that goal. Take the time to define your ideal life. See yourself living that life. Make a detailed list of every area you want changed and how, exactly, you want it to change. In basic psychology we are shown the figure called the pyramid of needs. Until our needs for food, water, and shelter are met, we cannot reach for our social needs to be met, and until our social needs are met, we cannot reach out for the need of entertainment. Similarly, as you define your ideal paradigm, you will first focus on your most basic need that is not currently met. Once that need is met, our horizons expand and we see that we desire much, much more. The process will not be a one-time session of determining your inner desires, but rather it will be time and again examining what changes you currently desire. Therefore, define your ideal life like stair steps to a final goal. Try to picture after you make it to your first step, what your second step will be, after reaching your second step what your third will be and so on. Place an order of importance upon your desires. If you could only have one, what would it be? If you had that one, what would be next?

When Diana graduated from college, she was given practice with how to answer job interview questions. One of the most commonly asked questions was, "Where do you see yourself in five years? In 10 years? In 20 years?" All the graduates learned to answer these questions based on what they believed the hiring companies wanted to hear. Few answered these questions for themselves.

At best most people spend a little time of introspection around New Year's Day. They come up with a few goals or a short list of changes they intend to make in the coming year. Most people don't have the resolve or a practical plan so they fail to make the changes or meet the goals that they set.

A wise man asks, "How do you eat an elephant?" And the wise answer is, "One bite at a time." This insight is why so many fail at the task of determining their inner desires and passions and then turning these dreams into reality. They try to eat the elephant in one meal instead of in bite-size chunks. Changing your life is a big task; break that task into smaller chunks and you will succeed.

Your ideal paradigm is the ideal life that you desire to live right now. To define this paradigm you must break your life into pieces. Often the easiest way to picture the pieces of this jigsaw puzzle is to list all the functions, desires, or roles that you have or would like to have. These include your relationships to others as well as to yourself.

For instance, Diana is a wife, mother, business owner, author, speaker, daughter, sister, friend, American citizen, and more. The relationship most people forget to consider is the primary relationship that each one has with themselves. In all your relationships or roles, your relationship with yourself is always a factor in how well you perform that function. It is not selfish to attend to your physical, social, emotional, mental, and spiritual well-being. When your self-needs are met, you are free to attend to the needs of others and to fulfill the mission you have in each of these arenas.

Once you identify your primary personas, you can discover your desired realities for each. Assume that all the resources are available in abundance and let passion, not practicality, guide your quest. In each role you have, dream about the ideal day, week, month, year, and outcome of each relationship or function. An excellent exercise is to write a mission statement for each relationship or function you have.

As a mother, Diana wrote this mission statement: "I guide my children to their marks through wise and kind instruction. I communicate love to my children by sharing quality time on a regular basis, by consistent, open and honest, deep communication, and through loving affection."

Mission statements can be used as a guide for setting specific goals or developing desired patterns of behavior. For instance, Diana has referred to her mothering mission statement to help make important parenting decisions. When living in an area where the quality of the school system was poor, Diana chose to home school to assure that her children received wise and kind instruction. Monthly, family excursions have become a practice in order to provide the opportunities for quality time and consistent, open and honest, deep communication. Despite her own unaffectionate upbringing, Diana makes a special effort to hug her children and display loving affection to them daily.

Several years ago, Diana wrote this mission statement in regard to her relationship to the world and people in general. "My purpose is to set people free from bondage by correcting wrong thinking and making paradigm shifts in the minds of people through sharing the revelation and wisdom that I have obtained in my life."

This quest was accomplished through sharing with friends and family that were open to new ideas. Many members of the groups that Diana and Larry have been a part of have sought their opinions and insight. This book was written to further

Diana's original mission statement to its next logical level; but when this mission statement was written, speaking engagements and books were not even considered. Diana's world mission statement directed Diana's and Larry's paths to a place where they could fulfill this dream on a higher level, a level that gives lasting purpose and meaning to their lives.

Do you remember the song "If I Were A Rich Man" from the movie, *Fiddler on the Roof?* Make up your own verses by picturing who you would be and what you would do if you had an endless supply of financial, poker chips. After the hoopla dies down, what passions remain that are worth investing your life pursuing? Many people find their passions by completing sentences of strong emotion. "I can't stand it when . . ." Or "It really brings me joy when . . ."

Lindsay found her passions by being honest with herself. She earned her income by desktop publishing but her passion was in nature. Soon she found a way to combine that passion with her work. She started publishing a newsletter for Tree People, and then she started contributing articles on nature hikes and walks. When her two children were born, she wanted to have a close-knit family, so she chose to home school. She took her children on these nature walks and began writing curriculum for them. The Los Angeles School District became interested in her work, and she is now writing the environmental, education curriculum for the Los Angeles School System.

What you currently think is your ideal paradigm will change as you gain more information and begin to live your dream. Doors of opportunity will open before you and expand the horizons of your thinking. This is similar to the pyramid of needs phenomenon. Once you meet your ideal in one area, you become free to fine-tune your ideal in that area or to meet the ideal in the other areas of your life.

For instance, your definition of your ideal looks may start from a low self-esteem and grow to a place of self-satisfaction. A person could start with the goals of fixing a tooth, removing a mole, and losing ten pounds, which are the areas of glaring imperfection in his mind. Once these are fixed, that same person may set goals to have healthier skin, improved muscle tone, and have Lasik surgery so that he doesn't need glasses any more. As we change, our perspective changes and our goals and ideals change too.

Knowing your passions, discovering your ideals, and defining your mission statements for each relationship you have, including the one you have with yourself, is the first step toward changing your reality and living your dream. The next step is taking practical measures to organize, plan, and take action to accomplish these goals and dreams. So, let's get practical!

"Everything should be made as simple as possible, but not simpler."

Albert Einstein

Chapter 14

MATERIAL AND RELATIONAL SUCCESS

Let's Get Practical

The magnetic force of faith works by aligning the energy of your imagination, thoughts, words, and actions in the same direction. Defining your ideal paradigm gave you the direction you desire to go for each area and role of your life. You had to use your imagination, your thoughts, and maybe even your words, if you wrote down your mission statements or discussed your ideals with someone. Your compass is now pointing in the right direction, but you have to walk it out in order to find yourself in a new place.

The reality that you are currently living and your attitudes toward life were created by the energy released from your words, thoughts, and imagination. To make a change in your reality, you must first change the words that come out of your mouth. As your brain ponders thoughts, they carve an image in your imagination. Once the image is formed in your imagination you speak forth the words that make what you have imagined your new reality. The easiest way to create your desired reality is to speak it. Writing down a summarized version of what you desire your new reality to be and speaking out loud the words you have written will cause the thoughts that your brain ponders to be the words that you have spoken. Then the image that is carved in your imagination will be the reality that you have chosen. After awhile the only words that will come from your mouth will be the words that form your desired reality. The length of time it takes to form your new reality depends upon how solid your current reality is, and how strong your desire is to change it.

Knowing what you want is only the first step in obtaining what you want. When you're hungry and you figure out you want pizza, you still need to decide if you're willing to follow through by calling in your order and paying the deliveryman. If you make a quality decision it requires action—in this case making the call and paying. Quality decisions are powerful and have impact. Quality decisions always require action and result in change. Change is stressful for many people so they avoid making decisions.

Most decisions start in the soul realm. We utilize our reason and enforce it with our willpower, or we react based on emotions. The soul is comprised of the mind, will, and emotions and is the center of decision-making. Occasionally, decisions come from an intuitive revelation, but the will must still be utilized to enforce the decision. Physical limitations may play a part in our reasoning or instigate a reaction to avoid pain, but rarely do decisions develop from the physical realm.

A quality decision ideally involves all three components of the soul to bring about the conviction and consistency of corresponding action resulting in change. If one reasons that he should eliminate chocolate from his diet but he loves the taste of chocolate, that individual may lack the willpower when his emotions are strong. Similarly if infatuation spawns a relationship, when feelings wane, there may not be enough reasons to continue the relationship. Therefore, examine your ideal paradigm for the areas of change that you truly desire by reason and emotion. Success in these areas is more likely since your mind, will, and emotions can act in harmony to attain this goal.

If you have a goal that is important to you because you

know it is best, but your emotions are against it, you can grit it out. In twenty-one days you can develop a new habit, and in ten days of fasting from a particular item, like coffee or chocolate, your body will stop craving that item. The trick is all or nothing for ten to twenty-one days to break the bondage of addictions or change destructive habits. Find someone who will support your goal to keep you accountable. Be careful not to substitute one bad habit for another. Do not cold turkey addictive drugs without professional help because in some cases the dosage must be slowly reduced to prevent harm to the body.

Decisions always involve a choice for something and against something else. If you choose to order pizza, you're deciding against Mexican and Chinese food. An honest evaluation of your capabilities is prudent. Can you walk and chew gum at the same time? Can you drive and talk on your cell phone at the same time? Are you good at planning a large meal and having the main course ready at the same time as the side dishes? You must know yourself. How many rings can you manage successfully in your "three ring" circus?

Many of us are capable of running a five-ring circus. Some of us can keep the schedules of our children in our head, work diligently on the project our boss assigned us, plan a romantic evening with our spouse, and keep up with a rigorous exercise program. However, some of us are mere mortals, who find the laundry constantly piling up, our beds not made, and the car keys disappeared once again. Only you know how much energy and time you can devote to pursuing the top desires of your heart. With training and practice you can increase your circus size; however, it is best to start with manageable goals to ensure success.

Often our lives are consumed with maintenance. Our lawns must be mowed. Our houses must be cleaned. Meals must be prepared. Laundry must be done. Showers must be taken. Maintenance, maintenance, maintenance. And the cycle never stops. Your time can be freed up by hiring out many things like yard work and house cleaning. If you currently lack the money to hire out tasks that you do not enjoy, make that a high priority goal to attain. Also, you can redeem the time of maintenance work by making it your classroom, a time for positive confessions, or a time for gaining intuitive insight. You can set up a cassette player in your laundry room or by the kitchen sink and play teaching tapes while you perform maintenance tasks. Laminate or tape over confession cards or pictures by your bathroom sink or even in your shower. Let them remind you to make positive confessions, or use your imagination, to attain your goals. The shower can be a peaceful place to find intuitive insight for solving problems or gaining greater revelation. Turn times that you tend to let your mind wonder or worry into times that you purposely use your words, thoughts, and imagination to generate positive energy toward desired change.

Diana had a tendency to be a perfectionist when it came to housecleaning. She once spent over three hours cleaning the bathroom with an old toothbrush. After working hard on the house, she felt justified in yelling at her children if they messed it up. Hiring a maid was money well spent in Diana's house. Diana was able to relax about the imperfections because keeping the house cleaned became someone else's responsibility. Diana could easily tell herself, "The housecleaning woman will take care of that mess on Thursday." In this case, hiring out the maintenance of housecleaning not only freed up Diana's time, it also brought a greater peace to her household. If certain tasks cause you undue stress, make them someone else's responsibility either within your family or by hiring out that task.

A delicate balance is required to maintain a successful career and prosperous family. Though people have within them enormous untapped resources, we can only be and do a finite number of things. Therefore, we need to consistently prioritize and monitor our activities to obtain the best life possible.

Start with defining your top ten goals for change. Each

should be concise and clear. Each should also be in the first person and the present tense. Each should be two sentences or less. For instance, "I am the ideal weight and shape. I look good and feel good all the time." It is best if you can choose wording that is clever or appealing in some way. Write each of your top ten on a separate 3" by 5" index card. Sort them in order of importance to you. Define a minimum goal for yourself like, "I will read these cards out loud every night before I go to bed". If you are ambitious, morning, noon, and night is better, but consistency is far more important than frequency. If you find that you do not have the time and energy for ten, shorten your stack and set aside the less important goals. Choose three to emphasize. Find pictures that help you imagine that goal is achieved in your life. Tape those pictures to your mirror or to your refrigerator door. It is important to keep your imagination focused on what you desire.

If you have done your homework to define your ideal life you have far more than you can work on at one time. At most you should focus on ten areas of change at once. You can create a card file to organize your goals under each role. This method can help define a long-term plan for your life in every area.

You may wish to focus on one role. Perhaps, you would like to focus on one important goal for each role. Or, you may decide to pick five easy short-term goals and five challenging long-term goals. If a particular goal seems "unattainable", consider what small steps you would need to achieve to progress on the path to the greater goal. View the smaller steps as your initial goals; that way you are at least making progress. Because there is such a great sense of victory associated with successfully obtaining one of your goals, be sure to include at least three goals that you consider "do-able" from your current mindset. Reward yourself with a victory party every time one of your goals is met.

Your primary goal should always be to improve yourself. At least one of your top ten goals should target a goal that will increase your physical, social, emotional, mental, or spiritual well-being. Since your self-esteem is the primary mindset that governs your actions, it is extremely important to take control of this crucial area of your life. If your self-esteem is low, you may wish to devote your entire top ten to achieve your ideal self-esteem before you tackle the other areas.

It's like sharpening a knife before cutting vegetables. The job is faster and easier because you took the time to maintain the quality of your knife. If you're not physically fit, your energy is depleted quickly. If you're emotionally wounded, then your emotional energy is drained quickly. If your self-esteem is low, how others treat you will dictate how you feel about yourself and your social well-being will suffer. The common denominator in meeting all your goals is you, so you are the highest priority in obtaining your dream life.

If you allow contrary forces to work against your goals all day long, don't think that making positive confessions morning and evening will be enough to change your life. If you love to sing-along to sad songs of loneliness and lost love, your confessions of enjoying a great relationship with the soul mate of your dreams just won't work. The music, movies, novels, and other input you allow into your life will affect your life. Is it worth the entertainment value to allow input that works against your goals? Think about the studies that have been done proving that watching comical films can purge the body of sickness. You can choose to surround yourself with uplifting and encouraging entertainment and eliminate negative input, but your cost may be giving up your favorite soap operas, your favorite country-western compact disc, or the horror films that you enjoy.

Don't underestimate the power of even the simplest change. One change can break a link in a chain that has held you captive. One change can divert your course to a new heading. The difference may seem imperceptible at first, but like two ships that started in the same place but were on different compass settings, you end up in an entirely different place with just a small adjustment in your heading. This effect is not linear but exponential. Like a snowball rolling down a hill or a sound that starts an avalanche, if you change a small thing, you can affect your entire life.

Therapists have noted that people that schedule an appointment to see them actually start improving their situation just by making the choice to do something about it. Our spirits know intuitively how to solve the problem and once the decision to change has been made we intuitively start making the necessary adjustments to improve our situations. A quality choice followed by a small corresponding action will change your course every time. In one survey two-thirds of those questioned reported concrete changes between the call for therapy and the first appointment. Most people don't need therapy; they just need to make a quality decision to change.

The theories of Sigmund Freud have affected the way people seek to resolve problems in their lives. Freud postulated that the key to every problem lay in the past and that, by identifying how a problem started, one can solve the problem. This is erroneous. Analyzing what caused your problem in the past does not lead to solutions. Dwelling on negative past experiences will increase your current problems by creating negative images, thoughts, and feelings. Instead, leave the past behind and seek solutions in the present.

Often the key is to identify times when the problem occurs, times when it does not, and then determine the difference between these times. There is no need to analyze the past, just examine the present. Eliminate the triggers that cause problems, and do more of what brings happiness. Don't wait for, or expect, others to change; change yourself. When you change, it will break the cycle of negative interpersonal action and reaction, and others will respond to this change.

Some people have the philosophy that if they expect the worst, they can't be disappointed regardless of what happens. This may seem logical, but this philosophy disregards the possibility that our expectation will affect the outcome. A psychology researcher, Robert Rosenthal, performed several experiments that proved that an individual's expectation impacted the outcome of the experiment. In one experiment, he had students run rats through a maze. The students that were told their rats were bright found that their rats excelled beyond the performance of the rats given to the students who were told that their rats were dumb. Rosenthal concluded that the students' expectations influenced their handling of the rats, which impacted the rats' performances. However, it is more likely that the expectations of the students were communicated to the rats on a subliminal level.

In another experiment, Rosenthal gave elementary students a standardized IQ test. He randomly selected twenty percent of the students and informed their teachers that the students were of superior intelligence. At the end of the school year, he retested all the students and found that the twenty percent showed a significantly greater gain than the other students. This experiment clearly shows that our expectations of others do influence their behavior.

Larry's father, Bob, was forced to work at a very young age making it impossible for Bob to attend high school. Bob was embarrassed that he never graduated from high school and this negatively impacted his self-esteem. For any of his boys to graduate from high school would cause further injury to his already bruised self-esteem. Although it was never spoken that Larry and his brothers should not graduate from high school, it was always downplayed as though education was unimportant. All of Larry's three sisters graduated from high school just like their mother, but out of the three boys, Larry was the only one who pursued a high school education. Although Larry never considered dropping out of high school as an option, Larry graduated from high school with a 2.5 average having never applied himself nor even considering education to be of any real value. When Larry went to college he graduated with a 3.6 grade point average although the coursework was far more difficult than high school. He realized at this point that the reason his high school grades were so low was because his parents never expected him to do well in school. But when he expected it of himself, he easily excelled.

Diana's parents were exactly the opposite of Larry's. Diana's parents continually communicated to Diana that they highly valued education and that good grades were expected of her. When she entered junior high school, the school did not want to put Diana into honors classes because her IQ tests didn't indicate that she could handle these classes, but Diana excelled and earned straight 'A's. The school later allowed her to take honors classes and gifted classes because she proved her scholastic aptitude. In these classes she also made 'A's. If Diana received anything less than an A, she would burst into tears, and although she never received praise for her hard work she continued to receive straight A's because she knew it was expected of her. Diana graduated from high school, received a bachelor's degree, and a master's degree all with high honors.

As writer Norman Cousins observed, "We fear the worst, we expect the worst, we invite the worst." The converse is also true. When we believe the best, we expect the best, we attract the best. While pessimists are depressed more often and live in a constant state of frustration, optimists perceive setbacks as temporary challenges and refuse to lose hope when confronted by bad situations.

A potential for disappointment exists when believing for the best, but disappointment is almost guaranteed if we expect the worst. When disappointment comes, choose to move on quickly and choose to believe, like Michele Weiner Davis in *Fire Your Shrink* suggests, "There is no such thing as failure, only feedback as to how to modify your next step." Don't quit because of negative feelings; keep living the way of success and positive feelings will soon return.

Disappointment is a result of false expectations or preconceived ideas. To avoid disappointment and still seek high goals, avoid mapping out an inflexible game plan for achieving a goal. It is desirable to have specific, well-defined goals, but it is undesirable to specify exactly what path must be taken to achieve those goals. In addition, disappointment may come if goals are not met by a specified deadline.

When we use our words, thoughts, and imagination to achieve goals, we speak, think, and imagine the end result. We "see" the goal achieved. There is no defined path, and the time is now. Intuitively, we will begin to make the course corrections necessary to achieve that goal. If we convince ourselves that a particular method should work to achieve the goal, and continue to do the same thing over and over, we are bound to be disappointed. Why would you expect a different result by doing the same old thing? We must be open to trying something different.

Sherilyn has always felt very comfortable with rules. She likes to have a schedule so she can move down the list checking off items sequentially as they're completed. For Sherilyn rules were guidelines that brought her comfort. After all, Sherilyn believes it's much easier to do what your parents expect when their expectation is laid out clearly before you. Sherilyn didn't like punishment of any kind and avoided it by following the rules. However, when her brother Mitchell was born, she believed it was her responsibility to continually communicate the rules to Mitchell and was astounded when he chose not to follow them. After all, why would someone do something he knows would result in punishment? Still, Mitchell would rather be punished than to follow a rule communicated to him by his sister. Sherilyn's parents thought they had developed a universal parenting plan that they could implement with all their children, but they quickly discovered that what worked with Sherilyn wasn't going to work with Mitchell. The key to successful parenting is to find something that works and implement it.

Mitchell is a very intelligent boy. When shown how to play the game of chess he mastered it the first day. However, Mitchell's parents discovered that there was a direct correspondence between his relationship with his teachers and the level of his grade in their class. If Mitchell liked his teacher he received good grades in their class, but if he didn't like the teacher his grades were much lower. At home if Mitchell did something that was inappropriate, his parents would punish him by taking away something he liked or making him go to his room. What they discovered was that this punishment would increase the level of inappropriate behavior that Mitchell exhibited instead of decreasing it as they desired. It became obvious to them that they needed to modify their parenting method to deal appropriately with Mitchell's personality. Mitchell's parents decided to observe those times when Mitchell responded to them with positive behavior so that they can do more of what elicited that positive response from Mitchell. For Mitchell praise was the trigger for positive behavior, and punishment was the trigger for negative behavior. So Mitchell's parents decided to do more of what works instead of trying to get Mitchell to conform to their method. Mitchell's parents communicated to his teachers how praise motivates him. In turn the teachers became more sensitive to this when dealing with Mitchell, and everyone's lives became much happier.

Another practical tip is to act as if the goal in your life is already met—as much as possible. The results will amaze you as others line up to your expectations and your emotions align with your actions. A common area where you see this method used by most people is in job interviews. When an individual interviews for a job his primary purpose is to sell himself to the company where he is seeking employment. It doesn't matter what expectations the company may have for its future employee, you convince them that you are the one for the job. You proceed with dialogue to convince them that you can perform the task better than anyone else even if you're not sure what they are talking about. You don't view anything you have spoken in the interview as a lie because you're convinced that you can learn anything if they're willing to pay you enough.

People also "act as if it is" when dealing with customers. You don't want the customer to think for one minute that there is any product even remotely related to your products that cannot be provided by your company. Again it's not viewed as a lie because your company can provide that product if the purchaser of that product is willing to pay the price. Larry did something similar to this when he started his company. He had vendors lined up to manufacture his product line. Because Larry had worked for a company that manufactured a similar product, he also had a good idea what the price range was for such products. He began soliciting sales for his product and received the first order before the product line was even designed. This action jumped the product design phase to a whole, new, energy level. However, the product was delivered on time. If Larry had not acted as if he was prepared to do business, he would not have received the business.

A more personal example happened early in Larry and Diana's marriage. Larry and Diana came upon hard times and were forced to move in with Diana's single brother. This was a very embarrassing situation for Larry and Diana. They recognized as a married couple that privacy was vital to a good relationship. As they were looking for a place to move to, they found a home that they considered to be ideal for them at that stage in their life. The woman leasing the house communicated to Diana that in order for her to hold it for them she required the first and last month's rent and a security deposit by the following day or she was going to lease it to someone else. Diana told the woman that would be no problem; she will have it the next day as promised. However, Diana was acting as if she had the money when the facts dictated that Larry and Diana only had a few dollars between them. Amazingly, that afternoon they received in the mail a large, unexpected check that made their move possible.

Another situation where acting as if comes in handy is when dealing with multiple children. Larry and Diana have, many times, implied that they knew which one of the children performed a dirty deed when at the time they were clueless. However, by "acting as if", they knew the child responsible would confess his crime. "Acting as if" the desired goal is met is also especially effective for relationship goals and self-esteem goals. For instance, if you do the things you do when you feel good about yourself, the feelings will follow, and negative feelings of inadequacy or depression will leave. If you "act as if" you like a co-worker and they like you, you'll feel better and a co-worker will feel compelled to respond favorably towards you.

There are many things that can be done to make a person's life better, but nothing is accomplished until a choice is made to do something. Set a goal for yourself and make a commitment to take a step in that direction. If the step you made doesn't net the desired results, do something else while keeping the focus on your goal. What are you doing today to change tomorrow? Take a step and keep moving. If you keep moving while focusing on a goal, you'll get there. Movement is the key; you can make adjustments along the way. Have you ever noticed that you can't steer a parked car? The car has to be moving first and then you can make it go where you want it to go. Anyone who regularly goes sailing has, at some point, sailed directly into the wind. It is impossible to steer a sailboat when it is facing directly upwind. Still, there is a term for such a condition; the term used for this maneuver is called "in irons." Don't be like a sailboat sailing directly upwind. First, get your boat moving—it's easier to steer along the way. You may have to tack or even turn about to avoid certain obstacles, but if you keep your destination in focus through your words, thoughts, and imagination and you keep moving, you will reach your destination.

*"Sometimes one pays most
for the things one gets for nothing."*

Albert Einstein

Chapter 15

MATERIAL AND RELATIONAL SUCCESS

Consistency Will Change Your Life

In order to make a consistent change in our way of life, we need to develop habits and we need to network with like-minded individuals. Supportive people can help us to stay plugged into the process of success. Here we must examine to what groups we belong, with what people we associate, and with whom we hang out. There may be family members who pull us down or who oppose our goals, people that we cannot eliminate from our lives; still, we may be able to limit the time we spend with them. Most of our friends and our groups are chosen by our own free will, however, and should be analyzed as to the quality of the influence that they have on our lives. Many of us were trained at a young age to regularly attend religious organizations, and we do not feel right about ourselves if we neglect that responsibility. We must honestly examine how we feel at the end of a long sermon. Are we uplifted? Are we encouraged? Or have we been made to feel unworthy, guilty, and powerless? Four generations of your family may have attended the same religious organization, but if it tears down your self-esteem or holds back your ability to grow, it needs to be eliminated from your life. We must be brave enough to leave our comfort zones and to try out new places of worship, or socialization, that promote our goals and our desires for growth.

Friendships are an important part of people's lives. Having a friend that won't judge you no matter what you tell him, and won't repeat your conversation with the neighbor, is a great friend indeed. If you don't have a large enough network of friends, it would be good to start creating one now. If you are asking yourself how can I accomplish this, the answer is simple; in order to have friends, you must first be friendly. Find someone you think will make a good friend, and then invite him or her over for dinner, out to lunch, or even to your local, coffee shop. Enjoy the opportunity to converse and get to know them.

Friendship can spawn the exchange of needed material items. For instance, Larry gave a complete professional camera setup to a friend who was an aspiring photographer, another friend received a stereo system to use in his ministry, and Diana received two years of like-new baby clothes from one of her friends. A good network of friends is far more valuable than money. Friendships are a good example of a win-win scenario. Good friends can help you find favor in situations that would otherwise be difficult. Referrals from a friend can be priceless.

Larry and Diana have been referred by friends to doctors, lawyers, accountants, web site creators, desktop publishers, and to a multitude of other, valuable people who have also become friends. When Larry and Diana started their first company, they were introduced by friends to the Johnson's. The Johnson's showed Diana how to file all the necessary, tax forms for their new business. They gave her numerous referrals including an accountant and a lawyer. In addition to the referrals the Johnson's also offered business advice and direction.

The accountant and the lawyer became invaluable, business

associates and good friends. Although friendships can truly be wonderful, a mistake that many people make is to place too high a value on friendships—thinking that every friendship will continue forever. This belief is just not true. Hopefully, a few friends will remain through the many course-changes of life; however, it's a fact that most friendships are just for a season. A few examples of seasonal friendships are: single friends that can no longer relate to each other after one of them gets married; a friend that is of the opposite sex who you no longer associate with for the sake of your new marriage; the "married with children" who can no longer relate to their friends who are "married but childless"; people who have taken on many responsibilities and can no longer relate to those whose lifestyle is just one big party; and those who just made a quality decision to be different than the friends with whom they used to associate. Each new season changes your perception of reality and makes it more difficult to relate to those who are left behind.

When we make major changes in our lives, our friendships will change. When Larry was in the military service, he made a quality decision to stop abusing his body with smoking, excessive drinking, and drugs. At the time, he thought his friends would remain his friends—but that was not possible. His reality had changed but theirs had not. They continued to party, to get wasted, to get high. Partying was a big part of their lives. When Larry eliminated these things, his mind, his money, and his time was freed up from the pursuit of these addictions. His friends changed to include body builders, leaders, and those who were on a path of growth. It is good for you to realize that friends are for a season and you need not be afraid to lose your current friends in the process of change. It is a natural process that, as you grow from one season to another, the magnetic force associated with each new season will attract new friends that are also in that season. Many of the friends from your previous season will be repelled by your new magnetism.

If you're one who is coming out of a season of addiction,

it is important to avoid gathering together with those of a similar addiction who like to commiserate their addictive past. The Biblical lesson is true that it's easier to deliver the people from Egypt than it is to remove the mentality of Egypt from the people. The Israelites were delivered from their slavery in Egypt, but as soon as they were delivered, they longed to return to Egypt. It's not healthy to associate with those who still long for the slavery associated with their addictive past. Some groups offer accountability, and there may be members that can offer you encouragement. However, the fundamental premise of many twelve-step groups is to "confess the problem". Of course, it is necessary to admit that a problem exists in order to seek change; but "confessing the solution" is the answer. Associating with others that are already where you want to be is far better than the "misery loves company" scenario that commonly occurs when suffering people are gathered together. For example, "Alcohol no longer has a hold over me" or "I enjoy a freedom from all addictions" are far better confessions than "I am an alcoholic." Although it may seem invigorating to speak those words at first, the continual confession of being an alcoholic keeps you in a fight for survival from that addiction. If you struggle with alcoholism, then become friends with those people who choose not to drink alcohol and have never been alcoholics. At least then you'll find yourself in conversations that have nothing to do with alcohol because for those people it's never been a problem. Unfortunately, standard group methods keep you in a continual fight for survival. Developing friends that are magnetized to your new season will make you free, and freedom is always better.

One key to changing your life is to first believe that you can change. A good, first step is to change your self-image by using role models. Role models help to create within you a new image of who you want to be. When Larry was climbing the Tae Kwon Do ladder, it was easier for him to master the techniques involved in each belt level by imagining how Chuck Norris would accomplish that move. When Larry practiced a move from his perception of what Chuck Norris would do, it was as though he attained insight that he was incapable of receiving on his own. At the time Larry thought that being like Chuck Norris was everything he aspired to be, but he later discovered that it was just one piece in the puzzle that would make up his future self.

The imagination is a powerful tool, and when used properly, it will give you the ability to rise above many obstacles. If you don't have a clear image of your future self, then observe others and notice what you admire in other individuals. Visualize that you have those attributes. As each piece of your image is put into place, you'll gain a clearer picture of your future self. It may be that the image of your future self is the accumulation of many people. For example, one individual may be very outgoing and friendly but doesn't have a deep relationship with anyone. Another person has a romantic relationship with their spouse and has been married to the same person for twenty years, but they don't have children. Still another acquaintance has multiple children and is an exceptional parent. The person you want to be has many high-quality friendships, a successful marriage, and several well-adjusted children. Although you see some of your future self in each "role model" none of them by themselves are a good role model for you. The important thing is that you use your imagination to help you create a future self of which you can be proud.

Mentoring can be a beneficial tool to aid in the process of change. Mentoring creates the association between yourself and someone you want to be like. Mentoring helps you to become accountable and to change your magnetism to be like your mentor. In many cases a mentor relationship will make available to you a whole, new network of people, and many of your mentor's friends will also become your friends. Since Larry had the background that he did, he knew no one who could teach him how to become an executive. In Larry's youth he had obtained a vast array of knowledge. Unfortunately, most of the knowledge he obtained had little to do with the future he desired. He knew how to milk cows, pick watermelon, seine bait, weed beans, bale and stack hay, and operate and repair farm equipment. However, executives were not needed in the farming community where Larry was raised. Larry wanted to change, but he didn't know how.

Larry's mentors, David and Sonia Selley, paved the way for Larry to become an executive and business owner. David was a top executive for a major pharmaceutical company. He worked his way up the corporate ladder until he was making so much money that the company could hire five people for the price they were paying him. When the company decided to do just that, David started his own business with the knowledge he had obtained from his corporate experiences. When David was introduced to Larry, he was impressed and viewed Larry as a diamond in the rough. David recognized that Larry had the character traits required for success, but Larry needed a makeover.

David took Larry under his wing in a mentoring relationship. David recommended numerous books and tapes that Larry devoured like a starving man. David and Sonia adopted Larry like a son and even allowed him to live in their home during a period of transition. Before he met David, Larry had a low self-esteem; but David and Sonia brought Larry into their network of influential friends like he was someone special. When David wasn't teaching Larry how the business world worked, Sonia was showing him how to dress for success. David and Sonia acted like a rock tumbler. Like a rough diamond, Larry was thrown into the mentoring process, tumbled about, and came out sparkling like a gem. Larry will be forever grateful for the impact that their influence made in his life.

The popular movie *It's A Wonderful Life* helped many people who felt their lives were meaningless to realize that the small things in life can make a difference. Often life is not as bad as it may seem and a few small course-corrections will put life back on track. For many people there is a direct correlation between their occupation and their self-worth or self-esteem. After all, an individual's occupation encompasses their greatest expenditure of time. With introspection you can determine the level of value received for the time spent, and you can use this valuable insight to make a course-correction so that the future value for time spent is greater. Sometimes when people look back on their lives, if they don't feel that they have made a significant difference, they find themselves in a fight against depression or a "mid-life crisis." At this point people either look for ways to mask their feelings of inadequacy, or seek ways they can make their lives meaningful. Don't get bogged down with negative feelings of inadequacy. If you think a different occupation would make you feel better about yourself, then investigate that occupation. In this Internet age it's easy to gather information. Once you have found something you think would be worth your time, invest in yourself and your future by investigating that option.

The fact that you're reading this book separates you from the multitude because you are taking a step in the right direction. Buy a book or a tape series related to a new occupation or change your desire. At worst, you'll spend a little money to increase your knowledge base. Joining a chat room, attending a seminar, or a workshop will give you valuable information about your potential future. Chat rooms, seminars, and workshops will do more than increase your knowledge base; they also provide a platform through which you can network with other like-minded individuals. People love to talk about the positive and negative aspects of their occupation. By communicating with others who have already discovered the drawbacks of an occupation you will receive insight that can keep you from making an occupational decision that you would regret later. Making a career change by working for a different company or becoming self-employed is a significant course-correction in an individual's life. A little research can make a big difference in helping you choose a career path that is best suited to your personality.

Diana believed that she would make a great doctor. She liked the idea of helping people and felt that she could really make a difference. She gathered all the usual occupational information, but she believed the only way she could truly see what it would be like was to get involved. So, she volunteered some of her time at a local hospital. This gave her the opportunity to observe what it would be like to be in that environment. She interviewed several doctors who seemed to be happy in their field. In one interview she asked the question, "Do you ever regret becoming a doctor?" To her surprise he said, "Like you, I wanted to become a doctor because I believed that I could help people. It was that thought that helped me persevere through med school. However, what I discovered after I became a doctor was that people paid me to mask symptoms. I told them how to solve the true source of their problem but they rarely took my advice. You can only help people if they are willing to apply the advice you give. Most people won't put forth the effort. I found that, instead of really helping people, I was paid to listen to people whine about problems they had no intention of solving." The volunteer work, in combination with the doctor interviews, revealed to Diana the drawbacks of this occupation. This valuable insight redirected her thinking to another occupation that was better suited to her personality.

Larry had been an engineer for many years. But engineering no longer seemed to be exciting or challenging to him. Larry wanted to be involved in something where he could make a difference. Larry knew that computers were here to stay. As an engineer the problem solving aspects of computer networking appealed to Larry. He knew that to be happy in life, it was important to have an occupation that he would enjoy. It seemed that managing an Information Technology department for a large company would be a great match. Larry decided that, before he would seek a position as a network manager, he would gather information that would help him make a better decision. Larry purchased books and CDs related to computer networking. He gathered a tremendous amount of information about computers from their inception in the marketplace to current day applications.

Larry probed everyone he knew that was involved in a computer-related occupation for information. Although Larry liked the positive aspects of that occupation, the drawbacks were unacceptable to him. Larry discovered that most computer maintenance is done at night, and he didn't like the idea of always being on-call for some computer-related emergency. Sure it was an investment of time and money—only to discover that it wasn't for him; however, the knowledge Larry gained about computers became very valuable in setting up and maintaining a network of computers in his own company. It is better to count the costs and assess the gain before jumping into a new occupation with both feet and trying to make something work that isn't good for the long term.

Friends, mentors, books, tapes, seminars, and workshops can be a tremendously helpful resource to you as you are making course corrections in your life. Larry met an individual at a seminar named Keith who worked for IBM. In a conversation with Keith, Larry asked where he could find the best price on IBM computers. Keith told Larry that working for IBM had advantages. For instance, there was a program that allowed friends of IBM employees to buy computers at a drastically discounted rate. Keith made the necessary arrangements for Larry to become involved in this program. By being friendly with someone that Larry just met at a seminar, Larry saved a substantial amount of money when he bought computers for his office.

Workshops are great places to learn valuable skills and meet friends. When Diana married, she didn't know how to cook. Larry eagerly showed Diana how to cook many dishes. However, Diana was somewhat concerned about the nutritional value of Larry's dishes because Larry started each cooking session by plopping a cube of butter into a pan. Diana attended several cooking workshops. At one workshop, not only did she learn how to prepare a gourmet, turkey dinner, but she also met Rhonda. Rhonda was a fashion expert and shared many secrets with Diana—like how to properly color-coordinate her outfits and where she could find wonderful clothes at a great value.

The attainment of knowledge is never a waste of time. For instance, if you've always been interested in real estate, take a weekend course. Many realty companies offer complimentary courses so that time is your only investment. During the course you might discover that real estate agents work many nights and weekends. Suddenly being a real estate agent may not be as enticing as you originally thought. However, that knowledge creates a level of confidence in the subject studied. Perhaps you discovered that you were drawn to real estate from an investor standpoint and the weekend course gave you the confidence you needed to succeed as an investor.

It doesn't matter what topic an individual receives knowledge about, there is always an opportunity to apply that knowledge somewhere in the future. Learn something new everyday. Put yourself in a position where you can focus on learning those things that you believe will be valuable to your future. Once you are on the path you believe will net the best future results for your life, consistently find a way to apply what you have learned to your life. Remember that if what you thought was best for your future is not netting the desired results, do something different. Be steadfast in your efforts and stay in harmony with your goals.

Consistency is the result of a choice to maintain a constant, steady movement in the direction of your desired future. Consistency is a powerful force. Don't underestimate what ten minutes a day can do to change your life. You see this in the maintenance you have to do to keep your body in the shape. If you brush your teeth every day, you won't develop cavities; but if you only give your teeth a good brushing once a week, the decay will overpower your efforts.

Likewise, if an individual went to the gym once a month and worked out for six hours, that person would be very sore, and would net nothing. However, if that individual exercised half an hour twice a week their heart and their muscles would maintain a proper strength. In these examples you can see that it is not the amount of time that is spent on a task, but rather it is the repetition of the task that produces the results. It is important to develop good habits that become a consistent force of change in your life. Consistency is like a river that carves a path through rock. The rock is forced to change to accommodate the desired path of the consistently flowing river.

Set goals for the changes you desire. By continuously moving towards a positive change in your life you prevent negative changes from happening. Everyone knows that negative changes happen to those who are not moving in a positive direction. For example, a saggy midsection automatically happens to those who don't exercise. If you'd rather have a six-pack instead of a keg, then you need to implement a consistent, exercise routine. Don't view your new routine as something you're going to try, instead view it as a long-term lifestyle change. Even if you change your goals, don't change this new way of life. This way of life is the way of success and consistency will change your life.

Ray had what he considered to be a dead end job. Ray had a bachelor's degree in business administration but for the last five years he had a commission sales position with a major retail outlet. Ray was offered a management position with a nearby, plastic container company. It was a difficult choice for Ray. On the one hand, he could remain in the position he had for the last five years and hope that his commission remained steady. On the other hand, he could accept the new position that guaranteed the same wage but didn't offer the medical and dental benefits to which he had grown accustomed.

As Ray pondered the offer he became excited about the possibility of actually using his business administration skills. The night before Ray was required to give his answer he had a vivid dream. In the dream he was offered a gold shoe or a black shoe. The gold shoe was a representation of the reward that would be given as a result of diligent, consistent effort. The black shoe was a representation of a lesser reward that would be given but less would be required to receive the reward. To Ray that was the answer: why bother going for the black shoe when he could go for the gold. Ray gladly accepted the position with the plastic container company and gave a two-week notice to his previous employer.

Ray was excited from the start and he easily learned the requirements of his new position. For the first time in many years Ray felt like he was making a difference—he was going for the gold. Ray wasn't concerned about the medical and dental benefits he no longer had because the benefits that his wife received were even better than the benefits he received from his previous employer. However, several things happened that Ray did not expect. Because the company was small, the owners were constantly running errands and would leave their children at the office. Ray didn't feel that he could adequately run the office and checkup on their children at the same time. It was during this time that Ray's wife decided she wanted to have another child. Ray's wife quit her job to have the child and they no longer had the medical and dental benefits to which they had grown accustomed. Ray asked the owner of the plastic container company for a raise but the owner said he was unable to give him one at that time. A couple of weeks later Ray heard that the owners bought a new, big screen TV. Ray became discontented and went back to the owner stating that he had two jobs; one was running the office and the second job was watching the owner's children. Ray told the owner he needed to either hire someone to watch the children or pay him more money to do the job. The owner attempted to reassure Ray that he would receive an increase in pay, but he needed to be patient because it was impossible to raise his salary at that time.

Ray had lost sight of the gold shoe that he saw so clearly in his dream. The value of trying to be consistent didn't seem to be worth it. Ray decided to take a few days off to sort out his feelings. Ray told his wife to call the owner for him. The story they agreed upon was that Ray hurt his back and the doctor told him he needed to rest, and that Ray would not be able to make it in to the office until the following day. The day after that Ray called the owner to remind him of all the things that he did for him and to express again his need for a raise. The owner reiterated to Ray that he would receive a raise in the future, but he could not give him one now. Then Ray said to the owner, "I know you need me, you wouldn't know what to do without me." The owner warned Ray that if he allowed himself to become discontented to the extent that it destroyed the relationship, he would have no choice but to let him go. Ray answered angrily, "You don't have the balls to fire me." Needless to say, when Ray came to work on Monday a package was waiting for him that included final compensation along with all the items from his office. Within a year that small company became a leader in its industry. Somewhere along the line Ray lost sight of the fact that diligent, consistent effort would be required to obtain the gold shoe. If Ray had remained consistent, he would have that gold shoe. Unfortunately for Ray the gold shoe that was once in his sight was given to another who had proven his loyalty through diligent, consistent effort.

You can plug into a process of success through association with others and through continually learning new things. If you live in agreement with your goals, making steps on an undeviating path toward your goals, you will achieve them. The lifestyle of success is not something you try. Success comes from a steadfast effort to choose a higher life. Success is a way of life. Now is the time for action. Don't just talk to friends or mentors. Don't just listen to tapes or read books. Do something. Create movement in your life that will stimulate change. Although everyone should learn new things, the perpetual student never applies that knowledge to their life. So don't get stuck. Keep moving.

If you have been consistent in the path you have chosen but have not seen your desired results, you may feel you are going around in circles like someone lost in the woods. When you're at that place, it's important for you to find a mountain that allows you to see above the woods. Then you can regain your focus.

Everyone's life is made up of choices. If you're making a choice to proceed in one direction, you're canceling the choice that leads a different direction. Think of each choice you make in your life as a choice for the past, present, or future. The past is familiar to you because it is a representation of where you have been. The present you are now living is a result of choices that you have made to either allow your past to continue on or to bring your new future into the now, or a combination of the two. The choices you are now making will form your future. If you choose wisely, that future will be the ultimate life you desire to live.

The reason people feel like they're going around in circles is because they are making decisions that are based upon their familiar past. Current decisions based upon past results will net a future that will look very much like the past. The present is the crossroads that intersects the past and future. You're consistently making choices that will either lead back to the past or on to the future. If you don't like your past and want to move on to the future, then it's important to make decisions that are different from those that have brought you to your current present.

For example, an individual who wants to take a great vacation to an exotic location, but never has because they didn't believe they could afford it, will never make the trip as long as they maintain that mindset. However, if that same individual were to start planning that vacation, he would find a way to go. Nothing changed except for the choice to make that vacation a part of their future. Most people believe that their current choices are dictated to them by present circumstances, but those circumstances were created by the choices of their past. They make decisions based upon experiences that are familiar to them; however, if they want to change they must make decisions based on their desired futures. You must resist making decisions based on present circumstances or on past experiences. Choosing to do nothing will reap the results of past choices. What's in motion has a tendency to stay in motion. Changing the direction of that motion requires that you must make choices for a new future each day.

Changing the direction of a ball that is in motion requires that it must be met with equal or greater force. It's important to know what direction you want the ball to go before you stop its present movement. A ball that is stopped accomplishes nothing. You must keep the ball moving—that requires a constant force. Once the ball is moving in the direction you desire, directional corrections require less force or effort. You must develop routines that help you maintain the momentum. You can listen to positively charged, teaching tapes while putting on makeup, sorting laundry, or performing other, menial tasks. Daily positive confessions should become a habit—like eating healthy foods and exercising regularly. One key to developing positive routines is to imagine what future you desire and then to picture in your mind those things that you would do if you had already achieved that desired future. You can begin to do as many of those things as possible. As you're developing these new routines, resist focusing on the negative experiences of the past that elicit feelings of unforgiveness and guilt. These experiences slow your momentum by focusing on issues that are not a part of your desired future. Positive words, thoughts, and imagination increase the momentum toward your desired future.

Larry and Diana confess their top ten desired goals daily. Larry keeps his top ten in his PDA phone, and Diana has her top ten on 3x5 cards on her nightstand. You must make sure that your confessions speak of your desired goals as though they have already been attained. This process keeps your imagination working to make the words spoken from your mouth come to pass. If you desire to own a new Lexus, your confession should read, "I love my new Lexus, and I really enjoy driving it wherever I go", rather than, "I would like to buy a Lexus, and that's the car I will own someday". The first confession brings the Lexus from the future into the present. The second confession could bring you a used Lexus ten years down the road. Your imagination doesn't work to make it happen unless you place a demand on your mind. Some Jewish and some Christian people have sayings that are "positive confessions." These positive confessions are associated with regular activities, such as, every time they would pass through a doorway they would say to themselves, "I am blessed coming in and I am blessed going out". This is a good example of using the imagination to bring something into the present. The act of going through the doorway is a present tense action that creates an association in the mind of being blessed every time one walks through the door.

Another example of choosing to make choices that will net the future you desire is Larry and Diana's choice to have children. Many people considered it foolish to have children until they had achieved some level of financial security. However, Larry and Diana wanted to have four children, two boys and two girls. They did not allow their bankbook to dictate the time frame in which they began to have children. Larry and Diana made this choice based upon their desired future, and now have four wonderful children. They found a way to afford their children. If they would have made their choice based upon circumstances, it is very likely that they would have only had two children instead of the four. If you know what you want your future to be like, then take steps in that direction. If you're waiting for the circumstances to be perfect, you may miss the opportunity to have what you desire.

At only thirteen years of age, Larry and Diana's daughter understood this concept. She was assigned to write her most meaningful mantra on a poster and present it in her public speaking class. She wisely chose, "Success is a choice". Her poster showed the road of life with decision signs where one reality intersects with another. She explained that each and every day one must continually make the choice to succeed; therein, success becomes a way of life.

"One cannot help but be in awe
when one contemplates
the mysteries of eternity, of life,
of the marvelous structure
of reality, . . . It is enough if one
tries merely to comprehend a little
of this mystery each day."
Albert Einstein

Chapter 16

INTUITION AND BEYOND

Mysteries Of Faith

For purposes of this book the word "faith" does not refer to a set of religious beliefs. Rather, "faith" is acting on what you believe. Fear and faith are opposites. Fear is a twisted form of faith. Fear causes negative things to happen because we believe those things are going to happen. Faith causes positive things to happen because we believe those positive things are going to happen. You need to have faith that you can achieve your ideal reality. You must renounce your fear. This faith goes beyond believing that you can because you, in fact, act upon the belief. Your actions may be as simple as saying your top ten desired goals out loud, or your action may be to consciously take the time to imagine . . . with all your senses . . . the fulfillment of what you desire. You have the power to choose what you believe. You have the power to change what you believe.

There exists a check and balance system within your spirit. If what you choose to believe fulfills only your own selfish desires or is hurtful towards others, then your spirit will condemn you with guilt. The mystery of faith is a clear conscience. Without a clear conscience your goals cannot be realized. Though it is possible to sear your conscience and receive a goal that is selfish or hurtful toward another, it is unwise to do so. If you know in your heart that your desired goal will achieve good for you and for those around you, you will easily be able to receive what you believe. Some people experience a false sense of guilt because they desire good things. Often based in false religious beliefs, this guilt foils their success. If this is a stronghold for you, you must deal with it. No one should feel guilty that they wish to prosper. We should all desire to prosper as well as desire that those around us will prosper. It is a false concept that those persons that are wealthy are evil. Not every one who is rich hurt others to gain that wealth. Also, false humility will hurt your ability to achieve the desires of your heart. If the desires of your heart are not hurtful toward another then they are pure and good. What makes something selfish is that it ignores the needs and the desires of others.

For instance, you may believe that you will inherit the riches of a relative. In order for you to obtain the inheritance, this relative must die. It would be hard to make a positive confession in regard to receiving this inheritance because harm must come to another human being for the goal to be achieved. Would you want to apply your faith toward shortening another's life? Even if this individual is in great pain, there is a conflict of interest in believing for the person's wealth to come to you and believing the best for that person. At best a confession would have to be carefully worded that this individual has chosen to bless you with his possessions, but that his passing would be by his own free will after receiving a full and happy life. Your faith is then applied to lengthening this individual's life—which is contrary to your goal of receiving his money. You can see how this is a difficult goal to achieve. Your conscience condemns a selfish goal.

You may find a conflict with monetary situations where you desire to sell an item for a high price or buy one at a reduced price. While there is nothing wrong with believing for favor, your conscience may condemn you if you want to sell an item such that the buyer has to spend an unfair amount for the item. Similarly, you should not desire to cheat another by paying so little for an item that the vendor is selling it at a loss. Believe for win-win scenarios and favor. When Diana was looking for a great deal on wallpaper, she found an in-stock print she loved. The storekeeper was pleased to sell it to her at half price because the storekeeper needed to reduce her inventory. Both parties received benefit from the transaction.

If a particular goal stays in your confession stack for a long time, the two most common reasons are that your conscience is not clear or that you have caged your energy by defining a rigid path for the achievement of your goal. Larry and Diana desired to move back to California. Logically, they determined that they needed to sell their house in Arkansas before they could move. They priced their house at an amount they considered near top dollar. They believed it was a great value because the house was in cherry condition with many extra amenities. The house sat on the market. Many people showed a great interest in the home but bought another. After a while it became apparent that some force was resisting their faith. They evaluated the price and reduced it slightly. Still the house did not sell. While meditating on the problem, Larry and Diana realized that they had predetermined the path for their ultimate goal. As soon as they took the home off the market, a renter asked for a year lease, and Larry and Diana realized they truly desired to maintain the home as an asset and rent it rather than sell it. The other things necessary for their move fell into place, and their goal was realized. If your subconscious self is at odds with your confession, you will encounter resistance. Some would say that God is trying to show you a better way. Be open to intuitive insight and continue on your course until you receive the insight that may be an alternate approach to your goal. Some goals just require a tremendous amount of energy to fulfill. You must simply stay the course while being open to a better way.

When we work on a goal in the physical realm, we often

know the exact steps that it will take to achieve that goal. However, when we are changing our reality through the intuitive realm or the logical realm, the path is not often as clearly defined. It is a mistake to cage your energy by restraining it to a predefined path. One of Diana's goals was to see perfectly without the aid of contacts or glasses. She had gone to an eye specialist to find out if technology had advanced to a place that, by surgery, her vision could be corrected. She was told that she was not a candidate for refractive surgery. That goal was part of her top ten for many years. Diana's goal started as the confession, "I see perfectly without the aid of contacts, glasses, or medical intervention". She imagined waking up one morning with perfect vision as if she had been touched by a great prophet to receive her sight. Five years passed. As many of her goals had been realized, this goal stubbornly stayed in the stack of unfulfilled goals. She began to wonder why.

Diana was unaware that she had caged her energy by restricting the path of her goal fulfillment. As she pondered this goal, she realized that she had eliminated the possibility of achieving perfect sight through medical means. At that point she changed her index card to read, "I see perfectly without the aid of contacts or glasses". A few months after changing the wording, her family moved across country to Santa Barbara. She was looking through the phone book for an eye doctor for her children when an ad leaped off the page and grabbed her attention. If she had not changed her mindset to allow the path of medical intervention to achieve her goal of perfect eyesight, her mind and spirit would have been closed to the idea of eye surgery. But because she had un-caged her energy she was open to the possibility. She called and made an appointment for a free consultation with the doctor whose ad she had seen. Amazingly enough, this doctor had patented a new method to cut a thinner flap into the eye, leaving a greater thickness for correction. What was previously impossible for her had become possible. Very few doctors in the country could correct over ten diopters of near-sightedness with Lasik, but this particular doctor could. After a ten-minute painless procedure, the difficult goal of perfect eyesight without contacts or glasses was achieved. Interestingly, Diana originally felt that obtaining this goal through medical means would feel like a failure because she wanted to achieve the goal strictly through faith. However, it required a high level of faith to face a scary, laser surgery. Since eyeglasses had been a source of ridicule in her childhood, Diana even received a boost to her self-esteem when she attained her goal.

Achieving a goal through breaking down that goal into smaller goals is usually helpful; however, there are exceptions. When Larry and Diana found their first home, they were stepping out of their financial comfort zone. They had no problem believing that the house was theirs. When they tried to obtain financing, they met several obstacles. When Diana focused on the end result of living in that house, she found that easy to imagine. But when she considered the amount of down payment that the loan company was requiring, her mind staggered at the amount. Instead of applying her faith to the down payment—the logical, first step—she kept her focus on the end result. She reasoned that another loan company would be willing to accept a lower down, but she pushed the problem out of her mind and just focused on living in her new home. Larry and Diana's faith brought unexpected money for the down without specifically believing for it because they believed they could have that house. If you can believe for the end result, focus on that instead of taking smaller steps toward that goal. In some cases, this is actually easier, and there is less likelihood that you will cage your energy by predetermining a means to the desired end.

Similarly, when we believe for something that involves other people, we must not cage our energy by focusing on what other people are going to do. When we change, the people around us must respond to that change; however, they retain the right to react to that change in their own way. Every person has free will to determine their own actions and reactions; however, we can influence people and force people to make a decision because of our actions.

We all have a sphere of influence. Each of us impacts the reality of those around us. The amount of impact is dependent upon the closeness of the relationship we have with these people. As parents we will impact our children's lives. Innately children desire to please their parents. If we have fostered a relationship of love and trust, our children will be greatly influenced by our advice and our actions. Our adult friends, coworkers and even our spouse will not be as easily influenced as our children. However, if they trust, respect, and care for us, they will listen and be willing to change because of the relationship. It is important to realize that every human being has been given free will—the power to choose for him or her self. It is the choices that form the realities. We can impact other's lives by the choices we make. The following two examples will show how the choices made by the individuals caused two different outcomes from similar situations.

Shortly after marrying her husband, Carmen realized that Craig had a problem with alcohol. Years later, after several arrests for D.U.I. and then mandatory, court appointed, dry-out clinics, Carmen was struggling with her belief that Craig would ever change. Craig promised Carmen many times over the eight years of their marriage that she was important to him and that he would give up alcohol. Carmen stayed with him for the sake of their four children. Craig convinced Carmen that he would change. Craig admitted that he had a problem with alcohol, and claimed he would be faithful to Carmen. However, instead of getting better it appeared that Craig was getting worse. He was never there for Carmen or for the children. Many times Craig would stay out all night. It got to the point that when Craig was home, he was like a fifth child. He did nothing but lay around the house, expecting Carmen to wait on him hand and foot.

One day Carmen was cleaning the house and discovered several love letters to Craig from other women. Carmen confronted Craig with the letters and gave him an ultimatum. Carmen told him that he must be there to help her with the children, that he must get help to eliminate his alcohol problem, that he must agree to go to marriage counseling with her, and he must never flirt with another woman. Carmen's husband loved alcohol more than his family; therefore, he did not have the needed desire and willpower to make a change. Carmen made the choices that affected her reality, but she could not force her choices on her husband.

Carmen knew that for her to remain in the relationship with Craig, knowing that there was no hope of recovery, would negatively affect Carmen and her children. Carmen could give Craig the necessary support hoping to influence a change in his behavior, but he wasn't willing to change. Craig refused to agree with Carmen's terms. When Craig and Carmen were divorced, Carmen received full custody of the children. Craig has been married and divorced several times since then, and has not seen his children in over six years. Carmen, however, is enjoying a new life, free from the agony of living with an alcoholic.

Tom and Tammy loved each other very much but Tom came from a long line of alcoholics. Shortly after their marriage Tom increased his intake of alcohol. Tammy convinced herself that it was just a phase Tom was going through and eventually he would come around. Tammy supported Tom and his decision to finish college so that he could obtain his engineering degree. Tammy believed that once Tom had his degree he would settle into his profession and leave alcohol behind. Before Tom graduated from college, Tammy was pregnant with their first child. Shortly after Tom graduated their second child was on its way. Tom excelled in his profession as Tammy expected. However, Tom's alcohol consumption increased instead of decreased. Tom spent many nights away claiming that "yet another project" required his attention. They had been married for ten years, and their children were half grown when Tammy discovered that Tom had a one night fling with another woman.

Tammy decided to give Tom an ultimatum. Tammy told him that there would be no more late nights, that he must be there for her and the children, that he must get help to eliminate his alcohol problem, that he must agree to go to marriage counseling with her, and that he must promise her to be faithful. Tammy knew she would do well financially if he refused to accept her ultimatum because state law entitled her to half of everything he made. What Tammy really wanted was Tom back without a drinking problem.

The thought of losing Tammy was devastating to Tom. After Tammy gave him the ultimatum, Tom realized how much she truly meant to him, and felt horrible about the pain that he had brought to Tammy's life. Tom accepted all of Tammy's terms. It took diligent effort to revitalize their marriage, and for Tom to get rid of his alcohol addiction, but they did it. Many of the feelings they had for each other when they were first married have returned, and they are more confident than ever about their future together. Tammy made the choices that affected her reality, and her choices influenced a change in her husband. Tom loved his family more than alcohol or a promiscuous lifestyle; therefore, he had the needed desire and willpower to make the changes necessary to repair the relationship.

Major discoveries, like proving man can fly, breaking the sound barrier, or discovering that other galaxies exist, all had a global impact on the reality of others.

Still, though it is possible to impact others, our focus should simply be on improving ourselves. Three common approaches to influencing others do not achieve long-term results. These three are 1) lecturing, 2) guilt manipulation, and 3) playing the martyr. Lecturing extensively, a.k.a., nagging, reinforces the mindset that no matter what you do, it is impossible to please the person who constantly gives the unsolicited lectures, so why bother trying. Similarly, manipulation by guilt reinforces the negative mindset that another individual is responsible to make your life better; and that person is guilty of making you unhappy. Deep down we know that we are each responsible for our own happiness and we resist someone who is trying to exercise control over us. Similarly, playing the martyr is a form of manipulation where one makes unnecessary self-sacrifices hoping to make another person change. Many times this backfires because others are more than willing to allow you to carry the load that you have volunteered to carry.

Notice all three forms of manipulation—lecturing, guilt manipulation, and playing the martyr—invoke negative feelings in the person that you're trying to influence. That is why these techniques fail. People respond much better when you invoke positive feelings through your actions or words. For instance, instead of trying to make a teenager perform a task like taking out the trash, the parent can ask for help and express appreciation to them for doing things that help the household run efficiently. Because the teenager has been shown by his parents that these actions have worth and value, he gains a boost in self-esteem through the positive reinforcement received when doing the desired task. People want to feel needed, appreciated, valued, and accepted for whom they are. When we offer actions or words that evoke positive feelings, others are much more likely to respond favorably.

Have you ever heard the statement, "He who loves least controls the relationship?" That statement is very true in many cases. When an individual makes a choice to change regardless of what the "old crowd" might think, they changed the dynamics in the relationship. For example, as a child Diana desired to please her parents. She tried to prove herself to her parents by attaining straight "A" report cards and then becoming an engineer. Diana continuously tried to gain their approval and praise. She wanted them to demonstrate that they truly loved her. Diana's self-esteem was wrapped up in what they thought of her. After Diana and Larry were married, Diana initially still looked to her parents for their approval. In the second year of their marriage Diana's perspective changed, and she began to discover her own self-worth. Diana loved children and desired to get pregnant. Diana knew that if she got pregnant, she would have to deal with her parents' disapproval. They wanted Diana to continue with her career and told her to wait because she couldn't afford to have children. Diana did get pregnant and her parents criticized her, as expected, but Diana no longer cared. Diana quit her engineering position to stay at home with her newborn. She was happier with that decision. Once her parents lost control over her; they tried to win her favor by asking Larry and Diana to come over to their house for dinner once a week. Diana's relationship with her parents achieved a better balance because she was no longer seeking their constant approval.

This same phenomenon can also be seen in marriage. Marriage appears at times to be much like a seesaw. When one individual takes all responsibility in the area of relationship, the other individual abdicates their responsibility. Relationships that are faltering on the brink of divorce often have one pursuing and the other running. If the one pursuing stops chasing, the other partner will most often stop running and show a desire to work on the relationship.

Changing your reality will influence a change in those around you. If you don't know how to influence another to change in a desirable way, you may need to seek the answer by tapping into the intuitive realm. If your goal stubbornly remains in your confessions stack and you don't know why, then you need a fresh intuitive insight. But what if you don't know how to tap into this hidden resource? Let's explore some ways that others have used to find direction and insight.

**"I admit thoughts influence
the body."**

Albert Einstein

Chapter 17

INTUITION AND BEYOND

Tapping Into The Intuitive

A goal is a dream with specific and measurable parameters. In order to have a goal, we must be able to imagine that it is possible. Most goals have a deadline, but when forming a goal to change your reality, the timeframe is always now. You believe your reality is what your goal is. As you achieve that goal you will move to higher and higher goals. It is like climbing a mountain, and as you get to the peak, you see a range of new possibilities. When you believe beyond yourself, your ability to imagine increases and new choices are made available to you. It is like being on a road in your mind that has many intersections. The roads that branch off from these intersections are choices that can change your life. If the road you're currently on is bumpy, you may decide to choose a different route. Unfortunately, some of the roads at these intersections lead to dead ends. Other roads lead you to an interstate that will help you transition faster from one state of mind to the next bringing you to your destination sooner. It is important to learn how to bypass the roads that will take you to dead ends, and to choose the roads that will make the trip to your desired destination more pleasant. The wisdom to choose the proper road is accomplished through the process of thought and revelation from the intuitive realm.

There are certain methods of thinking that are common to all. For example, everyone has spent time daydreaming about someone they like or an anticipated future event. Most have experienced situations in life that shifted their brain into high gear to the extent that they just lay in bed at night without even a remote possibility of sleep. Women are said to have special intuitive thought capabilities called "women's intuition." This intuition is usually referred to as an insightful understanding of the family unit. Men are said to spend most of their time mulling. If they don't have the insight into a current situation, they remain silent until the answer is formulated in their brain. Although these common methods of thinking occasionally give us a glimpse into intuitive thought, many times these methods fall short of true revelation.

It requires the imagination in order to truly tap into a higher state of consciousness. This book has already focused on the impact of the imagination, but not on how the imagination can be used to achieve a higher state of consciousness. In the pursuit of higher consciousness many people over the years have used a method of thought known as meditation. Meditation comes in many different forms, and there are numerous ways that an individual can arrive at a meditative state.

Some Chinese and Native American Indian cultures sought this meditative state with the aid of drugs. The drugs these cultures used were based primarily on their availability. Therefore, the drug normally used by the Chinese was opium, and the drug normally used by Indian cultures for meditation was the peyote cactus, more commonly known as "mescaline". Under the influence of these drugs the body would begin to shut down, but the mind of the individual was brought to a higher state of awareness. Some believe that this state of awareness is an intersection between multiple realities, and it is at this meditative state of mind that the individual experiences increased intellectual capabilities. The two hemispheres of the brain achieve a greater level of balance making the thought processes more orderly, allowing the meditator to attain a level of awareness that is not normally achieved without meditation. However, if an individual chooses a different path from the intersection of realities in the mind, he can witness future or past events with astounding clarity. Drug-induced meditation in many cases will bypass the normal stages or levels of thought, plunging the mind into a deeper level of thought very rapidly. Drug induced meditation can be very dangerous because the individual's mind doesn't have time to prepare for the journey.

Some cultic rituals use forms of drug-induced meditation, along with chanting, to invite vile spirits into the body. This situation arises with the human chalice. A human chalice is an individual who allows his body to be taken over by vile spirits through the use of spells and incantations. People who are well versed in the use of such spells and incantations perform a ceremony that is supposed to give an individual supernatural power; unfortunately the downside is that they also give up control of their body as it is taken over by the vile spirits. There are many different kinds of vile spirits.

Any spirit is considered vile if it attempts to take control by usurping the will of an individual. There is a vile spirit associated with hard liquor. Have you ever noticed that most liquor stores have signs in their windows advertising wine and spirits, "spirits" referring to hard liquor? An excess of hard liquor causes an individual to lose self-control, which allows vile spirits of addiction, depression, suicide, promiscuity, or any other vile spirit to have access to the individual's body. No vile spirit can take over the control of an individual's body without the permission of that individual. Excessive consumption of hard liquor or drugs creates an opening for vile spirits to control the body. The spirit and body under the influence is subjected to anything those vile spirits desire.

Unfortunately, a vile spirit enslaved Frank. When Frank was not under the influence of the spirit of alcohol, he was one of the nicest guys that anyone would ever want to know. He was kind, generous, and would give the shirt off his back if you asked him for it. However, when Frank was influenced by the spirit of alcohol, he was literally not himself. It was a true Dr. Jekyll and Mr. Hyde scenario. Under the influence he would beat his children and his wife. One time, under the influence, he went into his bedroom looked in the closet and said to his wife, "I'm tired of never having a place to hang my clothes; this closet is full of your clothes, and I won't put up with it anymore." Then he proceeded to take all her clothes and throw them out the front door into the snow. The next day he apologized for the behavior, but the damage was already done. Company would only stay to visit when Frank was in control of his body. Although his wife Betty waited patiently for many years trying to help Frank get free from the spirit of alcohol, that vile spirit had too great of control over him. Eventually his children all moved out of the house, and Betty divorced him. Frank drank himself to death, dying young and alone in the house that was once occupied by his family.

In the early 1970's research related to an individual's ability to perceive without the use of the five physical senses was very popular. The research was directed into an arena called "Extrasensory Perception." "Extrasensory Perception" can be divided into four primary categories—Telepathy, Clairvoyance, Clairaudience, and Precognition. Telepathy is the ability to sense the thoughts or feelings of another individual. Clairvoyance is the ability to see beyond the physical range of vision. Clairaudience is the ability to hear beyond the physical range of sound. Precognition is the ability to receive knowledge of future events through the use of Telepathy, Clairvoyance, or Clairaudience. In some of the initial research studies, the participants would be given Phencyclidine "PCP" or another drug with similar hallucinogenic capabilities. Although there were some apparent successes, in many instances the participants were not prepared for this drug induced, meditative state. Several participants had difficulty differentiating between the different realities even after the drug was no longer in their system. In the mid-1970s "PCP", under the names of "angel dust" and "rocket fuel", was made available to teenagers who experimented with it on their own. Because of the ability of "PCP" to bring the individual to an altered state of consciousness, some of these teenagers walked in front of moving vehicles believing that they were invincible, jumped from buildings expecting to spread their wings and fly, while others claimed to see through solid objects as though they were transparent. Drug-induced meditation is not a good idea, but the research showed the power available in altered states of consciousness.

Most non-drug induced meditation allows the mind of an individual to go through the normal stages or levels of thought on its journey to a meditative state. This is much safer, because the brain has the opportunity to assimilate information as these deeper levels are achieved. Additionally, during non-drug induced meditation the individual retains their free will. However, guided meditation, including hypnosis, can be dangerous. If you're considering hypnosis or another form of guided meditation, take a trusted friend or family member to observe and to stop the procedure if he believes that continuing would no longer be in your best interest. During hypnosis the willpower of an individual is weakened, causing them to be extremely open to suggestion. That is why hypnosis works, but it is also why hypnosis can be dangerous. You may not receive the results you are looking for if the individual guiding the procedure has a different mindset, or goals, than you do.

Hypnotism is a common form of guided meditation. Hypnotism is usually performed by licensed professionals. Obviously, because of the rules and regulations that must be followed, hypnotism is considered to be a relatively safe form of guided meditation. Many have claimed to receive a tremendous benefit through the use of hypnotism, but even hypnotism as a form of guided meditation leaves the individual open to the suggestions of another. Hypnotism is like a sign that says, "Enter at your own risk". It may be that the hypnotist and process used are completely trustworthy and safe. It may be that hypnotism is the best method for you, but that's the risk you have to accept in order to receive a guided tour into a meditative state.

Graham was exposed to a form of guided meditation that was similar to the cultic ritual previously discussed that ushered in vile spirits. Graham was a confused individual who sought a deeper level of understanding. Graham had suffered from health problems and was seeking a way to become well. He heard that there was a form of meditation that would aid in the healing of an individual's body. Believing it was the answer to all his problems, Graham readily became a part of this group. The group immediately began teaching Graham different forms of meditation. Those who were teaching this meditation monitored Graham on an EEG machine that tracked the alpha activity of his brain to determine when he was in the proper, meditative state. When they considered Graham's brain to be at "the optimum meditative state," they told him to picture himself sitting inside a certain room. When Graham indicated that he had arrived at that place, they told Graham to invite someone else into the room with him so that that person could help him with his problems. Through this process Graham realized that they were actually asking him to invite a vile spirit into his body. Graham instinctively resisted and awoke from his meditative state. When he asked them politely what they were trying to accomplish through the process, they responded by ushering him out of the building and asked him not to return. Graham deduced that the purpose of the group was to bring an individual unknowingly to a place where he would receive a vile spirit into his body.

The safest place to meditate is somewhere that is familiar to you so that you feel comfortable, and the safest form of meditation is non-drug induced, non-guided meditation. Some of the techniques used to arrive at a meditative state are: saying a scripture verse over and over; speaking in tongues; making deep sounds that come from within; the repetitive chanting of words; and singing praise songs. When done properly there are many advantages to meditation. Through meditation people have been able to find lost items, tap into past, present, and future events in their own lives and in the lives of other people, provide a diagnosis of medical problems, and gain valuable insight into almost every area imaginable.

Jason and Julie used meditation to help them get a new minivan. Jason and Julie did not have the ability to purchase a new minivan in the natural physical realm. Finances were very tight, but their family had grown to a place where their small car was no longer adequate to transport their family. They believed that the only way they could afford a new minivan was to bring it in through the process of meditation. The first thing they did, before they began the process of meditation, was to determine the vehicle that met both of their desires. Once they had the vehicle in mind they were both able to focus on the same vehicle as they meditated. They believed that there is a greater force associated with agreement. Every night they set the stage for meditation by playing soft music, lighting a candle, and sitting together in a comfortable location. After three months, they were made aware of a deal regarding the vehicle they desired. The people who were selling it just wanted to bless a family and weren't concerned about the money. Jason and Julie received their vehicle at a price way below market price with a comfortable payment plan, and the people who owned the vehicle fulfilled their desire to bless a family in need.

An additional advantage to proper meditation is the healing offered to the body of the meditator, along with the peaceful state that one achieves through non-drug-induced meditation. It has been well documented that through meditation individuals have a greater balance between the two hemispheres of their brain, thus creating a greater level of order and intelligence in the functioning of their brain and improved overall mental capabilities. Other advantages to meditation are reduced stress and anxiety, improved self-confidence, improved relationships at home and work, and a sense of overall well-being. The Hebrew Rabbi Eleazar, when describing the process of meditation, said "Think of yourself as nothing and totally forget yourself as you pray. Only remember that you are praying for the divine presence. You may then enter the universe of thought, a state of consciousness which is beyond time."

The process of meditation that Joe likes to use is a combination of using deep tones while speaking in tongues. Speaking in tongues is a New Testament concept of uttering a language given by the Holy Spirit, but unknown to the individual. The state of meditation is brought to pass by either focusing on a stationary object, or keeping eyes closed while speaking in tongues. The positions that Joe most commonly uses are sitting in a comfortable position with hands pressed together palm to palm thumbs pressed under the chin and index fingers pressed at the bridge of the nose; he also likes laying flat on his back with the knees bent with his arms to the sides with his fingers interlocked over his stomach. The first sign that he is entering into a meditative state is a tingling that begins in the frontal lobes of his brain, then proceeds back to encompass the entire cerebral cortex and the temporal lobes. At other times this tingling sensation begins in the middle of the spine, moves all the way up into the Medulla and proceeds to encompass the cerebral cortex and the frontal and temporal lobes. Regardless of where the tingling starts, every time he has achieved a meditative state it involves this tingling sensation that encompasses the brain. This state of meditation is very peaceful—almost a sleep state for his body; however, Joe's mind becomes extremely active with a heightened sense of awareness. The Bogatz's believe that the reason most people use less than five percent of their brainpower is because the brain is designed to interface with the intuitive realm.

People commonly observe a tingling in their brain during meditation because a greater portion of the brain is being used to interface with the intuitive realm. Remember the spirit realm operates at a higher speed than the physical realm; therefore, the body must be removed from the equation while the activity of the brain must increase for an interface to be achieved.

In a state of meditation Joe can place his hand on an individual and in his mind he is able to see the condition of internal organs. Many times Joe has commanded an organ to conform to its original state and has witnessed the result of the words spoken. Through meditation Joe has been able to tap into the thinking of others over vast distances. Through meditation Joe has been able to receive information about a person's past.

When Joe was conducting interviews to hire a nanny for his children, Joe believed that he had found the perfect nanny—until he was checking references and heard something from a previous employer that concerned him. Anyone who would be in a position to care for Joe's most valued assets had to be of the highest moral standards. Joe needed to be sure that this person met that standard. Through the process of meditation Joe was able to visualize the individuals past experiences. Joe discovered that the woman had been abused by her father—which was a problem for a time—but she had worked through that problem and it was no longer an issue that affected her job performance. In another instance Joe's children were being cared for by their nanny while he was away on business. Joe sensed that something had happened; so he began to meditate in order to discover what had transpired. Joe discovered that his child had just scratched his arm while playing and Joe was reassured that the nanny was not negligent in her duties. Through meditation he has also been able to receive insights with regard to future events. In meditation Joe sensed that a world-changing event would happen on September 11th, 2001, though he did not know what would happen on that day. Many times he has received insight into the lives of other people, and later had the accuracy of the information received confirmed by the individual.

Sometimes Joe has tapped into the lives of others and received information about future events only to discover later that they didn't come to pass. Joe became confused with the fact that sometimes what he saw came to pass in the future, but that other times what he saw didn't come to pass, even though the process he used was the same. In meditation Joe discovered that the reason the future sometimes came to pass as he saw it, and other times did not, was because the future was not certain. Joe was only able to tap into a potential future based upon what that person was thinking at the time. If they had continued on that line of thinking, the future that they were thinking about would have come to pass. What an individual is thinking affects the choices that the individual makes. The future is based upon the choices that are made every day, and if those choices change, so does the future.

The extreme of what Joe experienced is a process known as remote viewing. The difference between his meditative viewing as opposed to remote viewing is that Joe's consciousness never leaves his body. Joe witnessed an example of remote viewing. One night he was walking past the foyer in his home. The hairs on the back of his neck stood up as he sensed that he was being watched by someone outside the entry door. Joe went to the window by the entry door, and quickly turned on the porch light. To Joe's surprise what he saw was a black cat that was sitting outside staring at the entryway. Joe perceived that it was more than just a black cat. He opened the door to send it on its way. When he walked out the front door he noticed that the cat was seemingly unafraid as it continued to sit there and stare at him. It wasn't until Joe ran towards the cat that it took flight. In Joe's quest to understand the situation he experienced with the cat, he discovered information about the process called "remote viewing".

A common practice in the occult is to drug a human chalice, so that a vile spirit can temporarily move out of the human body into an animal host body. The animal can be controlled by the vile spirit to spy on others. Black cats are used because they are not easily seen in the dark. These vile spirits have given rise to the superstitions associated with black cats. In this type of remote viewing a vile spirit, instead of the consciousness of the individual, leaves the body and then returns again with the information obtained during the remote viewing process.

The U.S. government heard about incidents where individuals have successfully achieved remote viewing. The process of remote viewing gave an individual the ability to separate their consciousness from their body and transfer it to a specific place or into the body of an animal for a period of time. During that time of separation the consciousness of the individual is able to witness conversations or incidents without being discovered. The U.S. government spent millions of dollars to develop a program with the remote viewing concept in mind; however, the governmental program was designed to use the concept of remote viewing without actually separating the consciousness of the individual from the body. The CIA and the U.S. Army were responsible for this joint research program that was named "Stargate". The primary focus of Stargate was to develop psychic spies with remote viewing capabilities that could be used by the government to locate targets for elimination. In November 1995 the Channel 10 news out of Sacramento, CA broadcast a story showing evidence of the Stargate psychic spying program. Whether the process used for the Stargate program involved drug-induced meditation is not known. However, some persons have suggested that remote viewing was used to discover the location of U.S. hostages in Iran during the Carter administration. Regardless of the process used, many say the results achieved through remote viewing have been undeniable.

In some instances of remote viewing the consciousness of

the individual leaves the body for a period of time. In those instances the process of remote viewing is similar to that of an out-of-body experience. Many individuals who have had an out-of-body experience claim that the five, physical senses remained intact although their consciousness was separated from their physical body. In 1982 a former parapsychologist by the name of Susan Blackmore received results from surveys that indicated that up to twenty percent of the population has had an out-of-body experience at some point during their lives. Research conducted by Dr. Olaf Blankeof the Geneva University in Switzerland discovered that electrical stimulation at the juncture of the temporal and parietal lobes will stimulate an out-of-body experience. Out-of-body experiences are one form of proof of the existence of a spirit that gives life to the body.

Make a habit of meditation in your life. Find a quiet and comfortable place for peaceful thought, reflection, or prayer. Your approach should be consistent with your beliefs. Expect insight from your spirit, from the spirit realm, and from the God that you worship. Solutions to problems, direction for your life, and profound revelation are awaiting you. If you take the time to tap into the intuitive realm, your life will be greatly enhanced. For many, meditation will open up a whole, new world of possibilities. Avoid the dangerous use of drugs and use caution with guided meditation, but do not be afraid of what your own spirit has to offer you through meditation. Your brain was made to interface with this realm, so explore this resource daily.

Some of the issues discussed here could be considered as "paranormal" occurrences. The classification of the paranormal experience is any occurrence that cannot be explained scientifically. Although it can be difficult to discuss meditation without some crossover into the paranormal, the primary focus is the power of the imagination, and how an individual can achieve a higher level of consciousness through the process of meditation. Just because some experiences cannot be explained scientifically, does not mean that they cannot be understood by the individual having those experiences. However, because paranormal experiences cannot be scientifically explained, an individual must be willing to open up their mind to a world that goes beyond science in order to gain understanding. A supernatural world exists that supersedes the world experienced by the five physical senses. If you're ready to discover the world that exists beyond the visible world, then step into the realm of the "paranormal".

"The tragedy of life is what dies inside a man while he lives."

Albert Einstein

Chapter 18

INTUITION AND BEYOND

The Impossible
Is Possible

The standard, average, usual, and natural are considered normal. What is exceptional, remarkable, miraculous, or supernatural is paranormal. Of course paranormal experiences are not scientifically explainable because the paranormal supersedes ordinary events in mysterious and astounding ways. The supernatural seems to transcend the laws of nature and the laws governing the universe, as we understand it. We can easily accept that dogs have a supernormal sense of smell or that cats have the extraordinary ability to see in the dark. What boggles the mind is when humans suggest that they have abilities beyond the physical realm.

Human beings, however, are body, soul, and spirit; therefore, it should not be surprising that they possess abilities beyond the physical. In recent years society has more readily accepted the abilities of the soulful man. Thought, willpower, and emotional energy are generally considered part of the normal resources of human beings. The spiritual and intuitive resources of mankind have barely been acknowledged, yet alone, explored.

The New Testament proclaims, "Nothing is impossible for those that believe." Yet, few understand the power of belief. In essence we are all prophets who speak our beliefs, and see the phenomenon of self-fulfilling prophecy come to pass. The human race is tapping into spiritual resources without understanding, and this lack of understanding causes us to perish. We utter curses over ourselves and others and allow fear to rule over our minds and spirits. If we understand the power of our imagination, we would immediately curtail our fearful illustrations that portray defeat, destruction, and death. We would dwell on the imagery of hope, victory, success, and life. We would put the force of faith to work for us and tap into the intuitive realm knowing that our spirits can reveal truth.

If you can imagine something, then it is possible for you. Your spirit will illuminate your mind with the revelations you need to make your imagined events a reality in the physical. Your spirit is the light that brings life to your body. Spirit is not subject to time or limited by its constraints. Spirit exists on a subatomic level unseen by human eyes and functions at the speed of light or greater.

The concept that spirit is quick and functions at the speed of light comes from the Biblical representation of God, who is spirit and light. Scripture says, "God is light and in Him is no darkness at all." Also, scripture said of an angel seen outside Jesus' tomb, "His countenance was like lightning." When man was thrown out of the Garden of Eden, it was guarded by "a flaming sword, which turned every way to guard the tree of life." The picture is like a laser beam that is both energy and light. As paranormal psychologists have studied aberrations, they have been able to measure an electromagnetic energy when a paranormal phenomenon occurs. This fact is perfectly understandable when you consider that the essence of light is found in electromagnetic waves. If you can imagine something, then it is possible for you. Most people would say that living a life free of sickness is impossible, but Larry and Diana's family is free from sickness because they believe that they can be.

People would easily understand the realm of the spirit if the speed at which it functions were slowed. Like the propeller on an aircraft, the blur becomes well-defined as the blades cease to spin.

Children with auditory perception difficulties are being taught through a new method. A computer program slows speech to a pace where the child can grasp the individual letter sounds and therein can learn to read and speak with clarity. As understanding increases, the program increases the speed of the auditory input to normal levels, and the child begins to function at the normal pace.

Since our bodies function at the speed of this visible world, they are subject to the materialistic constraints of this plane. We are like children with a spiritual perception problem who need help to discern the faster realm of intuition. If we are willing to accept the existence of this unseen realm and acknowledge the hidden resources that are available to us from this realm, we can experience the supernatural and the paranormal in our lives. Through meditation we increase our brain activity to interface with the spirit realm. It is there—in the spirit realm—that we experience the supernatural. The following are true-life experiences in the realm of the paranormal.

Larry and Diana have dared to believe in the impossible and have seen miraculous events take place. Their son was suffering from a high fever. They commanded the fever to leave and felt the immediate temperature change on their child's forehead as the fever left. The once clammy hands became suddenly dry. They do not tolerate sickness in their family because they believe that freedom from sickness is possible.

As Larry prayed over his family members, he has experienced greater levels of intuitive insight. Literally he has seen and diagnosed what is going on inside a person's body.

Emily, a friend, had suffered for years with lower back pain. She had seen many medical doctors and chiropractors but obtained no relief. As Larry prayed over Emily he saw a vision of her lower intestines twisted, so he commanded them to straighten. Over the next couple days, Emily eliminated excessive greenish, brown waste that had apparently been lodged in her intestinal tract. Before the week was over, she was free from the lower back pain that she had experienced for so long.

When their oldest son was just a toddler, Diana would help him put on his shoes and socks every morning. This ritual was performed on the living room couch sitting on the center cushion in the same manner every morning. Over the years Diana has learned to be sensitive to her inner, intuitive voice. One particular morning, Diana heard, "Sit on the rocking chair to put on your son's shoes." This wasn't a logical choice for such a task, but Diana followed that inner leading. As Diana was starting to put on her son's second shoe, a heavy, wooden, decorative beam fell from the ceiling and one end of the beam thudded into the center cushion of the couch. Her son's skull could have been shattered by that beam; but her sensitivity to the spirit realm saved his life.

During Larry's enlistment in the military he had an overseas tour in the Philippines. A man from the area asked Larry if he knew a soldier that he specified by name. Larry responded that he did know the person spoken of, and that the person was in the same battalion. The local man said the military man had left his ID in a local bar. He asked Larry to come to the bar and retrieve the lost ID so that Larry's fellow officer would be able to get back onto the base that night. With Larry following, the man turned into a dark alley. As the alley was approaching a mid-alley intersection, Larry heard, "Run!" from within his spirit. It was so impacting to Larry that he turned around and ran. When Larry looked back, he saw several angry men standing in the alleyway—men who had been ready to jump him at the intersection and rob him.

Graham was driving toward home on De Soto Avenue when his daughter yelled, "Stop!" Graham slammed on the brakes and skidded to a stop right before entering the intersection. The light was green and Graham had the right-of-way; but if he had proceeded into the intersection, a speeding car would have broadsided his vehicle. He turned to his young daughter and said, "I'm sure glad you saw that car and yelled, 'Stop' because I didn't see it." His daughter replied that she did not see the car and she didn't say anything. In fact, she didn't hear anyone yell, "Stop!" and wondered why her daddy had braked so suddenly.

While playing with the children in the park, Diana lost an earring. It was one of her favorites, so she asked Larry if he could find it. It was a large park that was covered with blades of Bermuda grass, so finding something that small in such a big park was clearly a ridiculous task. Larry decided to put his intuitive powers to the test; he meditated until he had a clear picture of where the earring was. Then he walked into the park to the exact point he saw in his mind, bent down, and picked up the earring—to the amazement of their four children.

Larry left his favorite pair of sunglasses sitting on the counter at a store in the mall. He returned to check with a storeowner, but no one had turned them in. Just to be sure, Larry's family checked their vehicle, all their coat pockets, and Diana even dumped the contents of her purse out on the bed to assure him that she didn't put his sunglasses into her bag. Larry asked the angels to return his lost sunglasses to him. A few days later when Diana reached into her purse for her car keys, there were Larry sunglasses right on top. Ordinary miracles.

Larry and Diana always ask the angels to protect them and their vehicles. On a vacation trip to De Gray Lake, just as the sun was setting, an elderly man was coming down a hill; he struck the right rear of their blue van as Larry was merging into the center lane to make a left turn. There were five vehicles involved in this accident, and it was a big, news event. What happened to their van defied physics. The steering wheel on Larry and Diana's van locked up and the van coasted safely to a stop on the right hand shoulder of the road. Any further to the right and the van would have gone over the embankment and crashed on the distant rocks below. If the van had proceeded to the left in the logical direction, it would have gone into oncoming traffic. Instead, when the elderly man hit the right rear of Larry and Diana's van, the van went to the right, and the elderly man's vehicle went to the left into a head-on collision with the oncoming vehicle. Both cars immediately burst into flames. The second, oncoming vehicle clipped the right rear of the first, oncoming vehicle as the third, oncoming vehicle rear ended the second, oncoming vehicle and slammed the second, oncoming vehicle into the ditch. As the second, oncoming vehicle hugged the ditch, the front left tire sheared off, and the rear axle was broken as the car became embedded in the dirt. All the other passengers were taken to the hospital, but no one in Larry and Diana's van was injured. The elderly man told the police that he struck a big, bright, white truck that came out of nowhere. Perhaps he saw the angels as they guided Larry and Diana's van to safety.

Have you ever taken authority over the elements? Sarah is a single mom who values her vacation time. Every year she believes for rain-free, perfect weather during her two weeks off. Regardless of the weather forecast, year after year, she gets her perfect weather.

Larry and Diana were adding a sunroom to their home. The contractor came and finished out the sunroom before the roofer had completed his job. At the last minute the roofer backed out on his commitment to finish the roof. There was not time to find a new roofer because the rain would destroy the wood floor, walls, and the decorative ceiling. Larry had roofing experience working in his father's roofing company so he tackled the job himself. Dark clouds rolled in and begin to spit raindrops. Larry told the clouds, "You will not rain." For five hours the rain held back while he finished the roofing job. As he descended from the ladder, he said, "Okay, you can rain now," and immediately a heavy downpour descended upon his newly finished roof.

Diana experienced the normal back and labor pain with her first two children. She decided to believe for pain-free labors with her next two children. She confessed throughout her pregnancy for pain-free labors and healthy babies. She delivered a nine-pound baby girl and a ten-pound baby boy without pain. Both children were born at home with midwives in attendance. There were no complications and no pain, just peace through the whole process.

In Larry's fastener company, he had a nut vendor that defaulted on a contract causing Larry's company to lose a sizable order worth well over $100,000. Larry had no proof that the engineer from Sylvania Lighting Corporation would have placed the order except for the man's word. By the time the case was brought to arbitration, the engineer from Sylvania had moved on to another company, and Larry lost his only witness. He proceeded anyway despite the advice of his lawyer who insisted that the case could not be won on hearsay evidence alone. Larry believed in his spirit that the truth would come forth, so he insisted on proceeding with the case. The lawyer representing the other side did not object to Larry's testimony—for no explainable reason. The judge awarded Larry the full profit the order would have grossed the first year of production—based upon his hearsay testimony.

Have you ever felt déjà vu? The Bogatz's believe the sensation that makes you feel as though you have been there before, or done that before, is a result of your spirit telling you in a dream what may happen in the future. Dreams can provide a tremendous insight or prepare you for a possible, future event.

Larry had an intense dream one night. In his dream he went to church. He was watching a woman playing the keyboard. After the service Larry went home with her to where her husband and children were waiting. Larry put his hands on her shoulders and commanded cancer to leave her body. She was healed. Before the dream Larry was not aware that there was anything wrong with this woman from the church, but this dream was so intense that Larry sat up in the bed, spoke out, "Yes, I will do that", and then went back to sleep.

The next morning Larry went to church. It appeared to be just as he dreamed except that immediately after the service the woman left—before Larry had an opportunity to speak with her. Because things did not happen exactly as Larry had dreamed, he wondered if it was just a déjà vu experience or if he was really supposed to go to their house. All afternoon he was unable to get the image out of his mind, so he called the woman, who he hardly knew, and invited himself over to her house. When he arrived, he sat down with her and her husband and told them his dream. They all began to weep. They said that they had been up very late the night before and they were asking God to send them someone who knew how to pray for the wholeness of her body. She had been diagnosed with cancer, and they had not known what else to do. They didn't even have insurance. Larry prayed for her and she felt an intense heat in the area where the cancer was. Larry also prayed for the rest of the family, speaking out things he perceived in the spiritual realm but could not possibly have known. It was a very emotional experience, and they all wept with joy knowing that something very special had taken place that day. The x-rays taken the following week showed no sign of cancer. The doctors claimed that there must have been something wrong with the original x-rays. Most likely the original x-ray showed a shadow from something because the doctors believed there was no way that cancer could be there one day and gone the next.

When dealing with the paranormal world, it's important to know and trust the source from which you're receiving information. For example, if you hear anything that is related to your demise, consider the source. Don't buy into the lie; no one has authority over your life unless you give it to him or her. When Larry was eleven years old, he was playing in the backyard with his younger brother, Bobby, who was nine. Their older brother, Jeff, was making fireworks in the gutted body of a 1957 Chevy. To keep his two, younger brothers away, Jeff gave each of them a sparkler. Jeff rolled up the windows of the car to make sure that no sparks got in while he was using gunpowder to make his own, special fireworks. However, Jeff was unaware that the left, front, wing window was open and Bobby threw his sparkler into the car. The sparkler instantly ignited the gunpowder that in turn caught Jeff's clothes and hair on fire. He ended up with second and third-degree burns over ninety percent of his body. While he was on fire, Jeff received a vision that indicated to him that he was going to burn to death in a car accident before he was thirty years old, but he would be spared for now.

Jeff was killed in a car accident at the age of twenty-six, when his car went off the road, slammed into a tree, and burst into flames. The police believe he died instantly, but they could not tell for sure because his body was burned beyond recognition. At the funeral Jeff's ex-girlfriend Suzanne related the story that filled in the blanks. Jeff loved Suzanne and wanted to marry her. However, because he loved her, he didn't believe it would be fair not to tell Suzanne what was going to happen to him in the future. He told her about the fire and the vision that he had. He told her that if she was willing to accept the fact that he was going to die before he was thirty, he would be happy to marry her. Relating the story to Jeff's family, Suzanne revealed that she believed that Jeff had fabricated an enormous lie with the intention of "blowing her off." Suzanne responded out of anger, and no longer accepted his telephone calls. She stopped seeing him after that night. Suzanne said things would have been different if she would have realized that Jeff was telling her the truth. The reason Jeff's vision came to pass is because he believed that it would happen the way that he saw it. Be careful what you believe. Jeff did not have to accept the vision as his destiny, but because he chose to believe the vision it became a self-fulfilling prophecy. You can choose to renounce the negative.

One day Larry and Diana went to Baskin-Robbins for frozen refreshments. After they received their order, they sat in a booth to consume their purchase. Larry and Diana were sitting side-by-side in the booth. In front of them there were two men sitting across from each other. One man was facing them, and the other man had his back to them. Larry sensed that the man who had his back to them was filled with a vile spirit. Larry communicated to Diana what he had perceived, but Diana said, "Yeah, right." Larry began silently speaking in tongues and the man with his back to them started to make strange movements. He stopped speaking to the man who was sitting with him as his back began to twitch violently. He whipped his head around, stared at Larry and Diana; then he whipped his head back and said to the other man, "We've got to go." The two men quickly stood up and left the building. Witnessing this, Diana believed what Larry had said about the man.

Cheryl had been confessing, "God has given his angels charge concerning me and vile spirits are not even allowed to speak to me." Cheryl had the opportunity to see the results of this confession. Cheryl was helping out with a marriage seminar. When they were finished taking their lunch break from the mainstream events, they were in a hurry to get back to the seminar. Cheryl asked a waitress to give her directions to the restroom. Although this waitress had no problem speaking to the individual before Cheryl, when Cheryl asked the question about the bathroom, the woman began to spasm and could not speak. Cheryl said to the woman, "That's okay. I don't need a vile spirit giving me directions to the bathroom." After Cheryl walked away from the woman, she looked back and saw the waitress speaking with another individual as though nothing had ever been wrong. Cheryl, however, knew a vile spirit controlled the waitress' body and that it was not allowed to speak because of Cheryl's confession.

The exceptional, the remarkable, the miraculous, the

supernatural, and the paranormal are possible if you believe. Don't let the limits of scientific discovery limit you. At one time people believed that the universe revolved around the earth—until scientists proved that it didn't. Now scientists are speculating that the universe is made up of sound waves or that the universe is really a hologram. Don't wait on them for your own personal discoveries. Just believe the impossible is possible for you, and start your journey to your ideal reality. As you grow in understanding, miracles will become your everyday reality, an ideal reality, where you are in charge of your perception, your reality.

"Whoever undertakes to set himself up as a judge of Truth and Knowledge is shipwrecked by the laughter of the gods."

Albert Einstein

APPENDIX I

REALITY ACCORDING TO HISTORICAL PHILOSOPHY

HISTORICAL REALITY

Through the ages many theories as to what reality is have been proposed. Most concepts of reality are made up of one or more of the following three basic realms. The first realm is referred to as intuition or spiritual nature. The second realm is our logical, soul nature. The soul is comprised of the mind, the will, and the emotions. The soul has been argued by some to be part of our spirit, but for ease of explanation, we will treat the soul as distinct from the spirit. The third realm is the physical senses of sight, hearing, touch, taste, and smell. It is interesting to note that only the third realm is tangible; the intuitive and logical elements are intangible. Just as wind is intangible, the intuitive and logical elements of our reality impact us without being seen.

Most documented thoughts on reality are rooted in philosophy. Everyone has their own set of values, attitudes toward life, view of society, and nature. All of these combined are encompassed in the popular phrase ones 'philosophy of life'. The theologian focuses on the spiritual realm and proposes that the true reality is spiritual only. The mathematician stresses the logical reality created by the mind. The empiricism view focuses only on the physical realm and the reality that is perceived by the five physical senses.

It's important to discuss philosophy in order to understand what has been previously perceived as reality. Prior to the 1700s, there was no distinction made between science and philosophy, before that time frame, physics was known as natural philosophy, and psychology was known as moral philosophy. Let's first look at the history of philosophy and the people who greatly influenced the world as we know it today.

EASTERN PHILOSOPHY

Although the focus of this book is upon the philosophers who have been the most influential contributors to the current reality of the Western Hemisphere, it is also important to note the eastern philosophers who have had a more recent impact upon the present western philosophy. The three primary eastern philosophers are Siddhartha Gautama (Buddha), Confucius, and Muhammad.

First, Siddhartha Gautama (Buddha) is considered by many to be the most significant Indian philosopher of all time. Gautama was born approximately 564 B.C. in Lumbini, a small village in the foothills of the Himalayas (Current day Nepal). At the birth of Gautama, a seer prophesied that he would either be a great King or save humanity. This was a choice Gautama would have to make when he was of age to make such decisions. In an effort to cause Gautama to choose the life of a warrior king like his father, his father raised Gautama in the palace not allowing him to see the suffering outside the Palace walls. At the age of twenty, Gautama married Princess Yasodhara. It is said at the age of twenty-nine, Gautama received four visions-the first was of an old man, the second a sick man, the third a human corpse, and the fourth a holy man.

Gautama believed the vision of the holy man was his commission to help humanity by learning how to end human suffering and teaching the people the result of this "Enlightenment." Gautama left his newborn son, Rahula, and his wife, Princess Yasodhara, to go on a quest for the answers, or the "Enlightenment" as he called it, that would give him the ability to fulfill his commission. Gautama's quest began by denying his physical body the luxury of eating until the point of death at which point he received the knowledge of what Gautama called the middle way. One way is to deny the physical body. Gautama said you shouldn't deny the physical body because that inhibits concentration. The second way is to give the physical body all it desires. Gautama said you shouldn't overindulge either because that is a distraction from concentration, so the middle way is choosing a path between the two. In approximately 528 B.C. Gautama fueled with his knowledge of the middle way began a process of yoga meditation.

It was through this meditation period that Gautama received "Enlightenment" gaining his philosophy of reality and the knowledge of how to end human suffering. It was at this point of "Enlightenment" that Gautama became known as Gautama Buddha that means Gautama the "Enlightened" or "Awakened One". Gautama Buddha became a monk teaching the people for forty-five years and died in Nepal at the age of eighty.

Buddha's philosophy was based upon what he called the "four noble truths". One, all human life is suffering. Two, suffering is caused by desire. Three, by ending the desire the suffering is ended. Four, desires are ended by implementing the eightfold noble path. The eightfold noble path is achieved by having the proper understanding, thought, speech, action, livelihood, effort, mindfulness, and concentration.

Buddha believed that everything in the universe was loosely linked. And the idea of a unique self was just an illusion. He believed that everything was composed of several almonds. These almonds come together and fall apart. He believed that everything was transient, full of sorrow and without a soul. Buddha believed that humans continue in a cycle of birth and rebirth until they fulfill the eightfold noble path at which time they and the cycle of suffering cease to exist.

Tibetan Buddhists believe that the Dalai Lama is a reincarnated Buddha. Claiming that when the one Buddha dies his soul is transferred to the body of a newborn boy who becomes the new Dalai Lama.

Second, K'ung Fu-tzu (Confucius), that in Latin means the great master Kong, is considered to be the most respected and influential Chinese philosophers of all-time. Confucius was born approximately 551 B.C. in the state of Lu (present-day Shandong). Confucius was born of the noble Kong clan. Even though Confucius was of noble birth, because his father died when he was only three years old, he was raised in poverty.

Confucius was educated as a nobleman of a lesser clan, meaning that his education was based primarily upon the classical writings. In his youth, Confucius performed menial labors for the Duke and his officers in the court to support his crippled brother. Confucius was married at the age of nineteen and had a son and two daughters. He continued menial labors to support his family until after his mother died, and then he became a teacher. At the age of fifty-one, Confucius was offered the position of Crime Minister in the state of Lu. Crime was almost completely eliminated during his administration. Confucius was crime minister until he retired from that office. Confucius was the first professional teacher of adults in ancient China. In 479 B.C. Confucius died in the state of Lu at the age of seventy-two.

Confucius described his life by saying, "At age fifteen, my mind was set on learning. At age thirty, my character had been formed. At forty, I had no more perplexities. At fifty, I knew the will of heaven. At sixty, I was at ease with whatever I heard. At seventy, I could follow my heart's desire without transgressing moral principles."

The primary focus of Confucius's philosophy was a good moral character. The highest level of good moral character that could be obtained from Confucius's perspective was that of a gentleman. In Confucius's terms a gentleman was not one of noble birth; instead he is one of noble actions who exercises propriety (a set of rules that separated the civilized man from the barbarian).

In order to be a gentleman one must live an exemplary life exhibiting kindness, uprightness, politeness, wisdom, and faithfulness. Confucius said, "The gentleman uses only such language as is proper to speak, and only speaks of what would be proper to carry out. The gentleman, and what he says, leaves nothing to mere chance." Confucius believed that a true gentleman understands the power of his spoken word; therefore, he chooses his words carefully.

Confucius believed in a higher all-powerful being or beings that he referred to as Heaven. Confucius believed it was man's responsibility to discover his destiny that Confucius referred to as the will of the Heavens. Once he discovered his destiny, it was man's responsibility to fulfill that destiny. Confucius said, "The important thing is at least to be working to improve oneself. The worst error is not to even make the attempt."

Third, Muhammad is considered by many to be the key to Islamic philosophy. The name Muhammad means praised one. Muhammad was born approximately 570 A.D. in Mecca. Muhammad was of noble birth descended from the respected Hashim clan of the Quraysh tribe.

Muhammad's father died before he was born and his mother died shortly after he turned six. Muhammad was raised by his Uncle Alu Telib who taught Muhammed how to raise sheep and camels. All who knew Muhammad believed him to be of the highest moral character, and they called him Al-Amin which means the trusted one.

At the age of twenty-five, Muhammad was asked to manage a business for a wealthy widow named Khadiji. Khadiji was so impressed with the way Muhammad handled himself and her business that she offered him marriage that same year. Muhammad accepted her offer of marriage, and they had three children.

It is said that when Muhammad was thirty-five, he received a visit from the angel Gabriel who commissioned Muhammad to proclaim God's message to his people. Muhammad's wife, Khadiji, became Muhammad's first disciple. Muhammad taught his philosophy in Mecca until both his wife, Khadiji, and his uncle Alu Telib died in the same year. After their death Muhammad was offered a position of leadership in the nearby town of Medina. Muhammad accepted this position and instituted many laws that brought order to Medina. The laws that were written included issues like ending the death of unwanted baby girls, and violence can only be used as a means of self-defense. Muhammad also required the people to make Islam (submission) to God. Muhammad died in Medina on June 8th in the year 632.

Muhammad believed that an all knowing divine being or God controlled the universe and communicated to him through angelic messengers, an intuitive inner voice, and sometimes by his spiritual presence. Muhammad believed that true knowledge of reality came through personal relationship with this divine creator of the universe who sits on his throne in the immaterial world of the spirit.

The Islamic world today is greatly influenced by the Qur'an that was believed to be a text originally in the form of a preserved tablet supposedly given to Muhammad by

God in the year 626. The Islamic people were taught from birth to live by this divinely revealed Qur'an.

WESTERN PHILOSOPHY

Western philosophy can be divided into five periods: ancient, ancient to medieval transitional, medieval, foundation of modern, and modern. Ancient philosophy lasted from approximately 600 B.C. to about 00 A.D.; ancient to medieval transitional philosophy lasted from approximately 00 A.D to about 400 A.D.; medieval philosophy lasted from approximately 400-1600 A.D.; the foundation of modern philosophy lasted from approximately 1600-1700 A.D.; and modern philosophy is from about the 1700 A.D to present day. For completeness, we are including a brief chronological synopsis of the great philosophers. The three most significant philosophers of the ancient world are Socrates, Plato, and Aristotle. It is important that we talk about them first, not just because they were among the first philosophers, but also because their philosophy still influences much of our present western philosophy.

ANCIENT PHILOSOPHY

Socrates was born in Athens, Greece approximately 469 B.C. Socrates developed what was known as the dialectical style of debate, which is the pursuit of truth utilizing a system of questions and answers. Socrates would enter into a conversation with someone who claimed to be wise. In the beginning of a conversation Socrates would pretend to be ignorant with regard to the subject discussed. Through the use of questions, Socrates would find out how much that person really knew. Because Socrates claimed to be ignorant in the beginning of a conversation, when it was discovered later in the conversation that he knew more than he originally claimed,

Socrates was considered to be the wiser of the two. Socrates believed that this was the most important method of obtaining knowledge so he spent much of his time in the public places of Athens teaching the young people his methods. These methods used by Socrates are known today as the Socratic method of philosophy.

Socrates found the young people of Athens to be very open to his concepts. Socrates taught them that they should not believe everything they were previously taught, instead they should discover for themselves what is the truth. Socrates refused to accept payment from his students claiming that the only thing he taught them was an awareness of their need for additional knowledge. He taught his students not to accept the moral standards of society; instead, they should choose for themselves what is moral and what is immoral. Socrates claimed that he received a divine revelation that kept him from partaking of the immoral acts of his fellow Athenians. Socrates annoyed many Athenians because of the way he spoke out in regard to their moral standards. In 399 B.C, at the age of seventy, Socrates was brought up on charges before the court. The charges were "not believing in the gods the state believed in, and introducing different new divine powers; and also for corrupting the young." At the trial the leaders irritated by Socrates and what they considered to be a mockery of the court sentenced him to death. Socrates spent his last day with his friends including his prized student Plato. In the evening of that day he drank a vial of hemlock, which was the death sentence administrated by the Athenians. Socrates primary philosophical focus was human character and ethics. Socrates believed that one could objectively understand the concepts of justice, love, and virtue. Socrates believed that people are only bad, because they don't have the knowledge of a defined good. Therefore when people receive the knowledge of good they will act according to that knowledge. Socrates believed in a separation between the soul and body. Socrates often spoke of a divine being that communicated to him through an inner voice. Socrates believed that true knowledge came through his relationship with this intuitive or spiritual nature; therefore, he considered that relationship to be of primary importance.

Plato was born in Athens, Greece approximately 428 B.C. Plato who gained much of his understanding from his teacher, Socrates, combined his philosophical ideas with politics. One of Plato's most famous dialogues is where he discusses how Socrates discovered that the beginning of wisdom is the knowledge that at least one knows that he does not know. Although Plato believed that knowledge was attainable by the individual without the need for an intuitive or spiritual nature, he also believed that true knowledge couldn't be attained through the five physical senses, because the perception of the senses are subject to continuous change. Plato believed that all true knowledge is based upon constant unchanging things. Plato believed that knowledge must be infallible, and that knowledge must be based upon that which is genuinely real in contrast to what just appears to be real. Only those things could be attributed as being true knowledge. He considered some of these constants to be truth, beauty, and goodness, all of which are only known by the mind. He called this use of constants, his theory of ideas or forms. Plato taught that only ideas are real, and that all other things are just a reflection of these ideas. This view later became known as idealism.

Plato believed that there were two levels of awareness— opinion and knowledge. Plato believed the perceptions received through the physical senses such as observations or theories of science are merely opinions. Although some opinions may be well thought out and backed by previous understanding, none of them count as true knowledge. Instead, true knowledge is achieved through the process of reason. Reason properly applied leads to intellectual insights that are constant and certain. These intellectual insights became what he called abiding universals, the internal forms or substances that constitute true reality. In one of his published works, *The*

Republic, Plato described humanity as chained prisoners in a cave of ignorance. They cannot see one another. All they can see are shadows on the wall that are mistaken for reality. In contrast the philosophers are the individuals who penetrate the cave wall to the outside world and receive an understanding of the true reality.

According to Plato the knowledge of good is the purpose of all inquiry, and he believed that people who have received the understanding of good must return to the world using this knowledge in everyday life to serve humanity. Plato also believed that the soul is immortal and that only the body passes away. His ideas contributed to the views about the body, soul, and internal things. Plato relied heavily upon mathematics and considered the logical or soul nature to be of primary importance in his attainment of knowledge and in the perception of one's reality.

Aristotle was born approximately 384 B.C. in Stagira, Macedonia. When Aristotle was seventeen he went off to Athens to become a student at Plato's Academy. He quickly achieved recognition as the top student of the Academy where he remained as student then a teacher until the death of Plato in 347 B.C. Aristotle became the tutor of a young Alexander the Great and continued to be his tutor until Alexander became king. After the death of Alexander the great the Athenians charged Aristotle with not believing in the same gods the state believed in, and showing a lack of reverence for the gods. Remembering how Socrates was brought up on similar charges and was sentenced to death Aristotle claimed he would not allow them to "sin twice against philosophy." Aristotle escaped to the city of Chalcis where he died in 322 B.C.

Because Aristotle was the son of a physician to the royal court, Aristotle's philosophy was deeply rooted in biology. He believed that every species on earth would grow towards self-realization in accordance with its species and that this process of growth was built into nature. Therefore, a specific species would receive its growth, purpose, and direction from nature in accordance with its species. Aristotle believed that all things in nature have some purpose; he also believed that the nature of each thing is determined by its purpose, and all things seek to fulfill their nature by carrying out these purposes. He believed the pinnacle of human existence is happiness, and that when an individual achieved happiness, they had discovered their purpose for being. Aristotle believed that the body cannot exist apart from the soul and that the soul was a separate non-physical entity. He believed there were two realms of reality and knowledge. Aristotle referred to these realms as the changing and unchanging realms. The most important unchanging things Aristotle referred to as God, which he considered to be the foundation of philosophy. Aristotle originally referred to the study of God as his first philosophy but he later referred to it as the science of theology. Aristotle said, "There is nothing in the intellect that was not first in the senses." Stating his belief that the substance of all true knowledge was derived through the interaction of the individuals' five physical senses with the physical material world.

ANCIENT TO MEDIEVAL TRANSISITIONAL PHILOSOPHY

One of the greatest and perhaps most controversial philosophers of all time was Jesus of Nazareth. Whether he is known by the individual as Lord, or teacher, one should not discount his value as a philosopher.

Jesus of Nazareth was born in Bethlehem, Judah approximately 00 A.D. Although not much is said about Jesus' education, many believe he was raised with the pharisaical philosophy of his day like his brother James. Jesus later became known as a teacher or rabbi, a position of distinction and accomplishment.

Like Socrates, Jesus taught his students or disciples that having something as a tradition doesn't make it true and they should not believe everything they were taught from birth. Jesus taught that each individual is responsible for what they believe. Therefore, they should seek to understand for themselves what truth is.

Jesus wanted the people to be free from the oppression of the religious leaders, the Roman government, and the cares of the world (sickness, poverty, guilt, lack, and death). Like Socrates, Jesus publicly spoke out against the leaders of his day, teaching all who would listen that the philosophies or traditions they were taught from birth were nothing more than heavy burdens that kept them bound from the truth. Jesus said, "You shall know the truth, and the truth shall make you free." People flocked to Jesus by the thousands to hear his teachings. Like Socrates, Jesus challenged the leaders and spoke out strongly against them saying things like, "Brood of Vipers! How can you, being evil, speak good things?" Jesus called them, "Blind guides, who strain out a gnat and swallow a camel!" and said that they were "like whitewashed tombs which indeed appear beautiful outwardly, but inside are full of dead men's bones and all uncleanliness." Jesus said that they brought "heavy burdens, hard to bear, and laid them on men's shoulders; but they themselves will not move them with one of their fingers."

Jesus communicated to the people that all the leaders wanted was to help themselves to the wealth of the people without offering anything in return except hypocrisy, and the leaders wanted to put him to death for it. Jesus also believed in a divine creator that spoke to him through divine revelation. Jesus was brought up on similar charges to that of Socrates and was also sentenced to death. The charges were that Jesus believed in a god that was different than the leaders believed, introduced new divine powers, and taught publicly this philosophy to the people. At the age of thirty-three, Jesus was sentenced to death by crucifixion. It was purported than on the third day after his death by crucifixion that Jesus conquered death. It is said that he first showed himself to his disciples and then to a multitude of people for forty days before ascending into heaven.

Jesus believed in life after death, and a separation between soul and body at death. He believed that the soul and the body would later be reunited in a glorified form. Jesus believed that true knowledge came through an intuitive relationship with a divine creator, an all-knowing personal God (whom he referred to as Father) and that knowledge of reality can only be obtained through a personal relationship with this divine creator. Jesus believed that there were two realms that exist simultaneously, the first realm is the unseen realm of the spirit, and the second realm is the visible realm experienced through the five physical senses. Each realm contained laws that were the structural foundation of that realm. An understanding of the physical realm would give insight into the intuitive or spiritual realm. However, understanding and interfacing with the intuitive or spiritual realm through a relationship with the divine creator was important, because all knowledge could be obtained through this relationship with the Father God, even knowledge to supersede the laws of the physical realm.

Many historical accounts indicate that Jesus did exercise authority over the five physical sense realm. Accounts were documented of Jesus walking on water, changing water to wine, producing money from a fish's mouth to pay his tax, stopping a storm, feeding 5000 men with two fish and five loaves of bread, healing the sick, and raising the dead. It was claimed by John who was one of Jesus' disciples that Jesus did so many things "which if they were written one by one, I suppose that even the world itself could not contain the books that could be written." Jesus claimed his ability to supersede the laws of the sense realm was derived from the knowledge he received through his intuitive relationship with the divine creator (Father God).

One of the most prominent students of Jesus was Saint Paul. Although it is said that Paul never met Jesus in the flesh, he was certainly a student of Jesus through the study of his works. Saint Paul was born approximately 3 A.D. in the city of Tarsus by the Mediterranean Sea (present-day Turkey). Paul's birth name was Saul, named after the first king of Israel. Saul was a Roman citizen by birth. As a requirement of Roman citizenship Saul was taught Greek Rhetoric by Roman teachers known as sophist. Greek Rhetoric was the philosophy of the Roman government at that time. However, since Saul was also of Jewish origin Saul's parents sent him to Jerusalem to be taught the philosophy of the Pharisees by the famous teacher Gamaliel the elder. Saul considered himself to be the "Pharisee of Pharisee's". As a young man, Saul persecuted anyone who believed in Jesus. However, Saul claimed when he was going to Damascus that a bright light blinded him. Saul perceived the light as a vision of Jesus. Saul claimed that Jesus had commissioned him into service that day on the road.

After Saul accepted the philosophy of Jesus, his family disowned him. Saul then changed his name to the similar sounding Latin name Paul. When Paul returned to Jerusalem, his own father brought charges against Paul sentencing him to death. Paul was brought to the place of sentencing, his father threw the first stone, and Paul was stoned to the point of death. Paul left Jerusalem to recover and later wrote the letters that encompass most of what is known as the New Testament. Many of the letters of Paul were written in the Greek Rhetoric style he learned from youth.

Years later, the religious leaders seized Paul based on the grounds that Paul violated the law and defiled the temple. As punishment for this crime they intended to put Paul to death. However, Paul announced that he was a Roman citizen, and as a citizen of Rome it was his right to be tried by Caesar in Rome. After several years in Rome, Paul was sentenced to death by the Emperor Nero and was beheaded in 62 A. D.

Paul believed that an interface with the intuitive realm required a mediator, and Paul claimed that Jesus of Nazareth was that mediator. Paul believed that the sacrifice of Jesus made it possible for man to interface with the divine creator. Paul believed that by using the name of Jesus one could gain access to the personal Father God who resides in the intuitive or spiritual realm. Like Jesus, Paul also believed that the knowledge an individual received through an intuitive relationship with the divine creator gave an individual the knowledge to supersede the laws of the physical realm. The goal of Jesus was to set people free including freedom from oppressive rules; whereas, Paul's goal was to organize the followers by developing a moral structure comprised of rules. Many of the letters that Paul wrote were preserved by the communities who received them. These letters provided the people in those communities a philosophy to live by but did not gain worldwide recognition until St. Augustine and Martin Luther later adopted them.

Neoplatonism is a revised version of Plato's ideas, combined with the works of St. Paul, and adopted by Plotinus, a third century A.D. philosopher from Egypt. Neoplatonism became very popular in the transitional period between ancient and medieval philosophy and set the course for a new perspective of philosophy. Neoplatonism taught the existence of an infinite, unknowable, perfect one that is in fact the ultimate reality. The perfect one guides the individual toward a unity, a oneness with God, which is a state of blessedness. Plotinus believed that the human soul yearns for reunion with God, which can only be achieved through a mystical experience. Some say that Neoplatonism provided the bridge between Greek philosophy and early Christian philosophy. It inspired the idea that the most important information is received by the individual through the direct human intuition of God. These things can be learned only through faith and God's influence, not by reason, and will empower the individual to transcend the limitations of a finite world. This was later to become known as mysticism. Mysticism was defined as an intuitive knowledge of God or of an ultimate reality attained through personal religious experience. Spawned from this transitional period of Neoplatonism came medieval philosophy. Medieval philosophy lasted from approximately 400 to 1600 A.D. The two greatest medieval philosophers were Saint Augustine and Saint Thomas Aquinas.

MEDIEVAL PHILOSOPHY

Saint Augustine was born on November 13, 354 A.D. in Tagaste, Numidia (present-day Algeria). St. Augustine was educated in North Africa in the art of rhetoric. Plato wrote, "Rhetoric is the universal act of winning the mind by argument." Many orators used rhetoric speech to stimulate feelings and influence the judgment of people. St. Augustine embraced several philosophical positions in his quest for truth including Manichaeism, Skepticism, Neo-Platonism, and a form of Christianity.

Manichaeism, those who held this philosophy believed that there was a division in the universe consisting of two realms, the realm of good or light was the spirit realm that was ruled by God, the realm of darkness, the physical world was ruled by Satan. Somewhere along the line the two realms were mixed and ever since that time, there has been a struggle to redeem the spirit of man, which became imprisoned in the human body. St. Augustine believed this philosophy for nine years, and then he turned to the philosophy of skepticism. Skeptics believed that knowledge of reality was impossible to attain and that happiness was achieved when one no longer pursued the knowledge of things such as reality, which were impossible to understand. Skeptics doubted everything and used broken logic as a means to disprove other philosophies. St. Augustine went to Milan, Italy where he became a teacher of Rhetoric. There St. Ambrose, the bishop of Milan who held the Neo-Platonist view of philosophy, influenced him.

Combining his previous understanding with Neo-Platonism, St. Augustine developed his own perspective of reality. Approximately November of 386 A.D. St. Augustine claimed he was standing over the scriptures when he heard a divine inner voice saying, "Take up and read," then St. Augustine picked it up and read, "Put on the Lord Jesus Christ, and make no provision for the flesh, to gratify its desires." From that day forward St. Augustine associated himself with Christianity. This was a big step for St. Augustine who less than four years before said, "Give me chastity and continence, but not just now."

St. Augustine believed that religious faith and philosophical understanding were both required in order to obtain true knowledge. St. Augustine believed in a divine creator who predestined the course of man but also continues to speak to man through an inner voice when an individual needed a course correction. St. Augustinian Skeptics held the perspective than in order for an individual to gain true knowledge he must first "believe in order to understand and understand in order to believe." In other words, St. Augustine believed that both faith and reason are required to gain the knowledge of reality and a union with the divine creator. In one of St. Augustine most famous books entitled the *City of God,* St. Augustine described the struggle of humanity between good and evil. The people of the City of God represented the good, the saints of God, and the earthly city or world represented evil or the people of Satan with their materialistic values. In the book, the people of the City of God will gain internal salvation, but the people of the world receive internal punishment. Both the Roman Catholic and Protestant doctrines are largely based on the works of St. Augustine. John Calvin and Martin Luther, who are known as leaders of the Christian reformation, were both students of St. Augustine.

St. Thomas Aquinas was born in 1225 A.D. of a noble family in Roccasecca, Italy. After his father's death he joined a Mendicant order. His mother infuriated by this decision locked him in the family castle over a year, until she saw that he was determined to stay the course. When she released him he traveled to Paris and became a student of the German philosopher Albertus Magnus. Because of his large size, the other students nicknamed Thomas the Dumb Ox, and Albertus recognizing Thomas as a fellow philosopher said, "This Ox will one day fill the world with his bellowing." Thomas accepted a position as professor of philosophy at the University of Paris until he left to become an adviser to Pope Alexander IV. Thomas Aquinas died in 1274 at the age of forty-nine.

In addition to his more than eighty published works he is also well recognized for his immense compilation of the combined works of Aristotle, Albert Magnus, and Saint Augustine. St. Thomas Aquinas believed that both faith in a divine creator and sense knowledge / experience were completely compatible and required to obtain true knowledge. For example the existence of a divine creator must be taken by faith or divine revelation and through experience with the material world equally in order to receive a complete knowledge of God's existence. However, the deeper understanding of God requires a divine revelation. The philosophy of St. Thomas Aquinas combined the theology of Saint Augustine with Aristotle's philosophy that the individual is born with a given nature and purpose that is discovered by one's interaction with the five physical sense realm through a process of self-realization. St. Thomas Aquinas's philosophy eventually became the official philosophy of the Roman Catholic Church.

FOUNDATION OF MODERN PHILOSOPHY

The Foundation of Modern philosophy, referred to by some as the age of reasoning or enlightenment, began in the 1600s and lasted until the late 1700s. During this period the philosopher's stress the use of reason as opposed to reliance on authority and structural revelation. Many consider Rene Descartes of France to be one of the founders of modern philosophy, and some have even called him the "father of modern philosophy". The other philosophers of this time period who had a significant impact upon modern philosophy were

John Locke, Sir Isaac Newton, George Berkley, David Hume, and Immanuel Kant.

Rene Descartes was born of noble descent in LaHaye, Torraine, France in 1596. Descartes being the son of a nobleman came from a long line of educated men. Descartes studied law at the University of Poitiers. After his graduation, Descartes devoted most of his life to solving problems of mathematics and philosophy. Descartes was a mathematician as well as a philosopher. He invented analytic geometry. Descartes was what was known as a mechanicist; that is he regarded all physical phenomenons as connected mechanically by laws of cause and effect. Descartes believed that the only true reality was that which could be proven logically. He said, "In our search for the direct road to truth, we should busy ourselves with no object about which we cannot attain a certitude equal to that of the demonstration of arithmetic and geometry." This meant that even ones existence could not be considered real, unless proven through logical thought. In the act of doubting his owned existence, Descartes found the logical proof for his existence. Thus came his famous quote, "I think, therefore I am." From this basic revelation, in combination with logical deduction, he could prove the laws of nature and the existence of a divine creator.

John Locke was born of noble descent on August 29, 1632 in Wrington, Somerset, England. Locke graduated from Oxford and he lectured there until his departure from Oxford in 1664. Locke received various governmental positions. His last appointment was made by King William III who made Locke a member of the trade board. Locke died in Oates, England in 1704. Locke believed that at birth the mind of an individual is blank waiting for input to be received through the five physical senses. Lock believed that all true knowledge came through the sense realm, and there was nothing innate nor could anything be received through intuition because the whole of one's existence was based solely upon the experiences received by the individual after birth. Lock believed what people call intuition was just a reflection upon prior experiences. Lock believed that the five physical senses provided knowledge of the external world, but reflection provided knowledge of the stored experiences of the mind.

Sir Isaac Newton was born on December 25, 1642 at Woolsthorpe, Lincolnshire, England. Newton received his bachelor's and master's degree from the University of Cambridge. Newton believed that true knowledge could be achieved through intuition received from a divine creator and through the process of mathematics and logical deduction. Because of this perspective, Newton devoted most of his life to the study of mathematics, theology, and natural philosophy (physics). Newton perceived reality as an enormous complex machine that could be understood through divine revelation and logical deduction based upon physical observation and experimentation. Newton claimed he discovered the law of universal gravitation while standing under an apple tree. An apple fell from the top of a very tall tree and hit the ground. When the apple hit the ground Newton looked up to see where the apple came from and saw the moon. At that time, he received an intuitive insight. Newton perceived if an apple through the force of gravity could fall to the ground from such a tall tree then perhaps the moon was also held in place by the same force. Newton is most commonly known for his discovery of universal gravitation, which states that, all bodies whether on earth or in space is affected by the same force of gravity. Newton discovered optics, which states that sunlight is a blend of multiple rays each having its own distinct color. Newton also formulated the law of dynamics and invented calculus. Just before his death in 1727, Newton was quoted, "I do not know what I may appear to the world, but to myself I seem to have been only like a boy playing on the seashore, and diverting myself in now and then finding a smoother pebble or a prettier shell than ordinary, whilst the great notion of truth lay all undiscovered before me."

George Berkeley was born on March 12, 1685 in Kilkenny,

Ireland. Berkeley was educated at Trinity College in Dublin, Ireland. Berkeley graduated from Trinity College and became a fellow of the College. Berkeley was later given the position as Dean of Derry and he became the Bishop of Cloyne, a position he held until he retired. Berkeley died shortly after he retired in 1753. In 1878 the city of Berkeley, California was incorporated, named in honor of George Berkeley and home of the famous University of California at Berkeley. Berkeley believed that the information received by the five physical senses was nothing more than perception of the mind, and perceptions created in the mind have no material substance of their own. Therefore, nothing can exist independent of the mind. Berkeley believed that those things that appeared to exist independent of the mind are the result of a divine creator continually stimulating that perception in the human mind. Berkeley believe that true knowledge of reality is achieved through the perception of the mind and through the perceptions placed in the mind by an infinite omnipresent spirit, or a divine creator that perceives all that can be perceived.

David Hume was born May 7, 1711 in Edinburgh, Scotland and graduated from the University of Edinburgh. Hume published several philosophical works during his lifetime and died in Edinburgh in 1776. Unlike Descartes, Hume believed that there was no proof that anything existed. Hume argued that individuals don't have a constant perception of their own existence. Therefore, there is no proof of their existence; instead he said humans "are nothing but a bundle or collection of different perceptions." Hume also believed that it was impossible to prove the existence of the individual, mind, spirit, or a divine creator. In essence Hume believed that it was impossible to gain knowledge of reality because nothing truly exists.

Immanuel Kant was born on April 22, 1724 in Konigsberg, present day Keliningrad, Russia. Kant studied physics and mathematics at the University of Konigsberg where he received his doctorate. Kant accepted a teaching position at the

University where he taught science and mathematics for 15 years. Kant later shifted his focus to philosophy and became the professor of logic and metaphysics at the University, a subject he taught for the next 27 years. Kant died in 1804 at the age of eighty. Kant's philosophy is known as transcendentalism. Transcendentalism is a variance from Plato's philosophy regarding transcendence. Transcendence refers to the concept that a higher reality exists that is far beyond human comprehension. Some philosophers have used the concept of transcendence to describe the unknowable reality of a divine creator. In line with the concept of transcendence, Kant's philosophy of transcendentalism presupposes that it was impossible to gain knowledge of the physical world because the objects that make up the physical world are only a reference point for the perception of reality as received through the five physical senses. The physical objects don't truly exist; even space and time is just a product of the mind. Therefore, there is no true reality; there is only the perception of reality. Kant believed that individuals exist through their own perception of existence, and he represented the idea of a divine creator as a moral standard conceived in the individual mind. Kant believed that the only reality an individual could know is the reality based upon experience and the method in which the individual mind categorized that experience. In line with his philosophy, Kant was quoted saying, "Act as if the maximum of your action were to become, through your will, a general natural law." Kant did not dismiss the possibility of a divine creator; instead he classified that issue under the category of transcendent. Stating that if there was a divine creator, it would be an entity outside the realm of human experience; therefore, it would be impossible to gain any knowledge about such a being.

"If the facts don't fit the theory, change the facts."

Albert Einstein

REALITY ACCORDING TO MODERN PHILOSOPHY AND FILM

PRESENT REALITY

THE ELEMENTS OF MODERN PHILOSOPHY

Today's modern philosophy has developed into an ever-changing quest to understand the mystery of existence and reality. Philosophy is an intellectual attempt to understand the nature of reality, what is truth and knowledge, and to define what the purpose of life is, and how it is valuable or important. It is agreed by most that modern philosophy is divided into five main branches. These branches are epistemology, logic, ethics, aesthetics, and metaphysics.

Epistemology attempts to determine the nature, basis, and extent of knowledge. Philosophers place knowledge into two categories priori and empirical. Priori knowledge is obtained through the process of thinking. Its conclusions are based upon what we have previously learned but not experienced. We receive empirical knowledge through retrospective observation of what we have previously experienced.

Logic uses what are considered to be sound principles and methods to establish matters of fact and to understand the laws of nature. The two main categories of reasoning are deductive and inductive reasoning. Deductive reasoning is accomplished through the accumulation of facts that support its conclusion. This is the method of reasoning used by the well-known character Sherlock Holmes. Inductive reasoning is accomplished through observation and perception. The purpose of inductive reasoning is to establish matters of fact and to understand the laws of nature without having to be deductively sound. An example of inductive reasoning would be an experiment of ten white mice. You give the mice a choice between two different kinds of food. If all ten mice selected the same food, inductive reasoning would conclude that all white mice would choose the same type of food.

Ethics seeks to understand issues related to moral principles such as human conduct, character, and values. Ethics is also the study of what is right and what is wrong, and seeks to distinguish between what is good and what is evil.

Aesthetics deals with notions such as what is beautiful, ugly, sublime, or comic. Aesthetics also provides the principles of justifying critical judgments concerning works of art.

Metaphysics is the category of philosophy that seeks to understand the fundamental nature of reality, existence and of the essence of things. Therefore, metaphysics is the main branch of philosophy pertinent to this book. Metaphysics is often divided into two areas—ontology and cosmology.

Ontology is the study of existence or being. Cosmology is the study of the physical universe, or the cosmos. Metaphysics ponders questions like what is real, as opposed to what just appears to be real, and how can you distinguish between appearance and reality. Before one can arrive at a conclusion they must first have a starting point. Therefore, over the years philosophers have developed theories as a point of reference to help them better understand what reality is. We refer to these theories as categories of metaphysics. We consider the five most significant categories of metaphysics to be materialism, mechanism, teleology, idealism, and realism. Materialism maintains that reality is comprised of physical objects and physical interactions. Materialism also maintains that matter exists independent of the mind and that only physical matter has real existence. Therefore, all thoughts, feelings, and perceptions of the mind are produced only through physical interaction with the materialistic world. Mechanism maintains that everything in existence was created by purely mechanical forces. Nothing came into existence on purpose, and neither the universe, the individual, nor anything else has a purpose for being. Teleology in contrast to mechanism maintains that the universe and everything in it, exists and occurs for some purpose. Idealism is the perspective that nothing exists unless it is first perceived by the mind, and that all physical objects were brought into being after the mind perceived them. Realism in contrast to idealism maintains that physical objects exist independent of the mind, but that the mind can become aware of those physical objects by the perception of their existence through the five physical senses.

A MODERN NATURAL PHILOSOPHER (PHYSICIST)

The most prevalent modern philosopher is Albert Einstein. Albert Einstein was born on March 14, 1879 in Ulm, Wurttemberg, Germany. Although Einstein didn't speak until he was three years old, he was always very curious about the unseen natural laws like wind, thunder, static electricity, and the magnetic attraction between the North and South Poles. At the age of five, Einstein was shown a compass by his father. Einstein was puzzled about what unseen force could be holding the compass needle in the northerly direction at all times. By age twelve Einstein showed an amazing understanding of difficult mathematical concepts, and he taught himself geometry.

At the age of seventeen, Einstein entered the Swiss Polytechnic Institute in Zürich where he studied mathematics and physics. Einstein disliked the structured environment at the Institute and he spent most of his time studying physics on his own instead of attending classes. However, Einstein's good friend and fellow classmate Marcel Grossman was an outstanding student who took excellent notes in class. After studying Marcel's notes, Einstein passed all his examinations and graduated from Polytechnic Institute. Einstein accepted a clerk position at the Swiss patent office in Bern, Switzerland. Einstein received his doctorate from the University of Zürich and was advanced to the position Examiner of patents.

Einstein accepted a position as professor of theoretical physics at the University of Zurich, and later accepted a similar position at the University of Prague, Germany. Einstein became the director of the Kaiser Wilhelm Institute for physics in Berlin, Germany. Einstein resigned as director when Adolf Hitler became the dictator of Germany. That same year Einstein accepted a position as a member of staff at the Institute for advanced study in Princeton, New Jersey. Einstein became an American citizen in 1940 and died in Princeton, New Jersey, on April 18th, 1955.

Einstein believed that two realities exist, the physical reality that we contact with the five physical senses and coexisting is an indestructible spiritual world or reality that can only be known through an intuitive knowledge of God. He believed that the physical world was subject to time but the spiritual world was not. Einstein expressed this concept when he said, "Everyone who is seriously involved in the pursuit of science becomes convinced that a spirit is manifest in the laws of the universe," and he also said, "A spirit vastly superior to that of man, and one in the face of which we with our modest powers must feel humble. In this way the pursuit of science leads to a religious feeling of a special sort, which is indeed quite different from the religiosity of someone more naïve." Einstein believed that in order to obtain true knowledge of reality one must embrace science and religion equally.

Einstein described science as "methodical thinking directed toward finding regulative connections between our sensual experiences," in other words, gaining an understanding of the five, physical sense realm. Einstein described religion as the area dealing with "goals and evaluations and in general, with the emotional foundation of human thinking and acting." In other words gaining a knowledge of the logical, intuitive, or spiritual realms.

Finally Einstein described the correlation between these realms in his book *The World As I See It* when he said, "Even though the realms of religion and science in themselves are clearly marked off from each other, nevertheless there existed between the two strong reciprocal relationships and dependencies. Though religion may be that which determines the goal, it has, nevertheless, learned from science, in the broadest sense, what means will contribute to the attainment of the goals it has set up. But science can only be created by those who are thoroughly imbued with the aspiration toward truth and understanding. This source of feeling, however, springs from the sphere of religion. To this there also belongs the faith in the possibility that the regulations valid for the world of existence are rational, that is, comprehensible to reason. I cannot conceive of a genuine scientist without that profound faith. The situation may be expressed by an image: science without religion is lame, religion without science is blind."

At the age of twenty-six while still working at the Swiss patent office, Einstein formulated his special theory of relativity. Einstein submitted three papers for publication that year. All three papers were of significant importance to the current day understanding of physics. The three papers were called Brownian motion, the special theory of relativity, and the photoelectric effect.

Interestingly, all three of Einstein's papers were related to the study of the atom. This focus on the value of the atom dates all the way back to the Atomist philosophers of 400 B.C. (the term "atom" comes from the Greek word "atomos" that means uncutable or indivisible). The Atomists believed that reality was made up of two parts, the atom and the void in which the atom travels. They believed that atoms are unlimited in number, and they believed the atoms vary greatly in size, shape, and substance, which dictated the atoms position and arrangement as a whole. They believed that change in the physical world was caused by an atom connecting or disconnecting with another atom. The Atomists also believed there were two realities functioning simultaneously—the underlying unseen reality of a spiritual world that is a constant unchanging substratum, and the seen physical world that is constantly changing.

Galileo took the Atomist view and deduced that since the atoms have definable parts (shape, size, etc.) that they are mathematically divisible. Galileo was the first to develop a mechanistic view of the universe. This view was later adopted by Benedict Spinoza (1632-1677) and later by Einstein. Einstein like Spinoza had a strong foundation in geometry. Einstein and Spinoza were both mechanist philosophers. Einstein believed that the universe is like an enormous machine. This machine, the universe, is completely made up of atoms. Einstein believed that the atom was the key that unlocked understanding and the knowledge of true reality. Like Spinoza, Einstein believed the universe was God. As Einstein said, "I believe in Spinoza's God who reveals himself in harmony of all that exists." Einstein viewed God as the ever-existing substance of all things. To Einstein, God was the all knowing, self-sufficient basis of all reality. As you read the following synopsis of his three papers you can see Einstein's effort to understand the core nature of the atom and his desire to substantiate his atomic theory of matter.

The Browning motion was named after the British botanist Robert Brown who discovered in 1827 that the world was made up of molecules. Combining this with John Dalton's theory of matter and atomic theory, Einstein set out to further these works. Like those before him Einstein discovered through experimentation that there was an irregular motion of microscopic particles when they were randomly distributed in a liquid or gas, and that this irregular motion was caused by the collision of the particles with the molecules of the liquid or gas. This gave credibility to the belief that molecules were actually made up of smaller more basic entities called atoms. Using this research Einstein was able to formulate a mathematical explanation of this phenomenon making it possible for him to integrate this information into kinetic theory. This was the evidence Einstein needed to confirm his atomic theory of matter.

The special theory of relativity was originally titled "The Electrodynamics of Moving Bodies". Einstein's theory was based upon two factors—one, that the relativity principle (physical laws remain constant regardless of application) applies to all phenomenons whether it is mechanical or electromagnetic, and two, that light has a uniform speed (186,282 miles per second) regardless of its position in the universe, or the frame of reference used to measure it. Physicist would describe the relativity theory by saying that if two systems moved uniformly relative to each other, then all the laws of mechanics are the same in both systems. In other words, a person on a smoothly flying airplane could be bouncing a ball on the floor or flying a Frisbee with the same results they would have on the ground. However, if the airplane encounters turbulence the systems are no longer in a relative uniformity, and you see different results. Instead of a straight up and down movement of the ball it may hit the airplane window in response to the changed relationship of the two systems. Another example that shows the results of a changing correlation between two systems is that a person traveling on an airplane might see something taking place on the ground as one simultaneous action, when in fact multiple actions were taking place on the ground.

The photoelectric effect viewed light as a stream of tiny particles that carry energy. Einstein called this energy a photon. Einstein believed that these photons that make up a beam of light are transferred in units he called quanta. Einstein discovered that when a bright beam of light came into contact with metal it caused the atoms of the metal to release electrons. Einstein called this process the photoelectric effect. In 1921 Einstein's paper on quanta and the photoelectric effect earned him the Nobel Peace Prize in physics. This paper was also of vital importance to the formulation of the current quantum theory of physics. This paper established the theoretical basis for the photoelectric cell or what is known as the "electronic eye". This device was instrumental to the development of many inventions including the television, and it revolutionized the motion picture industry by making it possible to add sound to motion pictures.

WESTERN MINDSET THROUGH FILM

The Western mindset can be gauged by the movies we produce and watch. As a culture, we are addicted to entertainment and films rank highest on our list. Films, however, are so much more than entertainment. Film is a median of communication that surpasses all other forms. With today's visual effects and technical capabilities anything that can be imagined can be portrayed. A discussion of reality theories would not be complete without examining the ideas contained in recent films.

Though a few movies contained a fatalistic predestination mindset, even these question the boundaries of fate. For instance, *Final Destination* explores whether death is predestined for a specific time, and whether through extra sensory perception and logic an individual can cheat death. *The Time Machine* concludes that even with time travel the main character cannot prevent the death of a loved one in the past, but also alludes to while the past is fixed, the future can be altered or transformed.

Mindset and willpower are frequent topics in movies showing an individual overcoming the obstacles of life. *The Rookie* demonstrated that a life set on a specific course can be radically changed if you believe in yourself and have the willpower to pursue your dream. The idea that failure occurs only when we give up is also prominent. In *The Soldier*, the main character is so programmed to a particular mindset that he acts regardless of fear and pain. Yet, when he is told his usefulness is over, he rises above procedure and conduct choosing his own path and destiny. *Total Recall* takes this concept even further with memory implantation determining our actions in a volatile struggle with our inner desire and willpower to achieve the passions of the heart.

The existence of parallel realities is often illustrated in film. In many of the *Star Trek* episodes and films, various continuums were shown to exist. This theme was fundamental in the *Back To The Future* trilogy. Doc Brown even explains in detail how a choice or action at a particular point in time will cause a paradigm shift to an alternate time line or reality that in turn impacts the future of the individual as well as his universe. *The One* declares that multiverses exist at the same time. The main character travels to each universe and kills his alternate self. Since the energy and matter balance must be maintained, when he eliminated an alternate ego, it would boost his essences energy. It is proposed that if he could harness all the energy, he would become a god.

Many of today's most popular movies have the message that what is unseen is just as real as or more real than what is seen. In *The Truman Show*, the director explains the reason why Truman had not discovered the truth was because, "We accept the reality of the world with which we are presented." *The Sixth Sense* illuminates the world of the spirit that coexists with the world of the physical. The main character has the gift of perception beyond the sense realm that initially frightens him until he receives insight on how to live with his power. *Men In Black* shows how humanity is lulled into a comfortable misconception that what is real is what we perceive with our senses. When Will Smith discovers life beyond our humanity, he can choose to go back to his life of comfortable ignorance or jump into an exciting world of unknown possibilities. A similar choice is given to the main character of *The Matrix* when he must choose between the blue pill that would return him to the false reality of life as usual or the red pill of true reality where risk and challenge awaits him. Matrix carries the idea that we are living a computer simulation as does the movie, *The 13th Floor*. *The 13th Floor* shows layers of parallel realities that are not as real as they seem. It also shows the possibility of moving from a false reality to a true reality as the soul is transferred from one body to another.

Many believe there is a depth to individuals beyond their limits of normal consciousness or genetics. In *Unbreakable*, the two main characters discover that they have a hidden purpose that they are destined to fulfill. Their opposing objectives collide and irrevocably change the course of their lives. In *Changing Lanes*, the impact from two colliding realities transforms the mindset and lives of two individuals and their sphere of influence. In *Gattaca* the concept that genetics determines your outcome is challenged by the force of one's will and desire.

Movies can be of a totally different nature yet teach a

similar lesson. For instance, *The Scorpion King* and *The Gift* both proclaim that your destiny is yours despite the glimpses of prophets or fortunetellers. A component of reality that is addressed repeatedly in film is how time affects our reality. *Frequency* declares that time can fall back upon itself allowing unalterable things to be altered. Time impacts reality because time is subject to change. Many of us view time as a constant, but if you take into consideration Einstein's theory of relativity which clearly indicates that a person traveling near the speed of light will age slower than someone standing on the earth, then time must have some flexibility.

This brief movie review has clearly shown that we are seeking answers to our existence, trying to define what reality is, and how we can alter our current reality. A whole book can be written on the fabulous insights movies offer. Movies express ideas and stimulate your imagination to change your reality; one way to exercise your imagination is to enjoy films.

"People like us, who believe in physics, know that the distinction between past, present, and future is only a stubbornly persistent illusion."

Albert Einstein

REALITY ACCORDING TO PHYSICS

MODERN NATURAL PHILOSOPHY (PHYSICS)

We stated at the beginning of the philosophy section that prior to the 1700s, there was no distinction made between science and philosophy. Before that timeframe, physics was known as natural philosophy, and psychology was part of what was known as moral philosophy. Up to this point, we have covered historical moral philosophy and talked about philosopher/physicist Albert Einstein and others who have greatly contributed to our present reality. However, any discussion on reality would not be complete without laying some groundwork towards a fundamental understanding of modern physics. Although there are more than twenty specialized categories of modern physics we will focus on atomic physics, electrodynamics, particle physics, and quantum physics because they are closely related to theories that makeup our current understanding of reality.

Until the end of the 1800s, Isaac Newton's three laws of motion and his law of gravity seemed to describe the material world completely. Newton's first law states that every object will either remain stationary, or if it's moving it will continue indefinitely at the same speed unless it encounters another force. Newton's second law states that when an object encounters a force, the force causes the object to accelerate in the direction of impact. The amount of acceleration is equal to the amount of force applied to the object divided by the mass of the object. Newton's third law states that for every force there is an equal opposite force, or for every action there is an equal and opposite reaction. Newton's laws of motion became the foundation of classical physics. Classical physics is rooted in the concept that every effect has a cause.

James Maxwell broadened the horizons of classical physics by providing an understanding of electricity and magnetism. He discovered that there is no such thing as a pure electric or a pure magnetic wave. Instead, these forces are interdependent. An electric wave creates a magnetic wave and vice versa. These electromagnetic waves are made up of charged particles. Maxwell discovered that all electromagnetic waves travel at the speed of light, which led to the conclusion that light consists of an electromagnetic wave.

Thomas Young proved that light travels in waves and he discovered that if two light waves with opposite wave patterns were combined, then the waves would cancel each other out, resulting in darkness. Adding two kinds of light together to produce darkness was the beginning of many seemingly illogical scientific truths. Next came the "ultraviolet catastrophe." According to classical physics, if heat were added to electromagnetic waves the radiation produced would intensify, forcing most of the radiant energy to be emitted in the ultraviolet region. However, by the 1890s experiments with blackbody radiation disproved this belief. A blackbody refers to any surface that completely absorbs all radiant energy until its capacity for containment has been exceeded. Contrary to the expectation of Classical Physics the radiant energy did not increase to the point that it was forced out of the blackbody as ultraviolet radiation. Instead, they discovered that increased temperature caused a reduction in the electromagnetic wavelength, which also resulted in a reduction in the amount of radiation being produced. When the blackbody reached peak temperature, the electromagnetic wavelength became so short that the radiation was essentially nonexistent. The result of these experiments proved that an effective explanation of the physical world could not be achieved through Classical Physics.

Classical Physics took its place in the background as a new age of physics was discovered in the atom. The study of the atomic and subatomic world became known Particle Physics. The most popular advanced theory of Particle Physics is known as Quantum Mechanics or Quantum Physics. In simplified terms Quantum Physics refers to the study of matter and radiation at the atomic and subatomic level. According to the Quantum Theory every object has a wave function that measures the probability of locating that object at a certain point in space and time. According to the Quantum Theory of matter, the material universe is made up of atoms and molecules. There are approximately 100 different types of atoms and from these atoms all matter known to man can be formed. On the outer part of the atoms are electrons that allow the atoms to interact with other atoms. As an electron of an atom comes into proximity with the electron of another atom they exchange a packet of energy called a photon or quanta and then repel each other. The instant of energy exchange is known by physicists as the "magnetic moment." The type of energy or force created in this quantum exchange is dependent upon the structure of the atom and its subatomic particles.

The Heisenberg uncertainty principle named after Werner Heisenberg states that it is impossible to know the velocity and position of a subatomic particle simultaneously. Werner

Heisenberg discovered through experimentation that when he accurately measured the momentum of a particle, he was unable to accurately measure the position of the particle at the same time. Therefore, the conclusion was that no one can determine with certainty when the "magnetic moment" will occur, or which electrons will be involved in the quantum exchange. Since the momentum and position of a particle must be known in order to determine a particle's motion, the Heisenberg Uncertainty Principle contradicts Sir Isaac Newton's belief that the motion of all particles in the universe could be mathematically predicted.

To further complicate the understanding of quantum physics there were two experimentally proven theories of light. The corpuscular theory which stated that light was comprised of a stream of particles, and the wave theory which stated that light was comprised of electromagnetic waves. However, it was later determined by physicists that both theories were correct. Experimentation indicated that the electrons of an atom appear to have a dual nature known as particle wave duality. This means that sometimes the electron is viewed as a particle and at other times it can be viewed as a wave. The Quantum Theory now states that everything at the quantum level does not exist in a finalized form, but in a transitionary state of both particle and wave until it is measured or observed. For example some experiments have shown that electrons shot at a panel started out as a particle converted into a wave pattern and then converted back into a particle before it hit the panel. Experiments such as these fascinated Albert Einstein who spent most of his life trying to discover an all-conclusive unified atomic theory of matter or unified field theory. Einstein sought to understand all the components that make up our physical universe. It was so important to him that he devoted the last 30 years of his life to its development, but sadly he died without achieving his goal.

Theodr Kaluza was a little known mathematician who united Einstein's theory of gravity with Maxwell's theory of light and created a five dimensional theory of matter that was comprised of four dimensions of space and one dimension of time. This became known as the Kaluza—Klien theory. Then physicists C.N. Yang and R.L. Mills proposed that there are taffy like substances that hold protons and neutrons together like glue. They named this substance the gluon. Believing that the weak and strong forces associated with photons were caused by the quantum exchange, they also expounded upon the Maxwell theory of light. From the results of their experiments they created a general theory of matter that became known as the Yang—Mills field theory. The Yang—Mills field theory became so popular in the physics world that a comprehensive theory of matter was created from this theory and is known today as the "Standard Model".

Most physicists today believe that the "Standard Model" explains all the data accumulated with regard to subatomic particles up to one trillion electron volts of energy. One trillion electron volts is the limitation of the current atom smashers. However, even with all this acclaim the American Physicist and Nobel Laureate Richard Feynman believes that the "Standard Model" is incomplete because it doesn't describe gravity. Without question the "Standard Model" has greatly influenced modern physics. However, most physicists agree that the "Standard Model" is lacking the symmetry necessary to provide the ultimate answer to the questions of quantum physics. Richard Feynman believes that true answers have a level of simplicity that immediately become obvious to the observer that it is the truth. The "Standard Model" is lacking that simplicity.

Quantum mechanics and Einstein's general relativity theory are the two primary theories of the universe that are widely accepted in the physics community. However, there are a number of conflicts between these two theories that has created difficulties when attempting to unite them. Perhaps the largest conflict between the two theories is related to gravity. According to quantum mechanics the universe is filled with infinite amounts of energy. According to the general relativity theory where there are infinite amounts of energy there would also be infinite amounts of gravity, but it is apparent that infinite amounts of gravity does not exist.

Many physicists believe that the conflicts associated with the quantum theory and Einstein's theory of gravity must be resolved before any viable theory of matter can exist. It is also believed that is necessary to unite these two theories in order to achieve an all-inclusive theory of matter known as a grand unification theory (GUT). The superstring theory is an attempt to do just that. According to the superstring theory, if an individual particle could be magnified enough, what would actually be seen is a vibrating string. In this magnified world, fermions and bosons are the two primary types of particles, which are grouped together into supermultiplets within a relational symmetry, or supersymmetry. In simplified terms this just means that the grouping together of these particles creates a uniform string like appearance. The supersymmetry associated with the string makes it a superstring. This vibrating superstring is believed to be 100 billion billion times smaller than a proton. According to the superstring theory all matter is formed as a result of the various vibrations of these superstrings. Just like there are an infinite number of possible harmonies on a stringed instrument, there are an infinite number of possible forms of matter that can be created by the superstring. The superstring theorists believed that like the sand on the seashore the universe is comprised of countless vibrating superstrings. The superstring theory is a quantum field theory that claims the resolution of the conflicts associated with uniting the quantum theory with Einstein's theory of gravity, but the superstring theory requires a ten dimensional framework to unite these two theories without conflict. The supporters of the superstring theory believe it to be a quantum theory that provides an accurate understanding of matter-energy and space-time. They believe the superstring theory provides an accurate explanation for all the fundamental laws of nature, and that even the famous double helix being a string-like DNA molecule validates the superstring theory. Unfortunately, the technology is not currently available to prove or disprove the theory of superstrings.

Another theory of reality based upon quantum physics is called the holographic reality. Like the superstrings theory the holographic reality also attempts to unite the quantum theory with Einstein's theory of gravity believing that the outcome provides a greater understanding of life, and the elements that make up reality. As we previously stated according to quantum physics when an electron of an atom comes into proximity with the electron of another atom they exchange a packet of energy called a photon or quanta. From a biological perspective the energy bond created through this quantum exchange is called photosynthesis. Photosynthesis is the foundation of known biological structures. Every cellular process is energized through the quantum exchange and the breaking of chemical bonds associated with this exchange process. According to the holographic reality, it has been theorized that cells in the body contain electronic solid-state physical properties similar to that of a semiconductor. According to the holographic reality, all visible objects are three-dimensional holographic images formed by stationery and moving electromagnetic waves, and consciousness is nothing more than a frame of electrical charges in motion. These frames of electrical charges are transformed into structured frames that are stored in the brain, and the individual personality is the culmination of circulating stored frames that are united and transformed into a pattern of behavior.

Stanford neurophysiologist Karl Pribram believes that the human brain is itself a hologram that receives a holographic array of frequencies as its primary form of input. The brain mathematically converts the frequencies into sensory perceptions, and constructs hard reality from these perceptions. A paper entitled the holographic concept of reality written by Richard Allen Miller, Bert Webb, and Darden Dickson described the holographic world in this way, "We propose that the 'reality hologram', which appears as a stable world of material objects, is the elementary particle which has a long-term existence and fairly simple rules of interaction. We also propose the existence of a 'biohologram' which appears as mobile and evolving, through the DNA molecule. This 'biohologram' projects a dynamic three-dimensional image that serves as a guiding matrix for the manipulation and organization of the 'reality hologram.' Thus, we have mobile self-organizing holograms moving through a relatively static simpler hologram. The possibility exists that such 'bioholograms' could achieve sufficient coherence to continue existence as a pattern of radiant energy apart from a material substate." University of London physicist David Bohm believes that there is sufficient proof to indicate that objective reality does not exist. Instead he believes that despite its solid appearance, the universe is an incredibly detailed hologram. Bohm believes the reason that subatomic particles are able to remain in contact with one another regardless of the distance separating them is because their separateness is an illusion. He believes that a deeper level of reality exists were all things in the universe are infinitely interconnected within a superhologram where the past, present, and future all exist simultaneously.

Some believe that the creation of the quantum computer will help us to gain a greater understanding of the subatomic world and answer once and for all the questions of quantum physics and ultimately that of reality. Others believe that the reality of the universe is a highly complex cosmic quantum computer program. Edward Fredkin published his thesis "finite nature" in 1992 with this concept in mind. In his thesis "finite nature", Fredkin postulates that many things appear to have continuous motion, but nothing is truly in continuous motion. Just like a motion picture appears to be in continuous motion but what is truly being seen are numerous individual frames that move so fast they appear to be in continual motion. However, no one can see the truth of this reality, because of our limited powers of observation. In Fredkin's perspective, there can be no evolution, since there is no actual movement. Therefore, there can be no transitioning from one state of being to the next. Instead a thing exists at one moment, and then exists at another moment just like two separate frames of a film. Furthermore, a number such as a zero or a one can completely and exactly describe all actions. The only type of transitioning that can take place is that which correlates with the process of computing. Taking one group of information represented by numbers, applying the various rules for changing the numbers, and the outcome of the equation is a different set of information based upon these numerical modifications. This program is called CA architecture. The CA architecture has the potential to produce all varieties of interactions in the natural world. The individual reality is a quantum unit that functions under the strict mathematical rules imposed by the CA architecture. The individual or quantum unit functions within the parameters of the CA architecture and interacts with its neighboring quantum units producing change in the system within the parameters imposed by the CA architecture.

The Big Bang Theory is another theory of reality specifically related to the initial stages of existence. The Big Bang Theory has been modified many times but has for many years remained the most popular scientific theory related to the origin of the universe. According to the Big Bang Theory it all began about 15 billion years ago. At that time, all matter and energy was contained in one finite location. Then a tremendous explosion occurred known today as the Big Bang. This explosion forced the condensed matter and energy to scatter and fill the expanding space with all the particles of the universe. Immediately after the Big Bang, the universe was tremendously hot, and there was an equal amount of matter and antimatter that began to crash into each other resulting in the creation of pure energy. As the universe began to cool, matter prevailed over antimatter and common particles that contained all the building blocks for life as we know it began to form. It has been discovered that since the time of the Big Bang, the universe has continued to expand in all directions simultaneously.

The concept of the Big Bang Theory implies that there was a beginning. Most who have adopted the Big Bang Theory of existence now believe that there is strong evidence indicating that the universe had a beginning. Of course according to the rules of cause and effect anything that has a beginning will also have an end. The Big Crunch, and The Big Chill or Big Freeze are the two primary theories related to the end of the universe. The Big Crunch is a closed universe theory having what is called tidal gravity. With the tidal gravity perspective, there is a curvature of space-time where gravity is stretching or squeezing objects giving a similar appearance to that of an ocean tide. Another analogy for the Big Crunch Theory would be to view the universe as expanding like a bungee cord, which after it has reached its maximum stretch, it snaps back upon itself. Like the bungee cord, the Big Crunch Theory indicates that the gravitational forces of the universe will slow, eventually stop, and then begin to cascade back upon itself. As the universe begins to collapse, it will force the collision of stars and planets causing the universe to compress. The compression of stars and planets cause the universe to heat exponentially and eventually implode into a black hole. At this time the curvature of space and time will stretch out infinitely and space-time will cease to exist.

Another theory related to the Big Bang is the Oscillating Universe. According to the Oscillating Universe Theory, the universe begins with a Big Bang causing the universe to expand to its full capacity and then the universe cascades back upon itself into a Big Crunch. This process becomes a never-ending cycle of Big Bangs and Big Crunches. The

Oscillating Universe Theory obviously derives its name from this repetition of events.

The Big Chill or Freeze is an open or flat universe theory indicating that the space-time expands across a never-ending universe. According to the Big Chill/Freeze the universe will not cascade back upon itself like the Big Crunch, instead it will continue on indefinably. However, the energy of the stars will eventually wane causing the universe to grow ever colder as it expands. The universe will eventually slow down to a near stop as it continues to grow very dark and extremely cold. Some who have adopted this view believe that the universe will eventually become so cold that it will result in a new Ice Age causing universal extinction. It doesn't seem to matter whether it is the Big Crunch or the Big Chill/Freeze, the consensus is the same, that the universe will one day come to an end and all life in the universe will become causalities of these universal events unless the Oscillating Universe Theory is applied, at which time life would be recreated once again.

Although the Big Bang has remained the most popular theory of existence, the Genesis account of the Bible is the oldest written explanation of the existence of life in our universe. Edwin Hubble who was the first to discover scientific proof that the universe was continuously expanding laid the foundation of the Big Bang Theory. Since the introduction of the Big Bang theory there has been tension between those having a hard-core religious interpretation of the Genesis account of the Bible and those having a hard-core scientific interpretation that is prevalent in the current day educational system. Those with a hard core scientific interpretation saw The Big Bang Theory as an opportunity to prove that there was no beginning as described in the Genesis account. Instead the hard-core scientific perspective was that the universe always existed and the Big Bang just stimulated life in the existing universe that began the transition into an evolutionary process of life. Those who originally adopted this theory believed The Big Bang Theory not only provided evidence that there was no creator, but it also eliminated the need for a creator because all life in the universe began as a result of this massive cosmic disturbance called the Big Bang.

Over the years many have taken hard-line stances either from a Biblical perspective or from a scientific perspective as though the two were completely separate from each other. In his book *The Science of God,* Gerald L. Schroeder addresses this issue when he says, "The thought that religion and science must be at odds is ill-conceived." Schroeder claims, "What appear to be diametrically opposed the Biblical and scientific descriptions of the creation of the universe, of the start of life on earth, and of our human origins are actually identical realities but viewed from vastly different perspectives. Once these perspectives are identified, they coexist comfortably with all the rigorous science and traditional belief anyone could demand".

Today the scientific community agrees that the universe itself did not exist prior to the Big Bang. Therefore, there was a beginning and all that exists was brought into being as a result of the cosmic disturbance known as The Big Bang. To agree that there was a beginning is not conclusive evidence that there was a creator, but an individual could derive as a plausible logical conclusion that a beginning implies the existence of a universe creator. The key to finding the truth is to keep an open mind and seek the truth without any preconceived notions. A popular anonymous quote says, "The mind is like a parachute, it only works if it's open." An individual who seeks to find information to back up what they already believe will without a doubt find information to back up his or her position, but it may not be the truth. Most of us have fallen prey to this error at some point in our life, even Albert Einstein made this mistake in his Unified Field Theory. Einstein believed that the universe was not expanding instead it was static. Contrary to his own published works on relativity and the works of other physicists who theorized that the universe was continuously expanding

Einstein developed his Unified Field Theory with the premise of a static universe in mind. When significant proof was found that the universe is in fact expanding, Einstein denounced that portion of his theory and described the incident to his colleague Max Born as "the biggest blunder of my life." Obviously, the better method is to gather all the facts without prejudice before we proclaim a conclusion.

There are many avenues of input available to us today, and a tremendous amount of information that can be assimilated. However, with all this information available there is not one theory that can provide conclusive proof of reality. All the information available is just a spin off of theories conceived in the minds of men. Everything you were taught from birth as being true and real are just theories. Most likely all of these theories contain an element of the truth, but none of them contain the whole truth. What we propose is that reality is what you make it, and your perception of reality is in fact your reality. Just like the electron may appear as a particle or a wave depending upon expectation and observation, so also your reality is formed by your expectations and perceptions.

"Great spirits have always found violent opposition from mediocre minds. The latter cannot understand it when a man does not thoughtlessly submit to hereditary prejudices but honestly and courageously uses his intelligence and fulfills the duty to express the results of his thoughts in clear form."

Albert Einstein

APPENDIX IV

About The Authors

Larry and Diana Bogatz are motivational speakers, teachers, and the founders of B&B Hardware, Inc. Larry and Diana have been speaking and teaching for over fifteen years on subjects ranging from parenting and marriage to technical presentations at Fortune 500 companies. Diana has a Masters in Mathematical Simulation and a Bachelors in Electrical Engineering. Larry has a Bachelors in Mechanical Engineering. Larry and Diana have designed a complete line of reusable self-sealing fasteners that are used on products ranging from the space shuttle to gas meters. As inventors, they hold multiple patents and trademarks. From humble but diverse backgrounds they have blended their unique qualities and experiences to forge this positive, forward thinking book. They are living examples of how someone can change their lives forever simply by applying the solid principles described so well in their book, *Theory of Reality*.

Diana

Diana Bogatz:

Diana Bogatz is a successful business owner and author. Diana is happily married and the mother of four, well-adjusted children. Diana is a talented, motivational speaker. She is also content simply driving her BMW and happily living in Santa Barbara, California. Who she is today does not seem possible given her life story. However, because Diana has overcome so much, she is well qualified to help others change their lives. Diana recreated her life and is living her dreams.

Her story, the personal details, will be helpful to you as you realize your own similarity to her path. Therein you will be reassured that you too can make large and lasting changes in your life.

Diana was born and raised in a suburb of Los Angeles with her older brother, Michael, back when orange groves and cornfields grew where concrete jungles now dominate. Her father was a nuclear engineer for a major aerospace company and her mother taught home economics at a middle school. Diana's father, Graham, was raised in poverty. Graham's father was an alcoholic and his mother had phobias. Once a bee stung Michael—Diana's Grandmother Bessie pressed Michael's face to her chest—nearly suffocating him—while shouting out in terror, "He's going to die, he's going to die!" During thunderstorms, Grandmother Bessie hid under her bed trembling with fear. In a later incident, Graham was driving in a snowy, mountainous region with Bessie in the back seat of the car. Bessie was so afraid that the car was going to fly off the cliff that she tried to open her door to jump from the moving vehicle.

Like Bessie, Graham had intense, irrational fears. Graham's fears caused stress which eventually caused a terminal illness. Graham was afraid of everything, even going out the front door. He managed to go to work despite his fears until illness and phobia overtook his willpower. Because of Graham's illness and fear, Diana's family lived like hermits. Diana spent most of her childhood cooped up at home, except for the time she spent at school. Family vacations for Diana and Michael were few and far between. Diana rarely was allowed to participate in extra-curricular activities, not even the Girl Scouts.

Due to the stresses associated with a dysfunctional family, verbal abuse was also prevalent in Diana's upbringing. She was told that she had no rhythm when she attempted to learn to play the piano. She was told she lacked the coordination to ride a bike or play table tennis. She was told it was a wonder that she could even run since she looked so awkward and funny when she did.

During elementary school, Diana was sheltered in a private school. According to her mother, Diana would do anything for a gold star. She was seeking the approval of her teachers, and she became every teacher's pet as well as an excellent student. She had only one friend—her opposite scholastically—who also had a challenging home life. Upon graduation from elementary school, Diana was voted the most likely to succeed and the most popular. Diana believed the first, but she considered the second to be a cruel joke.

For middle and high school Diana was thrust into a hellish, local, public school system where gang problems flourished. In middle school, Diana witnessed on her first day of class two girls, very high on pot, in the restroom. One of these girls lit the other girl's hair on fire, and they both laughed as if it was great fun while they fumbled with wet paper towels to blot the charred mop that remained. Her pleas to return to private school were ignored by her parents. Bullies tripped her in the halls, slammed her hand in her locker, stole her lunch money, and chased after her—taunting her with names. During her second year of middle school, her father retired for medical reasons and became known to the children as the "thread on the couch". The doctors incorrectly predicted he would not live through the year.

During her last year of middle school Diana was asked out on a date, which her mother encouraged her to accept. When she returned home from the date, her father refused to talk to her because she had gone against his *unexpressed* wishes that she not date until she was at least sixteen. Graham had been Diana's hero and her best friend until this betrayal. After a year of giving Diana the silent treatment, Graham started to call his daughter names like "bitch" and "whore", probably due to the dementia caused by his illness. Graham was very unstable during Diana's formative years. At times, he would confide in his daughter his most recent plan on how he would end his life. In one example, he explained in detail how he would stand in front of the tree in the backyard and shoot himself . . . that way the bullet couldn't harm anyone else. When Diana expressed how horrible it would be for her to find his dead body, Graham simply said that his plan could just as easily be executed at a park as long as it was nearly empty of people.

During high school, Diana escaped the frontal assault at home through a downward spiral of negative, boyfriend relationships. After dating a particular boy for a while, Diana tried to break off the relationship. This boy slugged her a few times and left bruises where they wouldn't be obvious. He stalked her and threatened to kill himself if she left him. He became sick every time she would bring up the subject of leaving him. Eventually, Diana gained the courage to demand he stay away. He joined the military service—from which he was dishonorably discharged due to mental instability.

During high school, Diana lived a dual life. At school, she was president of science club, straight "A" student, and a "Miss

Goody Two Shoes". Away from school, she accepted every opportunity to escape her home life whether that led her to drinking parties or the association with the most unsavory characters. Once she accompanied a boy to a drug dealer's residence so he could buy some marijuana for an upcoming concert she had agreed to attend with him. The dealer flipped out, pulled a gun from a cut in his mattress and waved it at them. Diana learned to be more careful, but she was very naïve and overly trusting.

"College is the only option after high school" was the resounding image ingrained in Diana's mind, imprinted there from her youth by her parents. Diana's parents placed great value on education—unless it affected their pocketbook. When it came time for Diana to prepare for college, they notified her that not only would she be paying for her college education on her own, but she would also be required to pay rent to continue living at her parent's house. Coincidentally, her monthly rent payment was identical to the monthly amount required to pay for Graham's new life insurance policy. Diana's expressed resentment fell on deaf ears. Soon after Diana started college, her father had a stroke and was hospitalized. When Graham briefly became conscious, he remarked that he understood the mechanical unit, pointing to the TV, but that he never understood the human unit. Graham recovered and lived another ten years.

In Diana's sophomore year, Diana's mother, attempting to deal with the years of neglect, reasoned that she should not desert her dying husband; but she could find comfort with another man. When Graham discovered that Diana's mother was having an affair, he threatened to kill her mother and her mother's lover. Diana's parents used her like a ping-pong ball to relay messages to each other that they were not brave enough to deliver in person. Diana felt used, unloved, and abandoned. Diana poured her energies into college. She chose to become an engineer because it was the one thing her father claimed she could never succeed in doing. She was awarded the Litton

Systems scholarship and the Hughes Aircraft Fellowship. She graduated top of her class with her Bachelor's of Electrical Engineering and top of her class with her Master's in Mathematical Simulation.

Diana made the choice to love her parents no matter what, and she started reading self-help books related to self-esteem. For a short while, Diana saw a psychologist, but found that her advice was shallow and ended by the clock without consideration of her needs. Diana found support groups to attend that helped her let go of unforgiveness, and that provided fellowship with women who genuinely seemed to care.

Her first engineering job was at Hughes Aircraft. A co-worker invited her to see his new home. After he had lured her there, he attacked and raped her. Initially, Diana attempted to deny the incident ever happened, but that was virtually impossible to accomplish when she had to work with this person frequently. After this devastating experience, Diana was tempted to label all males as scum. Instead, after much thought, she realized that she was attracting men that would hurt her. Somehow her experiences with her father had created an inward belief that she was unworthy of love. In her subconscious she believed that all men would hurt her and betray her, like her father had done. After recognizing these erroneous beliefs, Diana chose to believe that she was worthy of love and deserved a man that would treat her properly.

Diana met that special man at age twenty-three. They married and helped each other to remove all the detrimental effects of the past from their lives. Together they started a fastener company that is currently over a dozen years in business. They have two girls and two boys, ages six to thirteen. They enjoy many activities together including sailing, dancing, and weightlifting. Their family lives happily in Santa Barbara, California.

Diana has spent many years mending her self-esteem. She has learned the art of letting go of unforgiveness, hurt, bitterness, and guilt. Diana has achieved peace of mind and spirit. She has an aggressive nature. She refuses to give up and is often characterized as biting off more than she can chew, but astounding those around her by finding a way to chew it. Her writing reflects her tenacity, honesty, and understanding of life.

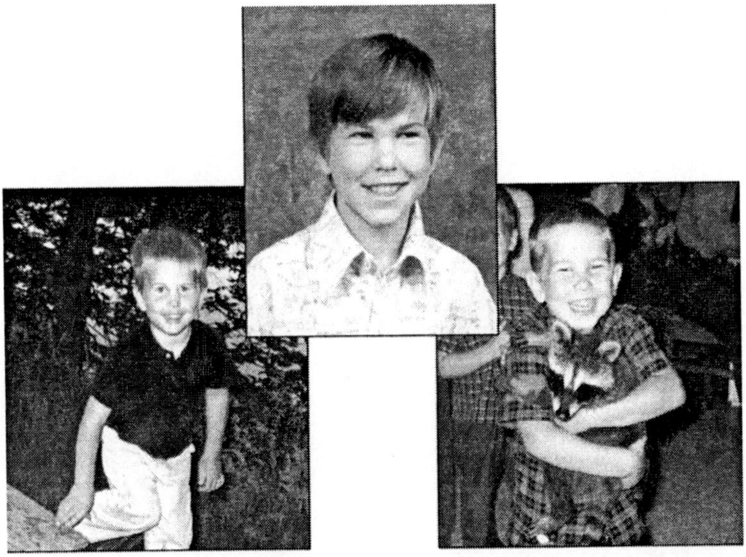

Larry

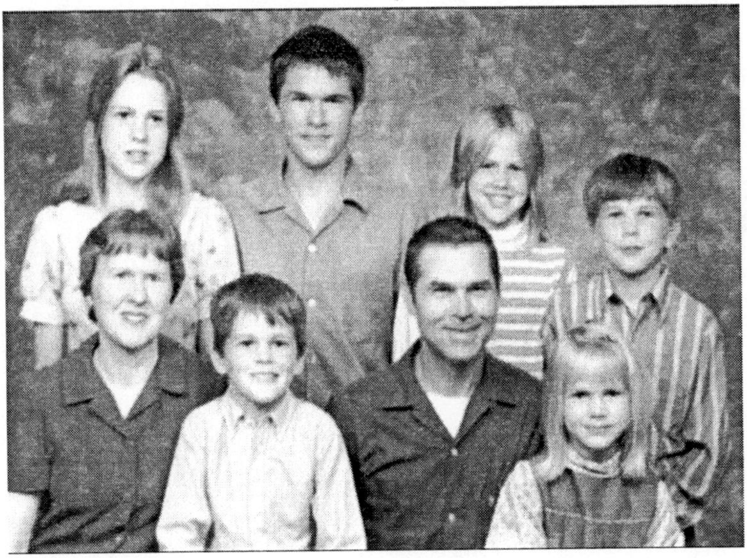

Larry Bogatz:

Larry Bogatz is the wonderful husband to Diana and father to their four children. He is the co-author of *Theory of Reality* and a successful business owner and investor. He has overcome many obstacles to become the person he is today. He lives in Santa Barbara, California, with his family. There he enjoys a freedom of time and money that few men ever achieve. His personal story and the resulting inspiration will empower you. Larry was born in Omaha, Nebraska. He is the middle child of six. He was raised in extreme poverty. When Larry was five, his parents found it difficult to pay the high rents in Omaha, so they bought an old, converted gas station and shop in the country. The house had no indoor plumbing, so the family shared an outhouse in the backyard. Even covered with fur, the seat was unbearably cold in the below freezing temperatures common with Nebraska winters. In the summer, the smell attracted insects of all kinds, especially wasps, who were continually trying to make the "one-hole amenity" their permanent home. Their water, which was carried in large pails up to the kitchen to be used for cooking and for washing dishes, came from "Armstrong", the red handled pump in the basement. Larry's handyman father, Bob, added the basic necessities, including running water and a bathroom, as quickly as he was able and finances would allow. During Larry's formative years, he took his showers in the school locker room to avoid waiting for the one shower his family of eight shared.

Upgrades to their house were slow because Bob was

working two, and sometimes three, jobs to make ends meet. The house was heated by propane when money was available. However, a woodstove was the primary source of heat in the winter. One of Larry's many duties was to cut, split, and stack the wood used to heat the house. Central heating was added after Larry left home to begin his military enlistment. While they had lived in Omaha, Larry's father allowed his younger brother's family of seven to live in their basement for a short while. After they moved to the country, Larry's impoverished uncle also moved to the country, built a house right across the street, and increased his family size to ten. At each meal, Larry's mother laid out the food, which was just enough to feed the family; but before they could gulp it down, their cousins, who lived next door, would arrive and start eating right off their plates. In Larry's childhood a special treat was getting candy for being quiet during Sunday mass or an orange in his stocking at Christmas. The many toys Larry saw advertised on television were rarely obtainable. However, Larry's parents usually managed to get him a plain label version of what he wanted for his birthday or the holidays.

Bob, Larry's father, suffered from a very wounded past. Bob's parents divorced, leaving him to be raised by a demanding mother. He was the oldest of three boys. At the age of fourteen, he left home and provided for himself. Bob felt guilty that he wasn't there to save his youngest brother, who was hit by a car and killed at the age of eight. Bob had difficulty handling the death of his younger brother. He joined the Navy at the age of eighteen. As an adult, Bob earned a high school equivalency diploma. Bob has the "man's man mentality" and was both verbally and physically abusive to his children. Because Larry had seen his father hit his older siblings, Larry learned to suppress his feelings and buried them deep inside to avoid conflict with his father. Larry was emotionally wounded from repeated times when his father would slap him on the back of the head and tell him that he was stupid and couldn't do anything right.

After his father bought and bragged about a new set of screwdrivers, which Larry perceived that his father loved more than him, Larry acted out his frustration in an unusual way. Bob locked the screwdrivers in the shop that was in the corner of the storeroom. Bob's shop didn't have a roof because it was inside the storeroom. Larry found a ladder, climbed over the wall of the locked shop, and took the new screwdrivers and a hammer. Larry pounded each of the new screwdrivers into the ground so far that his father never found them. As a child, this was the only way Larry knew how to let out his feelings of hurt and anger. Larry buried some memories so deep that for a time he didn't even remember them at all. Accessing them in later life has opened the door to great healings.

Larry was driven to make money at an unusually early age. His first business venture was to take abandoned railroad spikes and paint them with gold, spray paint. He persuaded his cutest cousin to sell them door to door for a commission. At the age of eight, Larry got his first, full-time summer job weeding beans with a machete. By the age of ten, Larry had moved up to bailing hay and cleaning horse stalls. By age twelve, he seined minnows and crawfish for a bait shop. At the age of sixteen, Larry claimed he was eighteen, so he could get a job with the state of Nebraska planting trees along the interstate and building rest stops. During the school year, Larry did every conceivable job that he could find. The money he earned went to buying decent shoes and clothes. At the age of seventeen, Larry joined the Seabees as a diesel mechanic on the delayed entry program, so that he would enter the service at the age of eighteen with a higher pay grade. In his senior year of high school, Larry was on the work-study program where he worked from 12 p.m. to 8 p.m. performing undesirable tasks for a diesel repair shop. Since the repair shop was not large enough for all the trucks to be inside the shop, Larry was delegated the unwanted tasks that required being outside during the cold, Nebraska winter.

In high school, Larry briefly dated a girl he found attractive. Their relationship ended abruptly when his "best friend" slept with the girlfriend. This painful experience fueled several erroneous beliefs that he had developed in his childhood. People couldn't be trusted. Men aggressively desired to hurt you and women passively let it happen. Larry's communication skills were greatly hampered. He had learned to keep his mouth shut, and he did not know how to properly express himself. The three girls in Larry's family were expected to graduate, but Larry was the only one of the three boys to graduate from high school. The August after graduation, Larry entered the Construction Battalion of the Navy to learn to be a diesel mechanic. Coming from a farming community, there was no greater aspiration than to be able to repair the farm equipment. He soon found that he enjoyed the mental challenge of the repair and maintenance of equipment, but he hated having to take three hour-long showers in order to feel somewhat clean. In the service, he expanded his horizons and went on to obtain a Bachelor of Science in Mechanical Engineering.

During his enlistment, his older brother died in a car accident that was mysterious and horrible. His brother was burned beyond recognition and his funeral was closed casket. Upon notification, Larry flew to his parent's house where he found that his father had been lying on the floor crying for two days. The first words that came out of his father's mouth were, "I never told him that I loved him"; Larry's brother was twenty-six when he died. This event marked a turning point in Larry's life. Since life could so suddenly and unexpectedly end, Larry was determined to make his life worth something. He changed many bad habits and started a journey to better himself from the inside out.

Shortly after the military, Larry met his wife-to-be, Diana. They knew each other as friends for about a year, meeting weekly at the singles coffee after Bible study on Friday nights. Larry liked Diana immediately, but he was struggling financially and was afraid to get involved with her when he didn't have the money to court her properly. Finally, when the time was right, Larry asked Diana out. In fact, on their first date Larry told her that he knew she was the one for him, and that he wanted to marry her. Less than a month later, he popped the question and seven months later they were married.

One night, after Larry was a married adult, he was dinning with his parents, his sister and her new husband. Out of frustration with his son-in-law, Bob smacked his son-in-law in the back of the head. The memories Larry had buried so deep came violently to the surface. The emotion was so great that Larry nearly vomited and excused himself to the restroom to regain composure. This incident opened an old wound. Over the next six months, Larry relived the countless times that his father had similarly struck him while criticizing him. Larry realized that much of his drive to succeed came from trying to prove his father wrong. Larry adjusted his attitude, talked with his father, forgave him, and was set free from many, past hurts. He became determined to succeed and to make something of himself because it was part of his dream, not because he needed to prove anything. Larry disagrees with the parenting methods of his father and mother, but he believes they truly did the best they knew how. Larry now has a good relationship with his parents.

After the military, Larry worked in technical sales. He was a territory, sales manager for an aerospace company selling specialty fasteners. Just five months after their first child was born, the aerospace industry suffered a tremendous cut back due to political changes in the country. Larry was laid off. He turned this negative into a positive by starting a fastener company of his own. In the beginning stages of the company, he sold the product and Diana did the product designs. Larry invented and patented three new fasteners, and their company has become a leader in its industry.

Larry is an industrious man. Besides his fastener company, Larry is an avid believer in learning new things. He has educated himself in philosophy, marketing, computers, law, and much more. He is well-versed in computer networking. He enjoys intellectual property law and has been involved in trademark and patent work. He is actively involved in real estate investments and property management. Larry is American Sailing Association certified and a certified diver. He has a brown belt in Tae-Kwan-Do and can bench press over three hundred pounds. He enjoys taking classes with his wife in everything from wine tasting to ballroom dance.

Larry has learned how to channel his energy in a positive way. For Larry, unforgiveness, guilt, and other emotional energy drainers are a thing of the past. Larry is a powerful, motivational speaker, full of wisdom and practical insight. He is candid, humorous, and engaging. Larry and Diana share their hearts through their book as well as their speaking engagements. Larry and Diana have been happily married for fifteen years. Together with their four children, they enjoy their dream life.

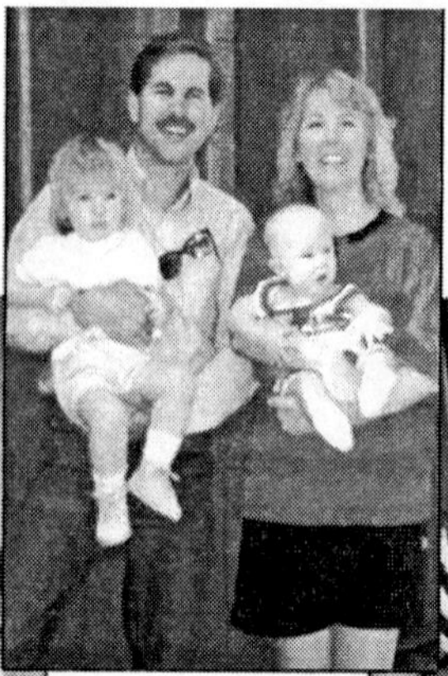
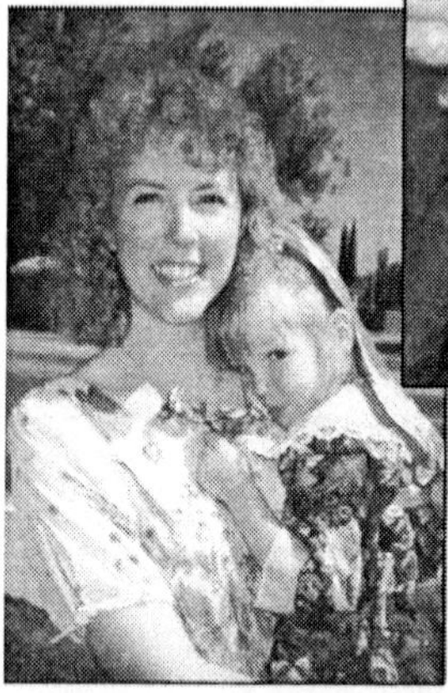
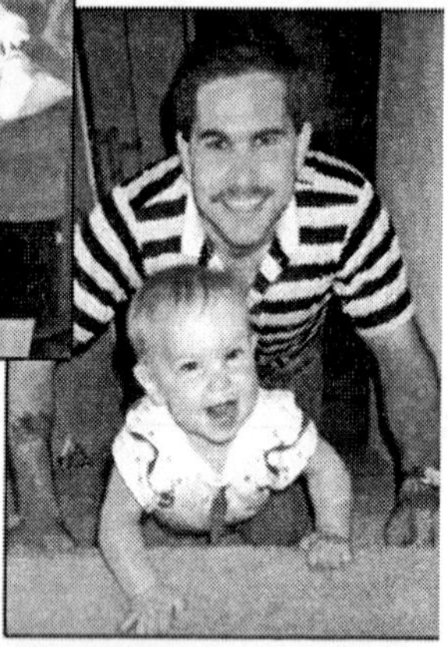
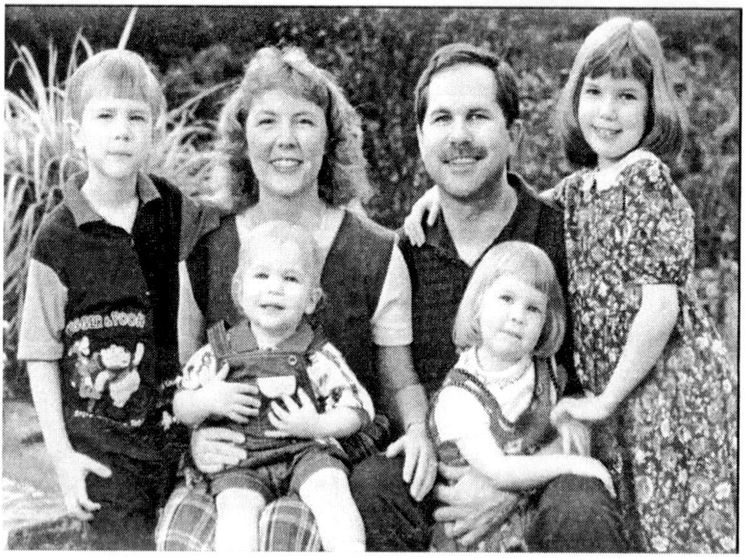

"If we knew what it was we were doing, it would not be called research, would it?"

Albert Einstein

APPENDIX V

Bibliography

Kiyosaki, Robert T. *Rich Dad Poor Dad.* New York: Warner Books, Inc., May, 2000.

Kiyosaki, Robert T. and Lechter, Sharon L. *Retire Young Retire Rich.* New York: Warner Books, Inc., 2002.

Roos, Dolf de. *Real Estate Riches.* New York: Warner Books, Inc., 2001

Davis, Michele Weiner. *Fire Your Shrink.* New York: Simon & Schuster, 1995.

Kaku, Michio. *HYPERSPACE.* New York: Anchor Books, Doubleday, 1995.

Kaufman, Steven. *Unified Reality Theory.* Milwaukee: Destiny Toad Press, November 1, 2001.

METAPHYSICS by Aristotle translated by W.D. Ross, 350 BC

Calaparice, Alice. *The Quotable Einstein*. Princeton: Princeton University Press, 1996.

Dukas, Helen, and Hoffman, Banesh. *Albert Einstein, The Human Side*. Princeton: Princeton University Press, 1979.

Bucky, Peter A., Einstein, Albert and Weakland, Allen G. *The Private Albert Einstein*. Kansas City: Andrews and McMeel. June, 1993.

Einstein, Albert. *The World As I See It*. Citadel Press; Reissue Edition. July, 1993.

Wall, Ernst L. *The Physics of Tachyons*. Palm Harbor: Hadronic Press, 1995.

Tompkins, Peter. *The Secret Life of Plants*. New York: Harper-Collins, March, 1989.

Christianson, Gale E. *In the Presence of the Creator: Isaac Newton and His Times*. Free Press, 1984.

Gribbin, John. *Quantum Physics*. New York: DK Publishing, Inc., 2002.

Spirit Filled Life Bible: New King James Version. Nashville: Thomas Nelson Publishers., 1991.

Harcourt. *Science*. Orlando: Harcourt School Publishers, 2002.

Sir William Thomson "The Wave Theory of Light" *Scientific Papers: The Harvard Classics*. (1914).

Deutsch, Hulton. "Rene Descartes." *Microsoft Encarta*, 1999. (CD ROM)

Duckworth, George E. "Rhetoric." *Microsoft Encarta,* 1999. (CD ROM)

Bornstein, Lawrence A. and Gamow, George. "Relativity." *Microsoft Encarta,* 1999. (CD ROM)

Martyn, Louis J. "Saint Paul." *Microsoft Encarta,* 1999. (CD ROM)

Gamow, George. "Quantum Theory." *Microsoft Encarta,* 1999. (CD ROM)

Linder, John. "Theory of Everything." *Microsoft Encarta,* 1999. (CD ROM)

Yang, Chen Ning. "Elementary Particles." *Microsoft Encarta,* 1999. (CD ROM)

Brumbaugh, Robert S. "Aristotle." *Microsoft Encarta,* 1999. (CD ROM)

Hesburgh, Theodore M. "Saint Augustine." *Microsoft Encarta,* 1999. (CD ROM)

Deutsch, Hulton. "Saint Thomas Aquinas." *Microsoft Encarta,* 1999. (CD ROM)

Deutsch, Hulton. "Immanuel Kant." *Microsoft Encarta,* 1999. (CD ROM)

West, Henry R. "Rationalism." *Microsoft Encarta,* 1999. (CD ROM)

Sandmel, Samuel. "Neoplatonism." *Microsoft Encarta,* 1999. (CD ROM)

O'Flaherty, Wendy Doniger. "Hinduism." *Microsoft Encarta*, 1999. (CD ROM)

Popkin, Richard H. "George Berkeley." *Microsoft Encarta*, 1999. (CD ROM)

Fuss, Peter. "Idealism." *Microsoft Encarta*, 1999. (CD ROM)

Westfall, Richard S. "Sir Isaac Newton." *Microsoft Encarta*, 1999. (CD ROM)

Westfall, Richard S. "Nicolai Hartmann." *Microsoft Encarta*, 1999. (CD ROM)

Jaffee, Dwight M. "Money." *Microsoft Encarta*, 1999. (CD ROM)

Eliade, Mircea. "Mysticism." *Microsoft Encarta*, 1999. (CD ROM)

Glasstone, Samuel. "Albert Einstein." *Microsoft Encarta*, 1999. (CD ROM)

Glatzer, Nahum Norbert. "Benedict Spinoza." *Microsoft Encarta*, 1999. (CD ROM)

Tripp, Thomas M. "Airplane." *Microsoft Encarta*, 1999. (CD ROM)

Webb Wilse B. "States of Consciousness." *Microsoft Encarta*, 1999. (CD ROM)

Petersen, Robert C. "Drug Dependence." *Microsoft Encarta*, 1999. (CD ROM)

"Chuck Yeager." *Microsoft Encarta*, 1999. (CD ROM)

"Physics." *Microsoft Encarta*, 1999. (CD ROM)

"Clocks and Watches." *Microsoft Encarta*, 1999. (CD ROM)

"Calendar." *Microsoft Encarta*, 1999. (CD ROM)

"Samuel Alexander." *Microsoft Encarta*, 1999. (CD ROM)

"Western Philosophy." *Microsoft Encarta*, 1999. (CD ROM)

"Manichaeism." *Microsoft Encarta*, 1999. (CD ROM)

"Francis Herbert Bradley." *Microsoft Encarta*, 1999. (CD ROM)

"Transcendentalism." *Microsoft Encarta*, 1999. (CD ROM)

"Empiricism." *Microsoft Encarta*, 1999. (CD ROM)

"John Locke." *Microsoft Encarta*, 1999. (CD ROM)

"Socrates." *Microsoft Encarta*, 1999. (CD ROM)

"Xenocrates." *Microsoft Encarta*, 1999. (CD ROM)

"Symmetry." *Microsoft Encarta*, 1999. (CD ROM)

"Metaphysics." *Microsoft Encarta*, 1999. (CD ROM)

"David Hume." *Microsoft Encarta*, 1999. (CD ROM)

"Causality." *Microsoft Encarta*, 1999. (CD ROM)

"Money Supply." *Microsoft Encarta*, 1999. (CD ROM)

"Saint Paul." *World Book Multimedia Encyclopedia*, 1997. (CD ROM)

Singer, Marcus G. "Philosophy." *World Book Multimedia Encyclopedia*, 1997. (CD ROM)

Huffman, Carl A. "Socrates." *World Book Multimedia Encyclopedia*, 1997. (CD ROM)

Brieske, Thomas J. "Sir Isaac Newton." *World Book Multimedia Encyclopedia*, 1997. (CD ROM)

Brieske, Thomas J. "Fourth Dimension." *World Book Multimedia Encyclopedia*, 1997. (CD ROM)

Morrissett, Irving. "Gold Standard." *World Book Multimedia Encyclopedia*, 1997. (CD ROM)

Doty, R. G. and Fischer, Stanley. "Money." *World Book Multimedia Encyclopedia*, 1997. (CD ROM)

Jespersen, James. "Time." *World Book Multimedia Encyclopedia*, 1997. (CD ROM)

Jesseph, Douglas. "Metaphysics." *World Book Multimedia Encyclopedia*, 1997. (CD ROM)

Hauffman, Carl A. "Atomism." *World Book Multimedia Encyclopedia*, 1997. (CD ROM)

Kevles, Daniel J. "Albert Einstein." *World Book Multimedia Encyclopedia*, 1997. (CD ROM)

Case, William B. "Relativity." *World Book Multimedia Encyclopedia*, 1997. (CD ROM)

Soll, Ivan. "Aristotle." *World Book Multimedia Encyclopedia*, 1997. (CD ROM)

Burrell, David B. "Saint Augustine." *World Book Multimedia Encyclopedia*, 1997. (CD ROM)

Miller, Richard A., Webb, Burt and Dickson, Darden "THE HOLOGRAPHIC CONCEPT OF REALITY" O.A.K.: *The Holographic Concept of Reality.* <http://www.geocities.com/nwbotanicals1/oak/holocon.html > (April 16, 2003).

"Reality-the Holographic Universe" Reality-the Holographic Universe. <http://www.keelynet.com/biology/reality.htm (March 16, 1997).

Rhodes, Ross "The Reality Program" *The Reality Program: chapter 9.* <http://www.keelynet.com/biology/reality.htm> (April 16, 2003).

Reasoner, Robert "The True Meaning of Self-Esteem" *The National Association for Self-Esteem.* <http://www.self-esteem-nase.org/whatisselfesteem.shtml> (April 12, 2003).

LaRocco, Chris, and Rothstein, Blair "The Big Bang: It Sure Was Big!!" *BIG BANG.* <http://www.umich.edu/~gs265/bigbang.htm> (April 16, 2003).

Pedley, Francis. "The Expanding Matrix" *Expanding Matrix and the Unification of Dynamics.* <http://www.members.tripod.com/Exmatrix/Part_1.html> (April 16, 2003).

Wilson, Joseph Bearwalker. "Magical Theory of Reality" *The Magical Theory of Reality.* <http://www.metista.com/shamanism/theory.htm> (April 16, 2003).

"The Big Crunch" *The Big Crunch Theory.* <http://ca.geocities.com/crankfiend138/tim1.html> (April 16, 2003).

Lindner, Henry H. "Against Quantum Theory: A Wave Theory of Light and Electrons." *Against Quantum Theory.* <http://www.geocities.com/hlindner/writings/quant/quant.html> (April 16, 2003).

"'M' Theory Stands for Magic, Matrix, Membrane, Mother, or Mystery" *'M' Theory Stands for Magic, Matrix, Membrane, Mother, or Mystery.* <http://www.2think.org/t000104312.shtml> article date (November 16, 1999).

Young, Rufus. "The Steady State Galaxy Theory an Alternative to The Big Bang Theory." *Steady State Galaxies-An Alternative to The Big Bang-by Rufus Young.* <http://personal.nbnet.nb.ca/galaxy/> article date (December 30, 1996).

"SUPERSTRINGS! Extra Dimensions" *SUPERSTRINGS.* <http://www.sukidog.com/jpierre/strings/extradim.htm> (April 4, 2003).

"SUPERSTRINGS! Supersymmetric Strings" *SUPERSTRINGS.* <http://www.sukidog.com/jpierre/strings/susy.htm> (April 4, 2003).

Thornton, Stephen. "Berkeley's Theory of Reality" *Berkeley's Theory of Reality.* <http://www.ul.ie/~philos/vol1/berkel.html> (September 13, 2002).

Sorokin, Pitirim A. "The Integral Theory of Truth and Reality" *The Integral Theory of Truth and Reality.* <http://www.intuition.org/sorokin.htm> article date (October 15, 1998).

"A brief History of Time Keeping" *Clock a History-Timekeepers.* <http://www.timekeepers.org/clock.htm> (September 13, 2002).

Suttle, Gary. "Albert Einstein" *PAN Lodestars-Albert Einstein.* <http://www.home.utm.net/pan/einstein.html> (November 8, 2002).

"Atomism" *Atomism.* <http://es.rice.edu/ES/humsoc/Galileo/Things/atomism.html> (November 21, 2002).

"Atomism" *Atomism.* <http://faculty.washington.edu/smcohen/320/atomism.htm> (November 21, 2002).

"The Story of Colonel Sanders" *The Story of Colonel Sanders.* <http://www.kentuckyfriedcosplay.com/ColSsanders/TheStory.html> (November 27, 2002).

Carroll, Robert T. "Remote Viewing" *The Skeptic's Dictionary.* <http://skepdic.com/remotevw.html> article dated (December 30, 2001).

Carroll, Robert T. "Astral Projection" *The Skeptic's Dictionary.* <http://skepdic.com/astralpr.html> article dated (December 30, 2001).

Carroll, Robert T. "Clairvoyance" *The Skeptic's Dictionary.* <http://skepdic.com/clairvoy.html> article dated (December 30, 2001).

Carroll, Robert T. "Clairaudience" *The Skeptic's Dictionary.* <http://skepdic.com/clairaudio.html> article dated (December 30, 2001).

Carroll, Robert T. "Paranormal" *The Skeptic's Dictionary.* <http://skepdic.com/paranormal.html> article dated (December 30, 2001).

Carroll, Robert T. "Telekinesis and Psychokinesis" *The Skeptic's Dictionary.* <http://skepdic.com/kinesis.html> article dated (December 30, 2001).

Carroll, Robert T. "dreams" *The Skeptic's Dictionary.* <http://skepdic.com/dreams.html> article dated (December 30, 2001).

Carroll, Robert T. "Dermo-optical perception" *The Skeptic's Dictionary.* <http://skepdic.com/dop.html> article dated (December 30, 2001).

Carroll, Robert T. "Out-of-body experience" *The Skeptic's Dictionary.* <http://skepdic.com/obe.html> article dated (December 30, 2001).

Carroll, Robert T. "Altered states of consciousness (ASC)" *The Skeptic's Dictionary.* <http://skepdic.com/altstates.html> article dated (December 30, 2001).

Carroll, Robert T. "ESP (extrasensory perception)" *The Skeptic's Dictionary.* <http://skepdic.com/esp.html> article dated (December 30, 2001).

Kat, Katie. "Life and Legend of Howard Hughes" *ChuckIII's College Resources.* <http://www.chuckiii.com/ reports / Biographies /

Life_and_Legend_of_Howard_Hughes.shtml> (November 27, 2002).

Greenstein, Albert. "Howard Hughes" *Howard Hughes.* <http://www.socalhistory.org/Biographies/h_hughes.htm> article dated (1999).

"Elvis Presley" *Elvis Presley Biography.* <http://www.leninimports.com/elvis_presley_bio.html> article dated (November 27, 2002).

"Gladys Presley" *Gladys Presley.* <http://www.elvispresleyonline.com.html/gladys_presley.html> (November 27, 2002).

*"The important thing
is not to stop questioning.
Curiosity has its own reason
for existing."*

Albert Einstein

APPENDIX VI

Suggested Reading

Financial Prosperity:

Kiyosaki, Robert T. *Rich Dad Poor Dad.* New York: Warner Books, Inc., May, 2000.

Kiyosaki, Robert T. and Lechter, Sharon L. *Retire Young Retire Rich.* New York: Warner Books, Inc., 2002.

Roos, Dolf de. *Real Estate Riches.* New York: Warner Books, Inc., 2001

Psychology:

Davis, Michele Weiner. *Fire Your Shrink.* New York: Simon & Schuster, 1995.

Physics:

Kaku, Michio. *HYPERSPACE.* New York: Anchor Books, Doubleday, 1995.

Kaku, Michio. *Introduction to Superstrings.* New York: Springer-Verlag, 1998.

Schroeder, Gerald. *The Science of God.* New York: First Broadway Books, 1998.

Hawking, Stephen W. *A Brief History in Time.* New York: Bantam, 1996.

Hawking, Stephen W. *The Universe in a Nutshell.* New York: Bantam, 2001.

Heisenberg, Werner. *Physics and Beyond.* New York: Harper Torchbooks, 1971.

Sagan, Carl. *Cosmos.* New York: Ballantine Publishing Group; Random House, 1980.

Marriage:

Harley, Willard F. Jr. *His Needs Her Needs.* Fleming H. Revell Co., April, 2001.

Wheat, Ed. *Love Life.* Zondervan, October, 1980.

DeAngelis, Barbara. *What Women Want Men To Know.* Hyperion, 2001

Parenting:

Ezzo, Gary and Anne Marie. *On Becoming Childwise.* Chatsworth: Growing Families International <http// www.gfi.org>

Christian:

Capps, Charles. *The Tongue a Creative Force.* Tulsa: Harrison House, 1987.

Capps, Charles. *Faith and Confession.* Tulsa: Harrison House, 1987.

Capps, Charles and Annette. *Tapes and Books.* <http// www.charlescapps.com>

Kenyon, E.W. *Advanced Bible Course.* Lynnwood: Kenyon's Gospel Publishing Society, 1970.

Kenyon, E.W. *The Bible in light of Our Redemption.* Lynnwood: Kenyon's Gospel Publishing Society, 1970.

*"People do not grow old
no matter how long we live.
We never cease to stand like
curious children before
the great Mystery into which
we were born."*

Albert Einstein

APPENDIX VII

Products

Motivational Aids, Mugs, Bags, Clothes, Mouse Pads, Clocks, and More.

Visit our online store at *www.TheoryOfReality.com.*

*"Common sense is the collection
of prejudices acquired
by age eighteen."*

Albert Einstein

Index

APPENDIX VIII

Q

R

S

Y

BVG